The Magical Christmas Cookbook

The Magical Christmas Cookbook

CREATE THE SPARKLE OF EUROPEAN CHRISTMAS
MARKETS AT HOME WITH 75 FESTIVE RECIPES

murdoch books
London | Sydney

Contents

Charles Dickens: Merry Christmas and a Happy New Year! ... 7

Heavenly starters and delicious bites

Cream of parsnip soup with thyme croutons ... 10
Button mushroom cream soup ... 13
Radicchio and rocket salad with cranberries and walnuts ... 14
Winter salad with bacon-coated prunes ... 17
Come Tomorrow, Girls and Boys ... 18
Rebecca S. Cooke: Merry, Merry Christmas! ... 19
Goat's cheese with orange honey and roast tomatoes ... 20
Beetroot carpaccio ... 23
Fredrik Vahle: A Snowflake's Weight ... 24
Hedwig Haberkern: Little Snowflake, Little Lace Dress ... 25
Honeyed balsamic carrots with hazelnuts and yoghurt ... 26
Roast pumpkin with rocket and feta ... 28
Classic potato cake ... 31
The Legend of Santa Claus ... 32
George Wither: A Christmas Carol (extract) ... 33
Spinach and salmon quiche ... 34
Carrot hummus with cumin ... 37
Saffron and almond butter ... 37
Garlic and porcini mushroom pull-apart bread with a feta and mushroom spread ... 38
Festive bruschetta two ways ... 41

Magical mains

Sophie Reinheimer: Ice Flowers ... 45
Pumpkin risotto with sage butter and caramelised chestnuts ... 46
Pumpkin gnocchi with beetroot in sage butter ... 49
Pumpkin and beetroot Wellingtons with kale pesto ... 50
Bread dumpling with mushroom ragout ... 53
Nut roast with sweet potato and chestnut mash ... 54
Winter vegetable gratin ... 57
The Brothers Grimm: The Elves and the Shoemaker ... 58
Salmon with potatoes and pea pesto ... 60
Gilthead bream in salt crust with pine nut butter and lemon and thyme potatoes ... 63
Christina G. Rossetti: A Christmas Carol ... 64
Walter de la Mare: Mistletoe ... 65
Fillets of lamb with rosemary and mashed celeriac ... 66
Leg of lamb with goat's cheese and herb salad ... 69
Kenneth Grahame: Carol ... 70

Ernst Anschütz: O Christmas Tree	71
Crispy pork belly with vegetables and potatoes	72
Duck breast with spiced orange red cabbage	75
Roast goose with potato dumplings and red cabbage	76
Charles Dickens: A Christmas Carol (extract)	78
Italian roast goose, Parma-style	80
German roast goose with gingerbread sauce	81
The Wassail Song	82
Karl Enslin: Ring, Little Bells	83
Pepper-crusted fillet of beef with sweet potato rosti	84
Swiss cheese fondue	87

Enticing desserts

Clement Clarke Moore: A Visit from St. Nicholas	90
Chestnut ice cream with vanilla and Amarena cherries	92
Roasted maple pears with almond praline and yoghurt	95
Honey parfait with mulled wine plums	96
White chocolate cream with raspberries	99
Maurice Reinhold von Stern: Winter Prayer	100
Emily and Fritz Koegel: The Baked Apple	101
Pannacotta with caramel sauce	102
Mousse au chocolat	105
Christmas cookie custard	106
Lemon sorbet	109
Orange mascarpone cream with slivered almonds	110
E.T.A. Hoffmann: The Nutcracker (extract)	112
Amaretto dessert	114
Gentleman's pudding	117
White chocolate and coconut parfait with red fruit jelly	118
Sweet fluffy dumplings with poppy seed butter	121
Joseph von Eichendorff: Christmas	122
Wilhelm Lobsien: Winter Night	123

Sweet Christmas baking

Vanilla crescents	126
Cinnamon stars	127
Butter biscuits	128
Almond shortbread nests	129
Coconut macaroons	132
Hazelnut rounds	133

Spiced biscuits	134
Layered domino biscuits	137
Black-and-white biscuits	138
Pecan biscuits with chocolate filling	141
Helen Maria Williams: To Mrs K___, on Her Sending Me an English Christmas Plum-Cake, at Paris	142
Cranberry shortbread	144
Apricot crumble gingerbread	145
German gingerbread biscuits	146
Flourless chocolate gingerbread	147
Nut triangles	150
Traditional stollen	153
Paula Dehmel: Christmas in the Pantry	154
Buttery quark stollen	156
Lemon and yoghurt Bundt cake	159
Tree log cake	160
Julius Kreis: Baking (extract)	163
Christmas cupcakes	164
Festive mud cakes	167

Festive drinks

Christmas forest berry punch	170
Mandarin punch	173
Hot apple punch	173
German flaming punch	174
White mulled wine	177
Red mulled wine	177
Christmas sangria	178
Jack Frost cocktail	181
Clementine and rosemary prosecco	182
Orange and chilli hot chocolate	185

Index of recipes 186

Index of ingredients 188

Unless otherwise stated, all recipes are for 4 people.

Charles Dickens
from *Sketches by Boz, Volume 1* (1836)

Merry Christmas and a Happy New Year!

There are people who will tell you that Christmas is not to them what it used to be. Never heed such dismal reminiscences. There are few men who have lived long enough in the world, who cannot call up such thoughts any day in the year. Then do not select the merriest of the three hundred and sixty-five for your doleful recollections. Reflect upon your present blessings — of which every man has many — not on your past misfortunes, of which all men have some. Fill your glass again, with a merry face and contented heart. Our life on it, but your Christmas shall be merry, and your new year a happy one!

Heavenly

starters and delicious bites

Cream of parsnip soup
with thyme croutons

1 large French shallot
500g (1lb 2oz) parsnips
1 tablespoon olive oil
1 litre (35fl oz) vegetable stock
100ml (3½fl oz) single (pure) cream
3 teaspoons horseradish (from a jar)
Salt
Freshly ground black pepper
1 pinch of cayenne pepper
200g (7oz) brioche buns
4 sprigs of thyme
2 tablespoons butter
Microgreens or cress, for garnish

Peel and dice the shallot. Peel and slice the parsnips.

Heat the olive oil in a saucepan, add the shallot and parsnip and sweat. Pour in the stock, cover and simmer for 20 minutes.

Thoroughly blend the soup, then stir in the cream and horseradish. Season with salt, pepper and cayenne pepper.

Dice the brioche buns or cut out Christmas shapes with a cookie cutter. Rinse the thyme, pat dry and pick off the leaves.

Heat the butter in a pan, add the brioche and toast briefly. Add the thyme and continue to toast the brioche, turning it continuously until the croutons are nice and crispy. Season with salt and pepper.

Divide the soup among bowls and serve topped with the croutons. Garnish with microgreens or cress and freshly ground pepper.

Button mushroom cream soup

Peel and dice the onion. Clean and trim the mushrooms and wipe them with kitchen paper, if necessary. Finely slice a few of the mushrooms and set them aside. Dice the rest.

Melt the butter in a saucepan, add the diced onion and sweat until translucent. Add in the diced mushrooms and fry for 2 minutes. Add the stock, white wine and cream and simmer for 10 minutes over low heat.

Blend the soup and season with salt, pepper and lemon juice. Divide among warmed bowls and serve garnished with the sliced mushrooms, wild greens, a tablespoon of olive oil and freshly ground pepper.

Tip: For this soup, be sure to buy button mushrooms with firm, white, fully closed heads.

1 small onion
400g (14oz) button mushrooms
2 tablespoons butter
1 litre (35fl oz) vegetable stock
100ml (3½fl oz) dry white wine
200ml (7fl oz) single (pure cream
Salt
Freshly ground white pepper
Juice of ½ lemon

Also

1 handful of wild greens
Olive oil

Radicchio and rocket salad
with cranberries and walnuts

For the salad

50g (1¾oz) walnuts
200g (7oz) rocket (arugula)
500g (1lb 2oz) radicchio
150g (5½oz) dried cranberries
30g (1oz) goat's cheese
50g (1¾oz) blueberries

For the dressing

5 tablespoons apple cider vinegar
4 tablespoons olive oil
1 tablespoon maple syrup
Salt
Freshly ground black pepper

Dry roast the walnuts in a pan until they become fragrant. Set aside.

Wash and spin dry the rocket leaves. Trim and quarter the radicchio, remove the tough core and slice the quarters into strips.

Whisk all the ingredients for the dressing together and season with salt and pepper.

Arrange the salad leaves on a platter together with the nuts and cranberries. Drizzle with the dressing. Top with the crumbled goat's cheese and blueberries.

Tip: If you like, serve this salad with slices of toasted baguette.

Winter salad

with bacon-coated prunes

Wash, spin dry and pick through the lamb's lettuce. Trim and finely slice the chicory and radicchio.

Cut the crown off the pomegranate and score the skin five times lengthways. Carefully break the fruit apart along the scored lines, separate the seeds from the pith and set aside. Peel and segment the orange and remove any pith.

In a bowl, thoroughly combine all the ingredients for the dressing.

Arrange all the salad ingredients on a platter and drizzle the dressing on top.

Wrap each prune in a slice of bacon. Heat a pan and fry until crisp on all sides, about 5 minutes. Serve with the salad.

For the salad

150g (5½oz) lamb's lettuce (or other salad leaves)
1 chicory (witlof)
1 small radicchio
1 pomegranate
1 orange

For the dressing

4 tablespoons honey
2 tablespoons mustard
2 tablespoons pomegranate juice
Juice of ½ lime
8 tablespoons olive oil
1 pinch of ground cinnamon
Chilli powder, to taste
Salt
Freshly ground black pepper

Also

8 prunes
8 slices of bacon

Come Tomorrow, Girls and Boys

Come tomorrow, girls and boys,
We'll have such a merry time!
Jubilation, cheer and joy
Will fill up our happy home!
One more sleep 'til we can say,
Wake up! It is Christmas day!

How the house will glow and sparkle;
Lights in all the rooms and halls.
Brighter than a crystal palace
Decorated for a ball.
Do you know from memory
How it feels on Christmas eve?

What a happy day's tomorrow.
All the pleasures that we know.
Our dear parents have been working
Long and hard to make it so.
Those who thank and love them least,
Don't deserve their Christmas feast!

Rebecca S. Cooke

Merry, Merry Christmas!

Merry, merry Christmas ev'rywhere!
Cheerily it ringeth through the air;
Christmas bells, Christmas trees,
Christmas odors on the breeze.
Merry, merry Christmas ev'rywhere!
Cheerily it ringeth through the air;
Why should we so joyfully
Sing, with grateful mirth?
See! the Sun of Righteousness
Beams upon the earth!

Merry, merry Christmas ev'rywhere!
Cheerily it ringeth through the air;
Christmas bells, Christmas trees,
Christmas odors on the breeze.
Merry, merry Christmas ev'rywhere!
Cheerily it ringeth through the air;
Light for weary wanderers,
Comfort for th' oppressed!
He will guide His trusting ones
Into perfect rest.

Merry, merry Christmas ev'rywhere!
Cheerily it ringeth through the air;
Christmas bells, Christmas trees,
Christmas odors on the breeze.
Merry, merry Christmas ev'rywhere!
Cheerily it ringeth through the air;
Deeds of Faith and Charity;
These our offerings be,
Leading ev'ry soul to sing,
Christ was born for me!

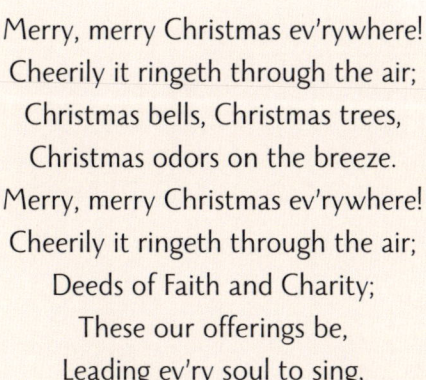

Goat's cheese

with orange honey and roast tomatoes

2 sprigs of thyme
50g (1¾oz) honey
250ml (9fl oz) orange juice
200g (7oz) cherry tomatoes
2 tablespoons olive oil
Salt
Freshly ground black pepper
1 tablespoon white wine vinegar
4 small rounds of goat's cheese
Orange zest, to taste
Freshly ground lemon pepper (optional)
Salad leaves, for garnish

Preheat the oven to 170°C (350°F/Gas 4). Rinse the thyme, pat dry and pick off the leaves. Heat the honey and orange juice in a small saucepan together with the thyme leaves. Simmer for about 12 minutes to reduce to a syrup.

Wash and pat dry the tomatoes. Drizzle with the olive oil, season with salt and pepper and spread on a baking tray. Bake in the oven for about 10 minutes. Remove from the oven, leave to cool, then toss with the vinegar.

Divide the goat's cheese rounds among 4 small plates and drizzle the honey and orange juice reduction on top. Garnish with orange zest to taste and sprinkle with lemon pepper or more freshly ground black pepper.

Serve with the roast cherry tomatoes, a few salad leaves and toasted white bread.

Beetroot carpaccio

Slice the beetroot (beets) very finely and arrange the slices on a large plate. Wash, trim and finely slice the spring onions. Arrange on top of the beetroot.

For the marinade, combine the red wine vinegar, oil and mustard and season with salt and pepper. Pour the marinade over the sliced beetroot and spring onions. Cover and set aside overnight to allow the flavour to develop.

Just before serving, pick through the lamb's lettuce. Wash and spin dry. Dry roast the pine nuts in a small pan. Top the carpaccio with the lettuce and garnish with the toasted pine nuts.

500g (1lb 2oz) cooked beetroot (beets)
2 spring onions (scallions)
4 tablespoons red wine vinegar
4 tablespoons olive oil
1 teaspoon mustard
Salt
Freshly ground black pepper
50g (1¾oz) lamb's lettuce (or other salad leaves)
40g (1½oz) pine nuts

Fredrik Vahle

A Snowflake's Weight

'It's snowing,' said the wolf.

'Nothing new there, old friend,' grumbled the bear.

'More than a thousand snowflakes,' said the fox, 'but I don't even feel them on my coat!'

'They melt on my hare's nose,' said the hare and then added pensively, 'you can't feel them. And yet they have a weight!'

'A single snowflake weighs less than nothing,' growled the wolf.

'And it has no power,' grumbled the bear.

'But it does weigh something, and it does have power,' objected the hare.

The animals started to argue about whether a snowflake had any weight or not.

'Let's count the snowflakes that fall on that fat old branch,' suggested the hare. 'Then we'll see whether a snowflake has any weight.'

The bear and the wolf laughed so loudly that their laughter reverberated throughout the forest. But then they helped the hare count, as they had nothing better to do. One ... two ... three ... four ... five ... six ... seven ... When they had counted to two thousand eight hundred and sixty-seven, there was a sudden, loud crack, and the fat old branch snapped.

'The hare is right,' growled the wolf, and even the bear was astounded about the snowflakes' power.

Hedwig Haberkern

Little Snowflake, Little Lace Dress

Little snowflake, little lace dress
Oh will you come down today?
You live in the snow clouds
It is such a long way.

Come and sit at the window,
You sweet little star,
Painting flowers and petals
What a dear friend you are.

Little snowflake make a blanket
Over our flowers' heads.
So they sleep safe and soundly
In their heavenly beds.

Little snowflake, little lace dress,
Our valley does call
Let us build a big snowman
And play with the ball.

Honeyed balsamic carrots
with hazelnuts and yoghurt

1.5kg (3lb 5oz) orange, red and yellow carrots
4 tablespoons olive oil, plus some extra for the yoghurt
2 tablespoons honey
1 tablespoon balsamic glaze
Sea salt
½ bunch of flat-leaf parsley
300g (10½oz) yoghurt
Juice of ½ lemon
100g (3½oz) blanched hazelnuts

Preheat the oven to 200°C (400°F/Gas 6). Wash and trim the carrots and cut them in half lengthways or leave whole if small. Add 3 tablespoons olive oil, the honey and balsamic glaze to a small bowl and whisk to combine.

Spread the carrots on a baking tray, drizzle the marinade on top and toss until coated. Season with sea salt and roast in the oven until caramelised and golden, about 40-50 minutes.

Rinse and pat dry the parsley. Pick off and coarsely chop the leaves. Combine the yoghurt with the parsley, a little oil, the lemon juice and 1 pinch of salt.

Coarsely chop the hazelnuts and roast in a frying pan with 1 tablespoon olive oil over medium heat until they start to take on colour.

Toss the carrots with the hazelnuts and serve with the yoghurt sauce on the side.

Roast pumpkin
with rocket and feta

800g (1lb 12oz) Hokkaido pumpkin (red kuri squash)
4 tablespoons olive oil
Salt
Freshly ground black pepper
1 garlic clove
1 tablespoon balsamic vinegar
1 teaspoon honey
150g (5½oz) rocket (arugula)
1 handful of walnut kernels
100g (3½oz) feta cheese
Microgreens or cress, for garnish

Preheat the oven to 200°C (400°F/Gas 6). Wash and trim the pumpkin, scoop out the seeds with a spoon and cut the flesh into thin wedges. Transfer to a baking tray and drizzle with 1 tablespoon olive oil. Season with salt and pepper and roast in the oven for 40 minutes.

Peel and mince the garlic. Whisk the balsamic vinegar, honey, garlic and remaining olive oil together in a large bowl.

Wash, pick through and spin dry the rocket. Transfer to the bowl and toss everything to combine. Divide the rocket among 4 plates and top with the roast pumpkin wedges.

Coarsely chop the walnuts and crumble the feta. Top the salad with the nuts and cheese and serve garnished with cress.

Classic potato cake

Peel and coarsely grate the potatoes. Peel and dice the onions. Rinse the chives, pat dry and slice thinly. Clean and trim the mushrooms and wipe them with kitchen paper, if necessary, then slice.

Whisk the eggs with the milk and flour in a bowl. Stir in the sliced chives. Season with salt, pepper and nutmeg.

Heat the butter in a large pan. Add the grated potatoes and diced onion and sweat. After 5 minutes, add the egg mixture and allow to set over low heat.

Heat the oil in another pan. Add the sliced mushrooms and fry. Season with salt and pepper. Add to the potato cake, then divide the potato cake and mushrooms among 4 plates to serve.

750g (1lb 10oz) waxy potatoes
2 onions
1 bunch of chives
400g (14oz) button mushrooms
3 eggs
250ml (9fl oz) milk
100g (3½oz) plain (all-purpose) flour
1 teaspoon salt
1 pinch of freshly ground black pepper
1 teaspoon freshly grated nutmeg
4 tablespoons butter
2 tablespoons vegetable oil

The Legend of Santa Claus

A very long time ago, around the year 270, a child named Nicholas was born in the city of Patara in Asia Minor.

The boy grew up in a very wealthy, loving family, and when his parents died of illness, they left him a great fortune in gold, silver, jewels, land, palaces and horses. But Nicholas, stricken with grief, did not know what to do with his wealth and began to share his possessions with the city's poor. One day, he heard of a poor man and his three daughters who had no money at all. Out of love for her sisters, the eldest daughter offered to leave home and work as a maid so that at least her two sisters would have enough money to survive. Hearing of this selfless offer, Nicholas snuck to the family's home at night and threw a small bag of gold through an open window. When the father found the gift on the floor the next morning, he was overjoyed because it meant that his family could stay together!

This good deed is the reason why many people still hang socks by the fireplace or leave shoes on the doorstep on the eve of St Nicholas Day. They won't find them filled with gold the next morning, but they will be stuffed with nuts, mandarins and other treats.

St Nicholas is the patron saint of children, but also of merchants and sailors. When, during a great famine, news spread that three of the emperor's ships, laden with wheat, were anchored in the port of the city of Myra, Nicholas asked the sailors to unload some of the grain and give it to the starving. But they refused, fearing that the emperor would notice — after all, the grain had been carefully weighed. But Nicholas told them, 'Everything will be all right! Do as I say and trust in God!' And indeed, the sailors gave him the grain he had asked for. Nicholas distributed it to the starving people in the city and in the countryside. Meanwhile, the three ships continued their journey, and the sailors were surprised that their cargo had not lost weight. And indeed, when the wheat was weighed, not a single grain was missing. News of the event rapidly spread throughout Asia Minor and beyond.

To this day, images of this miracle can be found in many churches, especially in port cities.

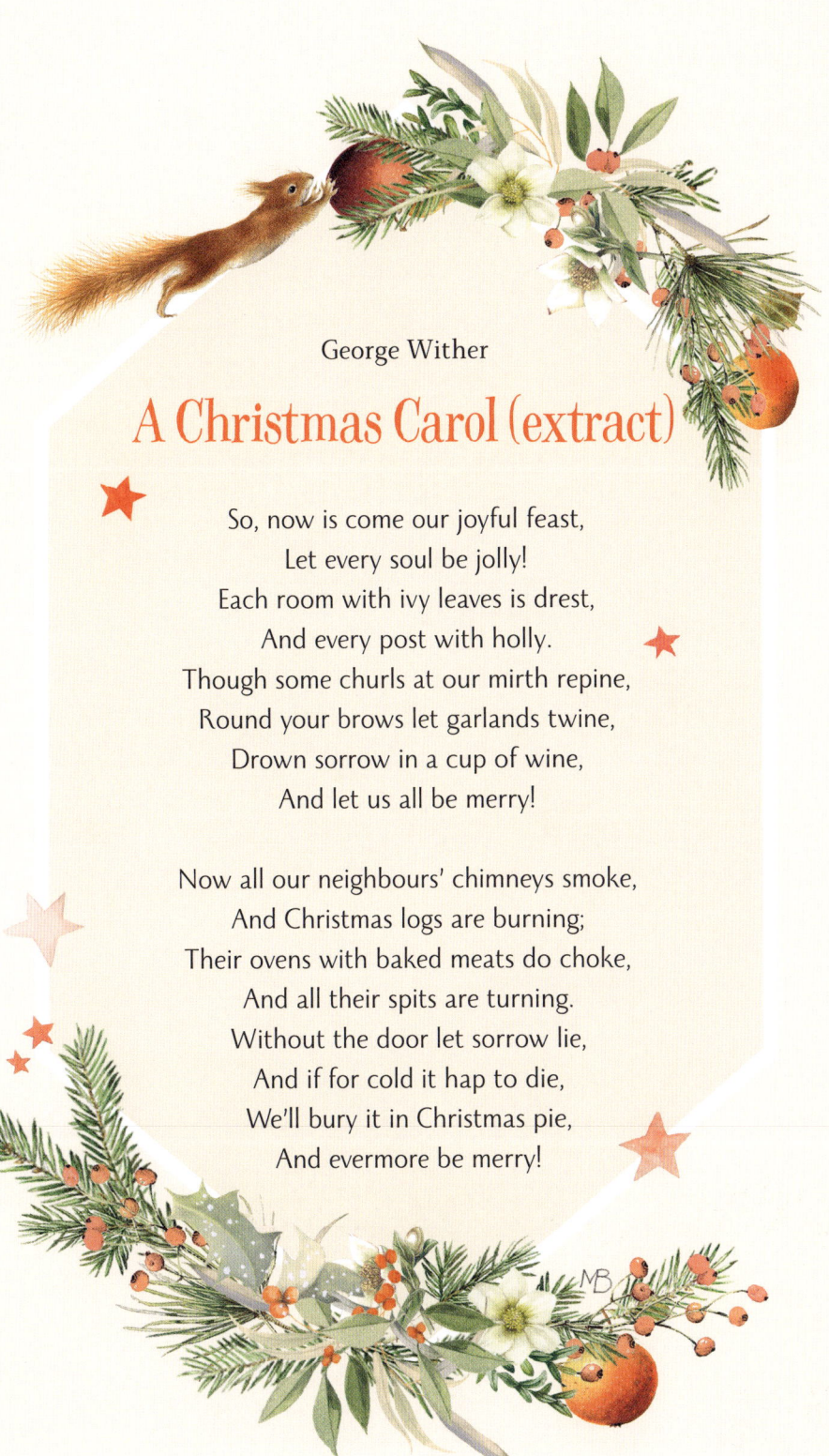

George Wither

A Christmas Carol (extract)

So, now is come our joyful feast,
Let every soul be jolly!
Each room with ivy leaves is drest,
And every post with holly.
Though some churls at our mirth repine,
Round your brows let garlands twine,
Drown sorrow in a cup of wine,
And let us all be merry!

Now all our neighbours' chimneys smoke,
And Christmas logs are burning;
Their ovens with baked meats do choke,
And all their spits are turning.
Without the door let sorrow lie,
And if for cold it hap to die,
We'll bury it in Christmas pie,
And evermore be merry!

Spinach and salmon quiche

½ bunch of parsley
3 eggs
250g (9oz) plain (all-purpose) flour
Salt
100g (3½oz) butter, at room temperature
500g (1lb 2oz) spinach (put a few leaves aside for garnish)
300g (10½oz) cream cheese
125ml (4fl oz) milk
100ml (3½fl oz) vegetable stock
100g (3½oz) sour cream
1 garlic clove
½ bunch of dill
Freshly ground black pepper
200g (7oz) smoked salmon

Also

Quiche dish

Rinse and pat dry the parsley. Pick off and chop the leaves. Separate 1 egg and set aside the egg white.

Combine the egg yolk, flour, 1 pinch of salt, butter, 6 tablespoons water and parsley in a bowl and knead to make a dough. Wrap the dough in cling film and refrigerate for 30 minutes.

Preheat the oven to 200°C (400°F/Gas 6).

Wash the spinach. Bring water to the boil in a large saucepan, add salt and blanch the spinach in the water for 2 minutes. Refresh under cold water, drain and chop coarsely.

Whisk the cream cheese, milk, vegetable stock, sour cream, egg white and 2 whole eggs in a bowl. Peel and mince the garlic. Rinse, pat dry and chop the dill. Stir the minced garlic and chopped dill into the cream cheese mixture. Season with salt and pepper.

Line a quiche dish with baking paper or grease with oil. Roll out the dough and transfer it to the dish, making sure to press it into the edges. Spread the spinach and salmon evenly across the pastry base and top with the cream cheese mixture. Bake in the oven for about 50 minutes.

Serve garnished with a few spinach leaves.

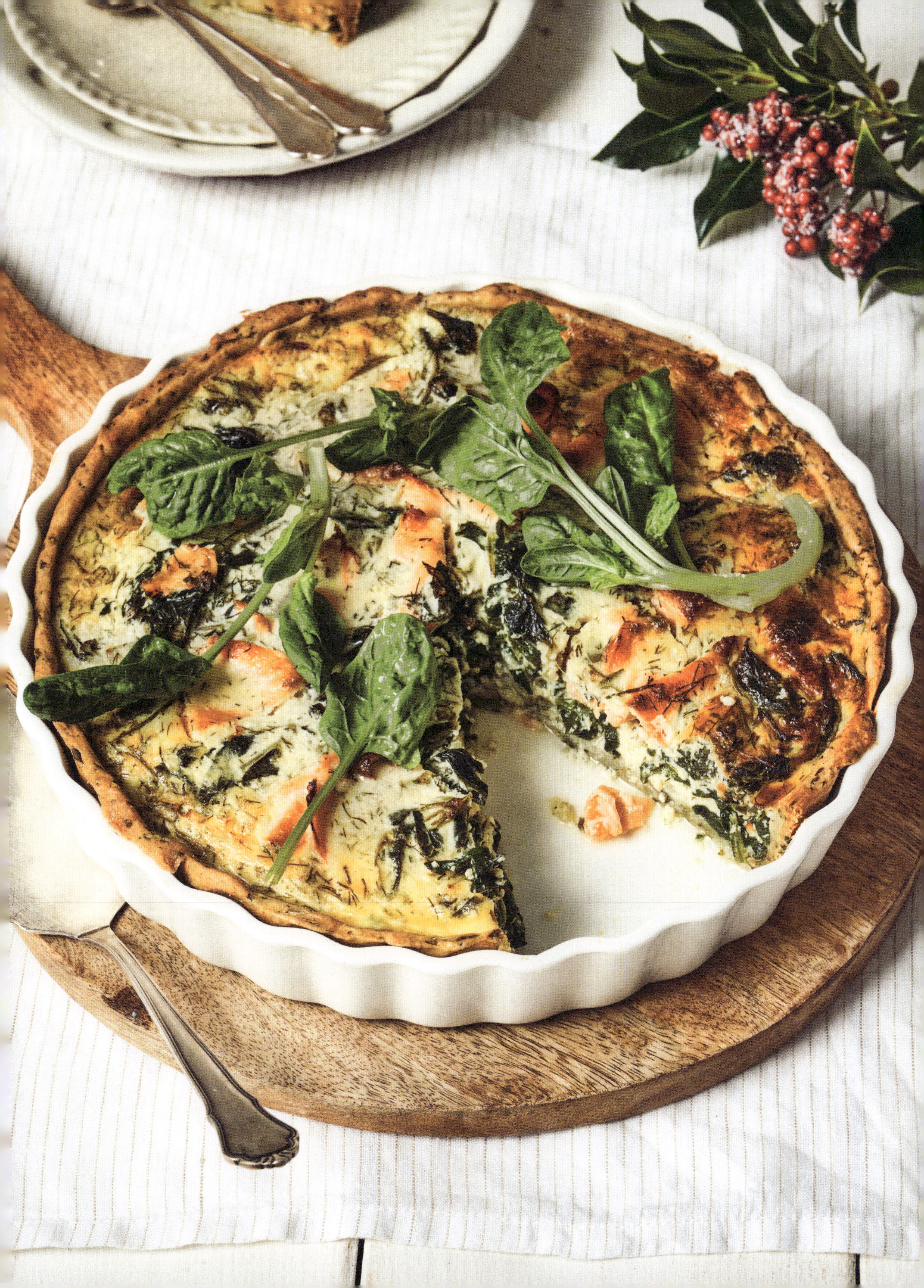

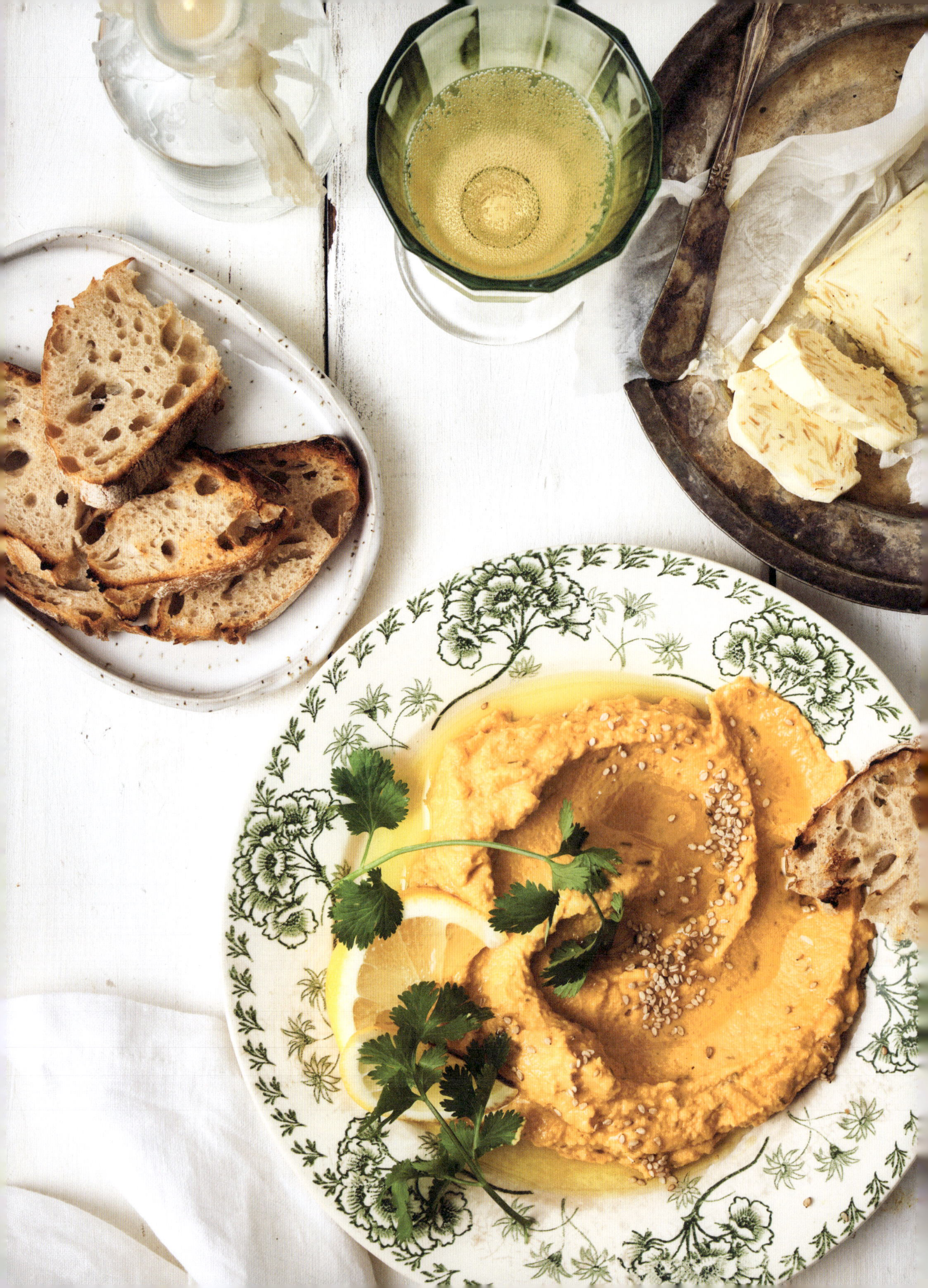

Carrot hummus
with cumin

Peel and coarsely chop the carrots. Transfer to a saucepan. Add enough water to just cover the carrots. Bring to a boil and cook until soft, about 8–10 minutes. Drain the carrots and season with salt and pepper.

Peel and coarsely chop the garlic. Rinse the chickpeas in a colander and drain well. Thoroughly blend the carrots, chickpeas, garlic, oil, tahini, lemon juice and cumin with a stick blender or in a food processor.

Garnish with coriander, sesame seeds and lemon wedges.

3 large carrots
Salt
Freshly ground black pepper
1 garlic clove
400g (14oz) chickpeas (from a tin)
3 tablespoons olive oil
2 tablespoons tahini (from a jar)
Juice of ½ lemon
1 teaspoon ground cumin
A little coriander (cilantro), sesame seeds and lemon wedges, for garnish

Saffron and almond butter

Finely chop the almonds. Combine the chopped almonds, oil and saffron threads in a small saucepan and warm for 1–2 minutes. Remove from the heat and set aside to cool.

Transfer the almond mixture to a bowl, add the butter and use a fork to combine everything well. Stir in the salt, lemon zest and juice to make a soft butter. Transfer the mixture onto a piece of parchment paper, shape into a log and seal the ends well. Refrigerate the butter for at least 1 hour to set before serving.

Tip: These spreads make a heavenly topping for ciabatta bread!

40g (1½oz) blanched almonds
1 teaspoon olive oil
½ teaspoon saffron threads
125g (4½oz) butter, at room temperature
½ teaspoon coarse sea salt
Zest and juice of ½ lemon

Garlic and porcini mushroom pull-apart bread

with a feta and mushroom spread

For the pull-apart bread

5 garlic cloves
4 spring onions (scallions)
150g (5½oz) butter, at room temperature
Salt
Freshly ground black pepper
250g (9oz) fresh porcini mushrooms
150g (5½oz) gouda cheese
1 loaf of rustic sourdough bread (750g/1lb 10oz)

For the feta and mushroom spread

100g (3½oz) button mushrooms
1 tablespoon butter
100g (3½oz) feta cheese
50g (1¾oz) crème fraîche
100g (3½oz) yoghurt
½ red onion
3 sprigs of basil
4 sprigs of flat-leaf parsley
Salt
Freshly ground black pepper
½ teaspoon chilli flakes
A little lemon juice

For the pull-apart bread, peel and very finely mince the garlic. Wash, trim and finely slice the spring onions. Combine both with the butter in a small bowl and season with salt and pepper. Trim the porcini mushrooms and wipe them with kitchen paper, if necessary, then slice. Grate the gouda cheese.

Preheat the oven to 180°C (350°F/Gas 4).

Score the bread in a grid pattern, making sure not to cut all the way through. Push the sliced mushrooms and grated cheese into the gaps. Spread the sides of the cuts and the top of the bread with the butter mixture. Bake in the oven for 20-25 minutes. If the bread starts to brown before the cheese has melted, cover it with aluminium foil.

For the spread, wipe the button mushrooms with kitchen paper, if necessary, then trim and finely chop. Heat the butter in a pan, add the mushrooms and fry briefly. Set aside to cool.

Crumble the feta into a bowl and combine with the crème fraîche and yoghurt. Peel and finely dice the onion. Rinse and pat dry the basil and parsley. Pick off and finely chop the leaves.

Stir the onion and herbs into the crème fraîche mixture, then add the chopped mushrooms. Season with salt, pepper, chilli flakes and lemon juice.

Remove the bread from the oven and serve immediately with the feta and mushroom spread.

Tip: If you can't source porcini muschrooms, it's fine to substitute chanterelle or king oyster mushrooms.

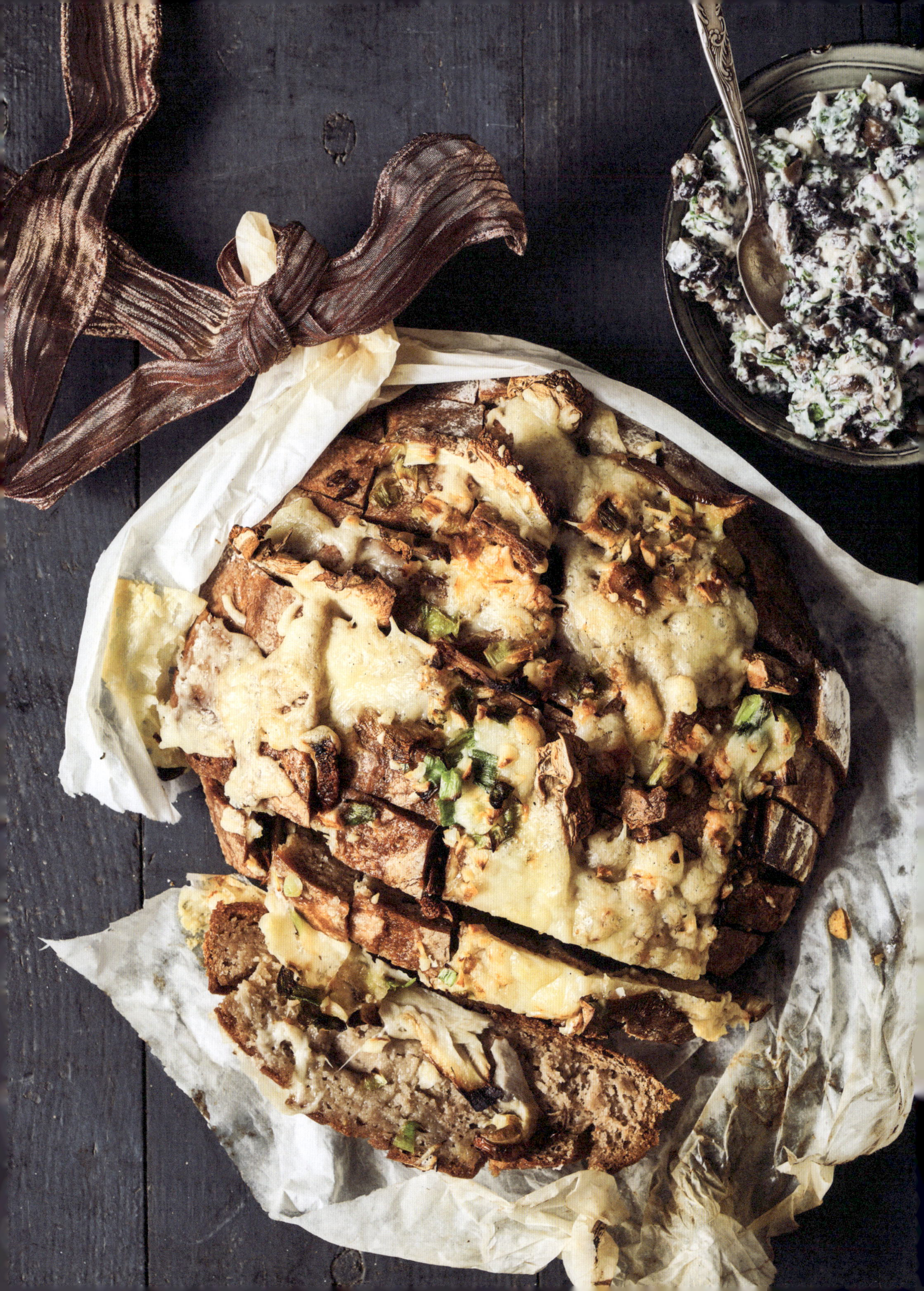

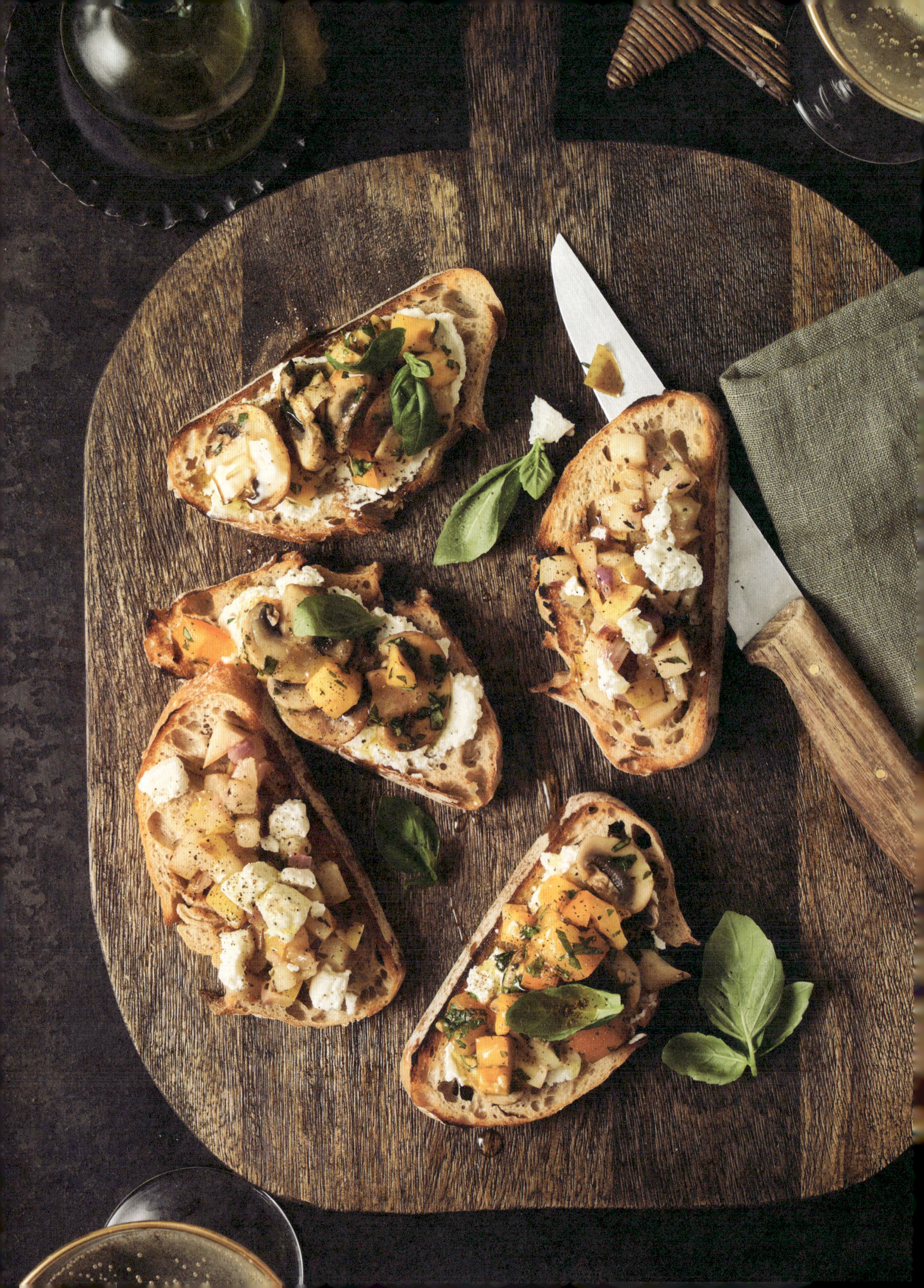

Festive bruschetta two ways

Bruschetta with pear and goat's cheese

Preheat the grill in the oven. Peel and halve the garlic clove.

Toast the baguette slices for about 5 minutes under the grill. Remove, rub with the garlic clove halves and drizzle with a little olive oil.

Rinse and pat dry the rosemary and thyme. Pick off the leaves and chop finely. Wash, core and finely dice the pear. Peel and finely dice the onion.

Melt the butter in a pan. Add the diced pear, onion, chopped rosemary and thyme and sweat. Season with salt and pepper.

Divide the mixture among the slices of baguette and crumble the goat's cheese on top.

1 garlic clove
8 slices of baguette
3 tablespoons olive oil
1 sprig of rosemary
1 sprig of thyme
1 pear
1 onion
1 teaspoon butter
Salt
Freshly ground black pepper
80g (2¾oz) goat's cheese

Tomato and mushroom bruschetta

Preheat the oven to 200°C (400°F/Gas 6). Peel and halve the garlic clove.

Drizzle 2 tablespoons olive oil over the baguette slices and rub them with the garlic clove halves. Transfer to a baking tray and toast in the oven until golden brown, about 10 minutes.

Wash the tomatoes, remove the stem bases and dice. Wipe the button mushrooms with kitchen paper, if necessary, then trim and slice.

Heat 2 tablespoons olive oil in a pan and briefly fry the mushrooms. Combine with the tomatoes in a bowl and season generously with salt and pepper.

Rinse and pat dry the basil. Pick off the leaves and chop finely. Add to the mushrooms together with the remaining olive oil. Spread the slices of baguette with the ricotta. Top with the tomatoes and mushrooms and serve.

1 garlic clove
8 slices of baguette
10 tablespoons olive oil
4 yellow tomatoes
100g (3½oz) button mushrooms
Salt
Freshly ground black pepper
1 bunch of basil
150g (5½oz) ricotta cheese

Tip: You can also toast the slices of baguette in a frying pan.

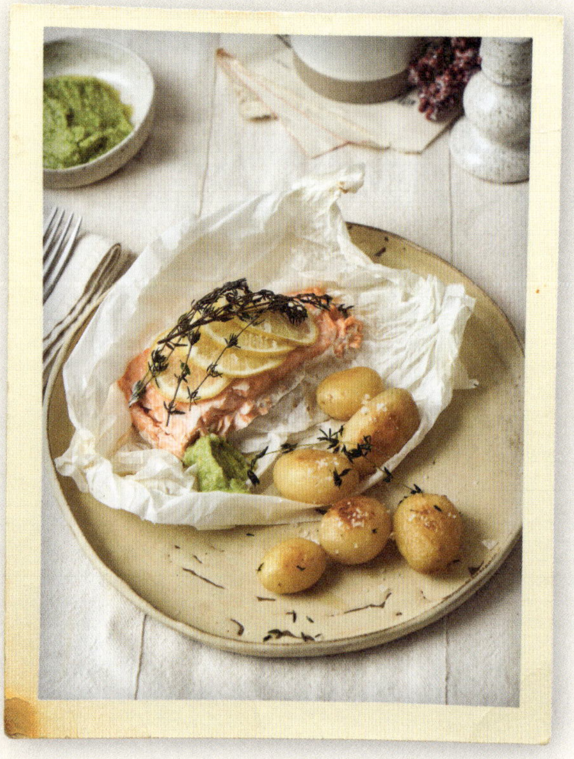

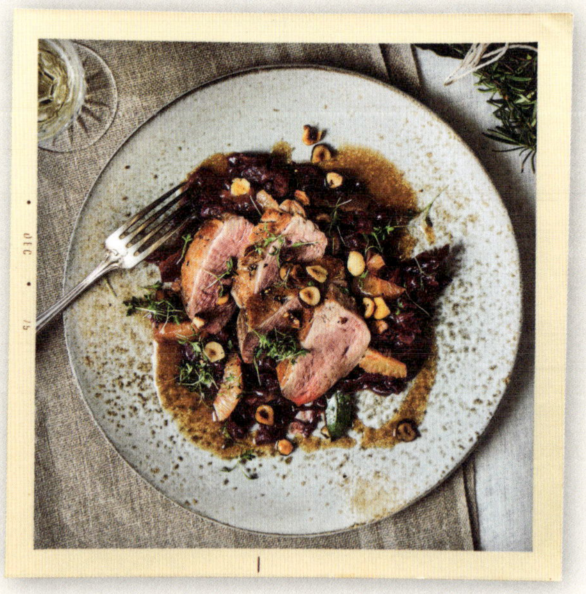

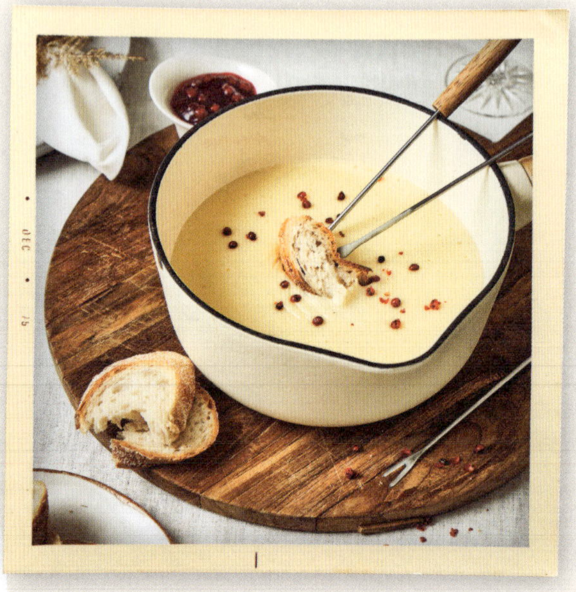

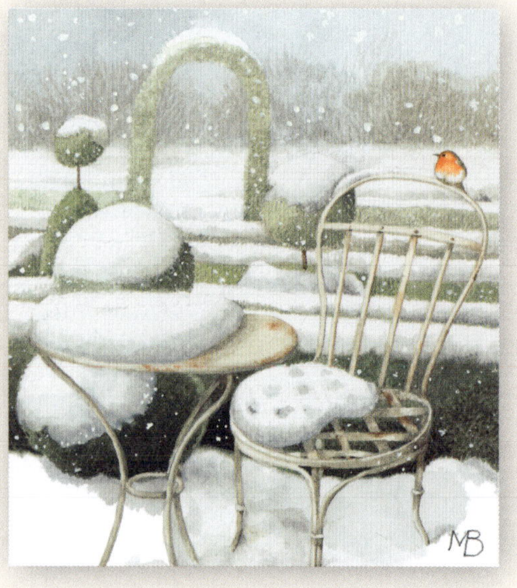

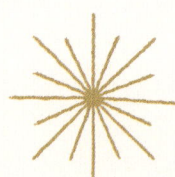

Magical
mains

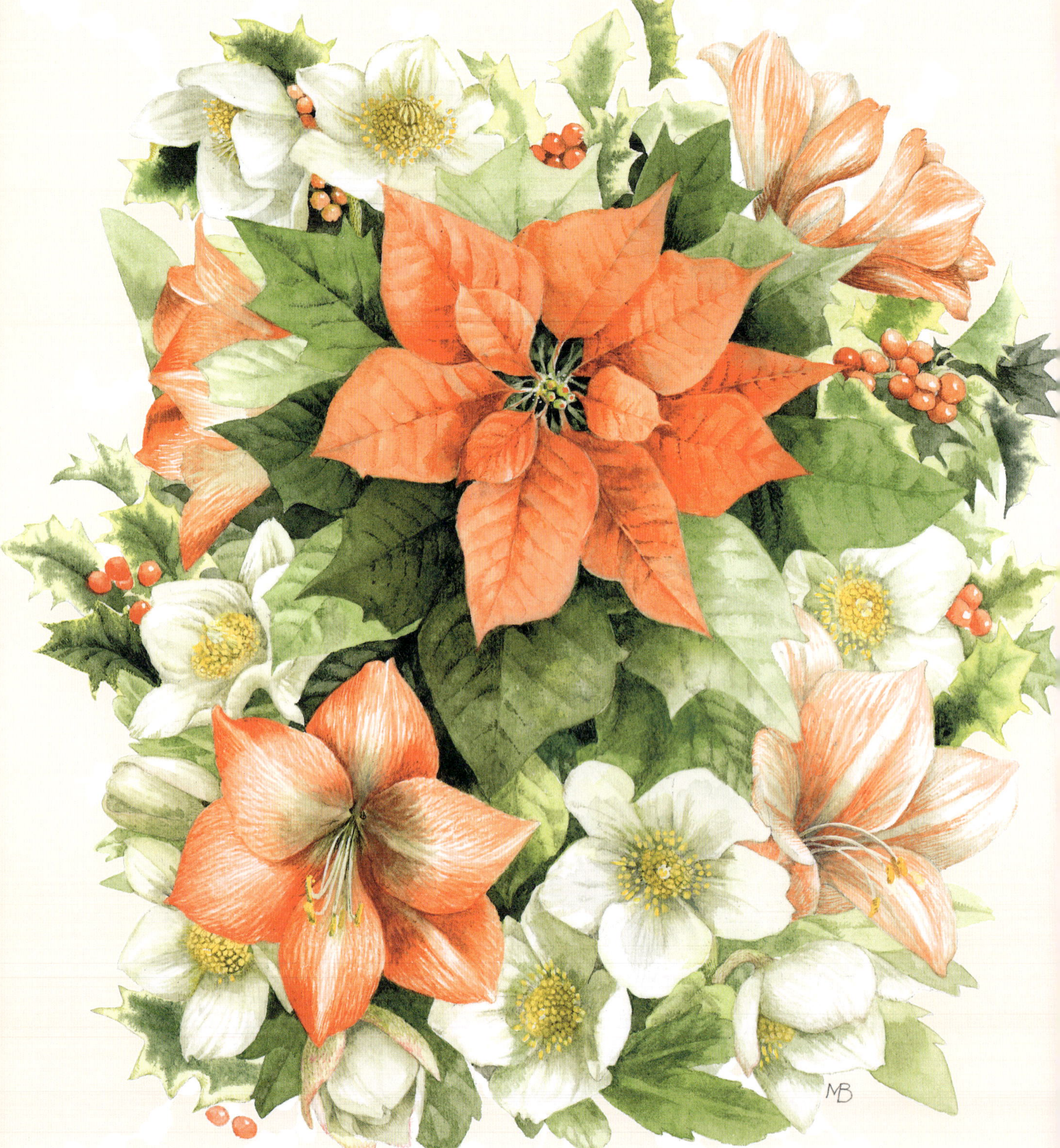
MB

Sophie Reinheimer

Ice Flowers

Now there was not a single colourful flower left outside, the garden beds had been covered with pine branches, the rose bushes had been tucked away under warm straw hoods, and the flowers outside the windows had long since withered and been taken away.

'What a shame,' said the sofa, which sat quite comfortably behind the large dining table in the living room and had a good view of the window. 'It was so nice when the flowers nodded at us and told us everything that was going on outside in the street.' The other furniture agreed. The table said we shouldn't complain, because this was just the beginning of the cosy time for the living room! In summer, people ran this way and that, out into the garden, the woods and the fields. In winter, however, they stayed together nicely in the living room, telling each other stories or reading to each other, and so they — the furniture — actually heard even more than when they relied on the flowers. That was true. But the room had looked nicer with the flowers, everyone agreed.

Now, listen to hear about the big surprise the furniture had one morning a few weeks later. It was bitterly cold outside, and it had even got very cold in the living room overnight, so cold that the furniture envied the beds in the bedroom, which had warm feather duvets to cover themselves with. Just as the cupboard woke up from its slumber, it made a loud cracking noise in surprise. This woke up all the other furniture, and what did they see? The whole window was covered from top to bottom with a snow-white, glittering crust. This was no ordinary, smooth ice. It made very unusual shapes like flowers, leaves, stems, but all mixed up, sometimes hard to make out.

'What could that be?' the sofa asked quietly. It was completely dazed by the glistening white splendour. 'Maybe the glazier came overnight and secretly changed the windows?'

'Maybe it's a bit like the witch's cottage in *Hansel and Gretel*,' said the mirror cabinet. 'I think the witch on my shelf has turned the glass into sugar.'

At the word 'sugar', the little black fly that also lived in the room quickly flew off, but it soon returned, disappointed. 'No — it's not sugar,' it said. 'It doesn't taste the tiniest bit sweet! But it's as rough as sugar, that's true.'

'I think it's flowers,' said the watering can.

The stovepipe, which was always a little up itself, cut in, 'Don't talk nonsense!' But everyone else in the room agreed with the little watering can. Indeed — but who had magically painted the windows with those strange snow-white flowers at the crack of dawn? The furniture would have loved to know! But the window, the only one that would have known first-hand, remained completely silent — whether because it was so enchanted, or because someone had bewitched it along with the white flowers, was impossible to say.

But listen — suddenly there was singing in the street, 'Winter has brought an abundance of flowers overnight. They're ice flowers, they're ice flowers — didn't you guess? Winter sent a whole load of them this morning, straight from the North Pole, freshly picked, freshly picked, as you can see! In the sunshine, Winter scatters them on every window. Oooh — the people marvel at their beauty! Hui hihi ...'

Pumpkin risotto
with sage butter and caramelised chestnuts

For the chestnuts

2 handfuls of chestnuts
1 tablespoon butter
2 tablespoons honey

For the risotto

1kg (2lb 4oz) Hokkaido pumpkin (red kuri squash)
1 cinnamon stick
5 tablespoons olive oil
1 garlic clove
1 onion
300g (10½oz) risotto rice
200ml (7fl oz) dry white wine
1 litre (35fl oz) hot vegetable stock
100g (3½oz) Parmesan cheese, plus more for serving
Salt
Freshly ground black pepper
1 bunch of sage
3-4 tablespoons butter

Preheat the oven to 200°C (400°F/Gas 6).

Score the chestnuts crossways and soak them in a bowl of water for 5-10 minutes. Place the chestnuts on a baking tray, scored side up, and bake them in the oven for 15-20 minutes. When the chestnuts are cool enough to handle, peel them by hand and coarsely chop them.

Melt the butter and honey in a pan, add the chopped chestnuts and caramelise over medium heat. Remove and set aside to cool.

Wash and trim the pumpkin, scoop out the seeds with a spoon, then cut the flesh into wedges. Break the cinnamon stick and finely grind it in a mortar. Brush the pumpkin wedges with 3 tablespoons olive oil. Transfer to a baking dish and sprinkle with the cinnamon. Cook in the oven for 40-45 minutes.

Peel and mince the garlic and onion. Heat the remaining oil in a large pan. Sauté the onion and garlic until translucent, add the rice, sauté briefly and then deglaze with the white wine.

Gradually add just enough stock to cover the rice. Cook the rice over medium heat, stirring continuously. As soon as the stock is almost absorbed by the rice, add more stock, ladle by ladle, until the rice is fully cooked.

Remove the pumpkin from the oven, cut into bite-sized pieces and add to the cooked rice. Remove the saucepan from the heat.

Grate the Parmesan, stir in and season everything with salt and pepper. Rinse the sage, pat dry and pick off the leaves. Melt the butter in a pan, then fry the sage leaves for 1-2 minutes.

Divide the pumpkin risotto among plates and sprinkle with the caramelised chestnuts, sage leaves and more Parmesan before serving.

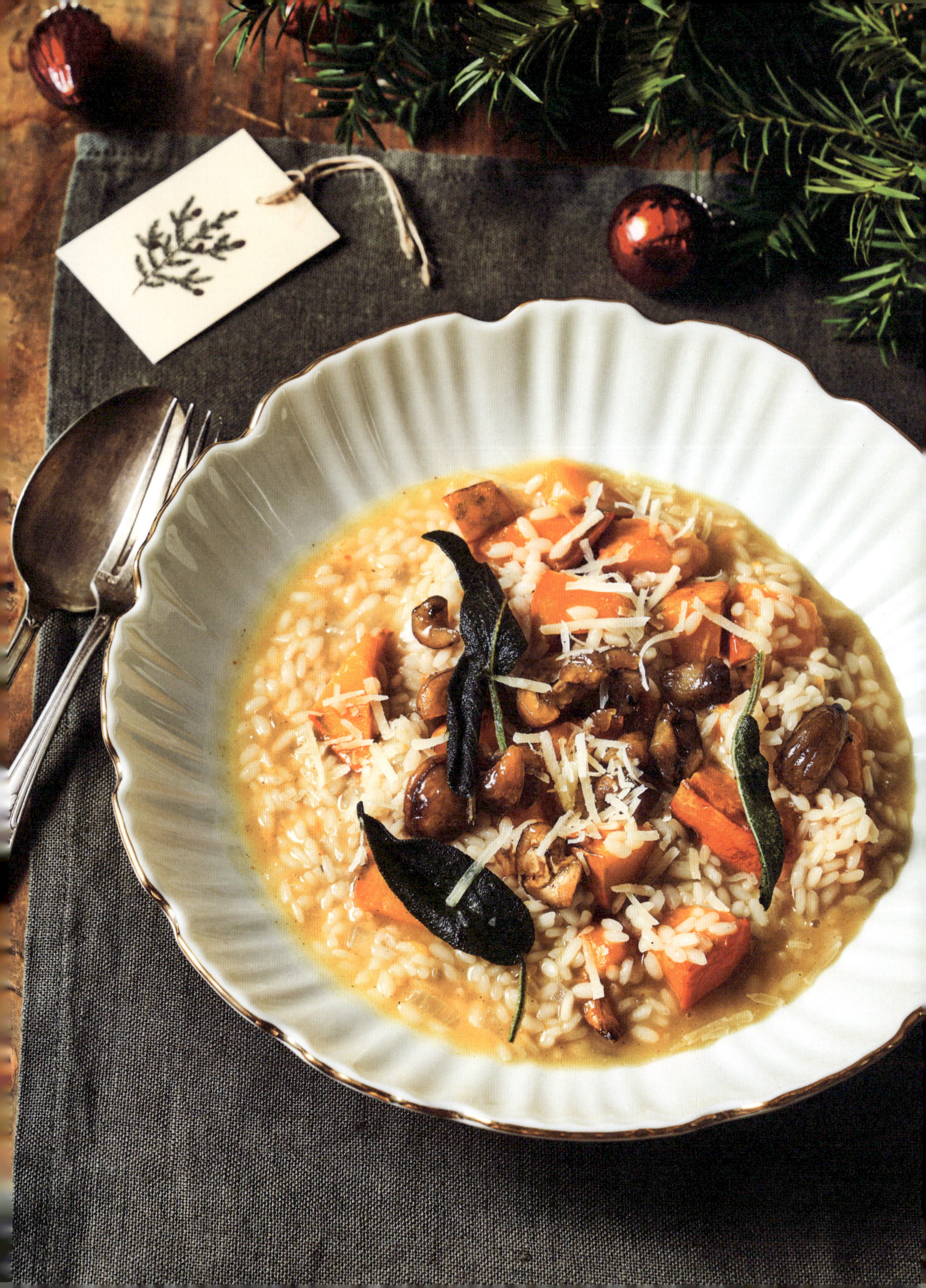

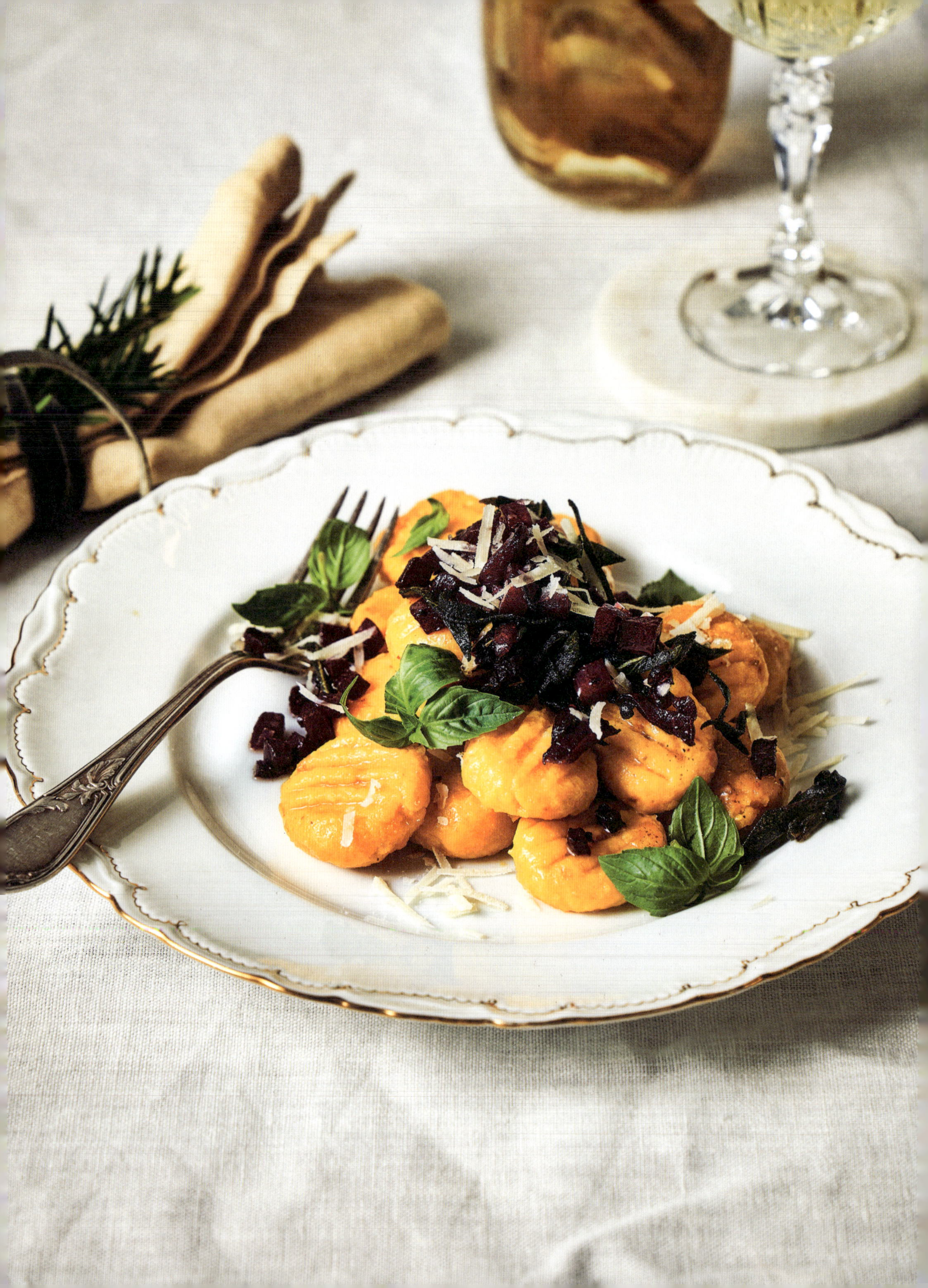

Pumpkin gnocchi with beetroot in sage butter

Preheat the oven to 200°C (400°F/Gas 6).

Wash and trim the pumpkin, scrape out the seeds with a spoon and cut the flesh into 6 wedges. Place the wedges on a baking tray lined with baking paper and bake in the oven for 35 minutes.

Meanwhile, bring a saucepan of salted water to the boil. Add the potatoes and boil them for 20 minutes. Drain, set aside to cool slightly, peel and press through a potato ricer into a bowl.

Remove the pumpkin from the oven, also set aside to cool slightly, then mash and add to the potatoes. Season with salt, pepper, nutmeg and lemon juice. Add the egg yolk and semolina and mix with a wooden spoon until well combined and pliable. If the mixture is too sticky, add a little flour.

Shape the potato and pumpkin mixture into several 2cm (¾ inch) thick logs, cut these into 2cm (¾ inch) pieces and shape the gnocchi into little pillows with floured palms. Transfer to a floured baking tray and gently roll the back of a fork across each pillow.

Bring a large pot of salted water to the boil. Cook the gnocchi in batches for 2–3 minutes each, until they rise to the surface. Remove with a slotted spoon and set aside to cool.

Dice the beetroot (beets). Peel and halve the garlic cloves. Crush gently with the back of a knife. Cut the sage leaves into strips. Rinse the basil and pat dry; grate the Parmesan into thin shavings.

Heat 1 tablespoon oil and 1 teaspoon butter in a pan. Add the beetroot, garlic and sage and fry for 5 minutes. Set aside. Wipe out the pan. Heat the remaining oil and butter and briefly toss the gnocchi in it.

Gently toss the beetroot with the gnocchi. Serve immediately, topped with the basil and Parmesan.

For the pumpkin gnocchi

1kg (2lb 4oz) Hokkaido pumpkin (red kuri squash)
Salt
500g (1lb 2oz) potatoes (all-purpose)
Freshly ground black pepper
Freshly grated nutmeg
1 dash of lemon juice
1 egg yolk
4 tablespoons semolina

For the beetroot

500g (1lb 2oz) cooked beetroot (beets)
2 garlic cloves
20 sage leaves
2 tablespoons oil
2 teaspoons butter

Also

Plain (all-purpose) flour, for dusting
10 basil leaves
120g (4¼oz) Parmesan cheese
Potato ricer

Pumpkin and beetroot Wellingtons
with kale pesto

For the pumpkin and beetroot Wellingtons

1 red onion
250g (9oz) beetroot (beets)
½ butternut pumpkin (squash) (about 400g/14oz)
5 garlic cloves
2 tablespoons olive oil
1 tablespoon dried thyme
1 tablespoon sumac, plus a little extra for garnish
250g (9oz) cooked Puy lentils
Salt
3 sheets of puff pastry (about 500g/1lb 2oz)
2 tablespoons almond milk

For the kale pesto

180g (6½oz) precooked chestnuts
½ lemon
100g (3½oz) kale
4 tablespoons olive oil
Sea salt

Preheat the oven to 190°C (375°F/Gas 5).

For the pumpkin and beetroot (beet) Wellingtons, peel the onion and cut it into 8 wedges. Peel and dice the beetroot; peel the pumpkin, scrape out the seeds with a spoon and dice the flesh. Gently crush the garlic cloves with the skin on and combine the vegetables with the garlic, olive oil, thyme and sumac in a bowl. Spread everything evenly on a baking tray and roast in the oven for 45 minutes.

When the vegetables are soft, peel and mash the garlic cloves. In a bowl, mix half of the mashed garlic with the lentils and roasted vegetables, season with salt and leave everything to cool completely.

For the kale pesto, roughly chop the chestnuts. Juice the lemon. Bring a small pan of water to the boil and blanch the kale for 2 minutes, then drain and squeeze out any excess water. Blend everything with the remaining garlic, olive oil and a little sea salt to make a thick pesto.

Preheat the oven again to 190°C (375°F/Gas 5).

For the Wellingtons, join and then cut the three sheets of puff pastry to make two rectangles. Spread one half of each rectangle with the kale pesto and top with the lentil and vegetable filling. Brush the edges with a little almond milk, fold over and seal well.

Transfer the Wellingtons to a baking tray lined with baking paper. Brush with almond milk, sprinkle with sumac and bake in the oven for 30-40 minutes until golden brown.

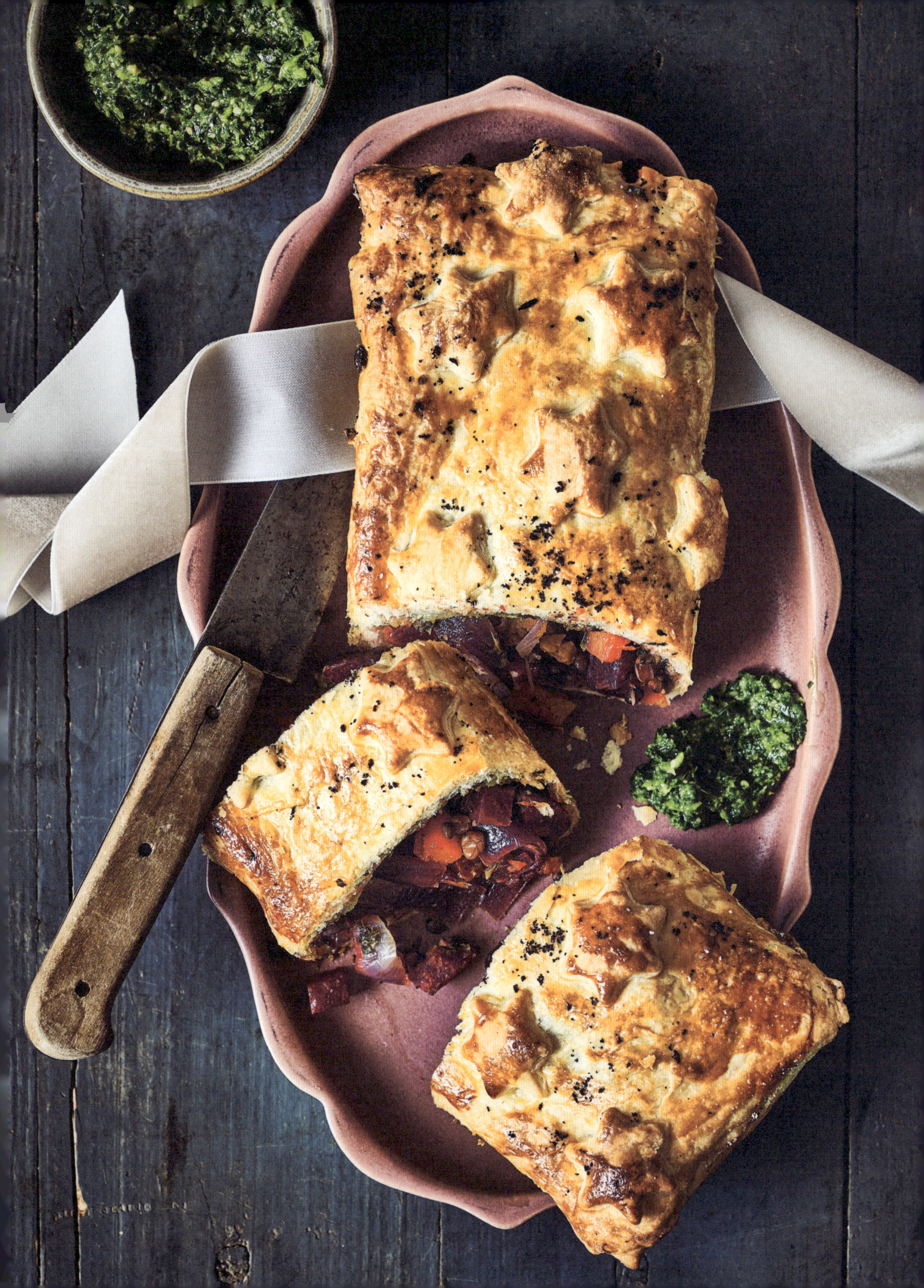

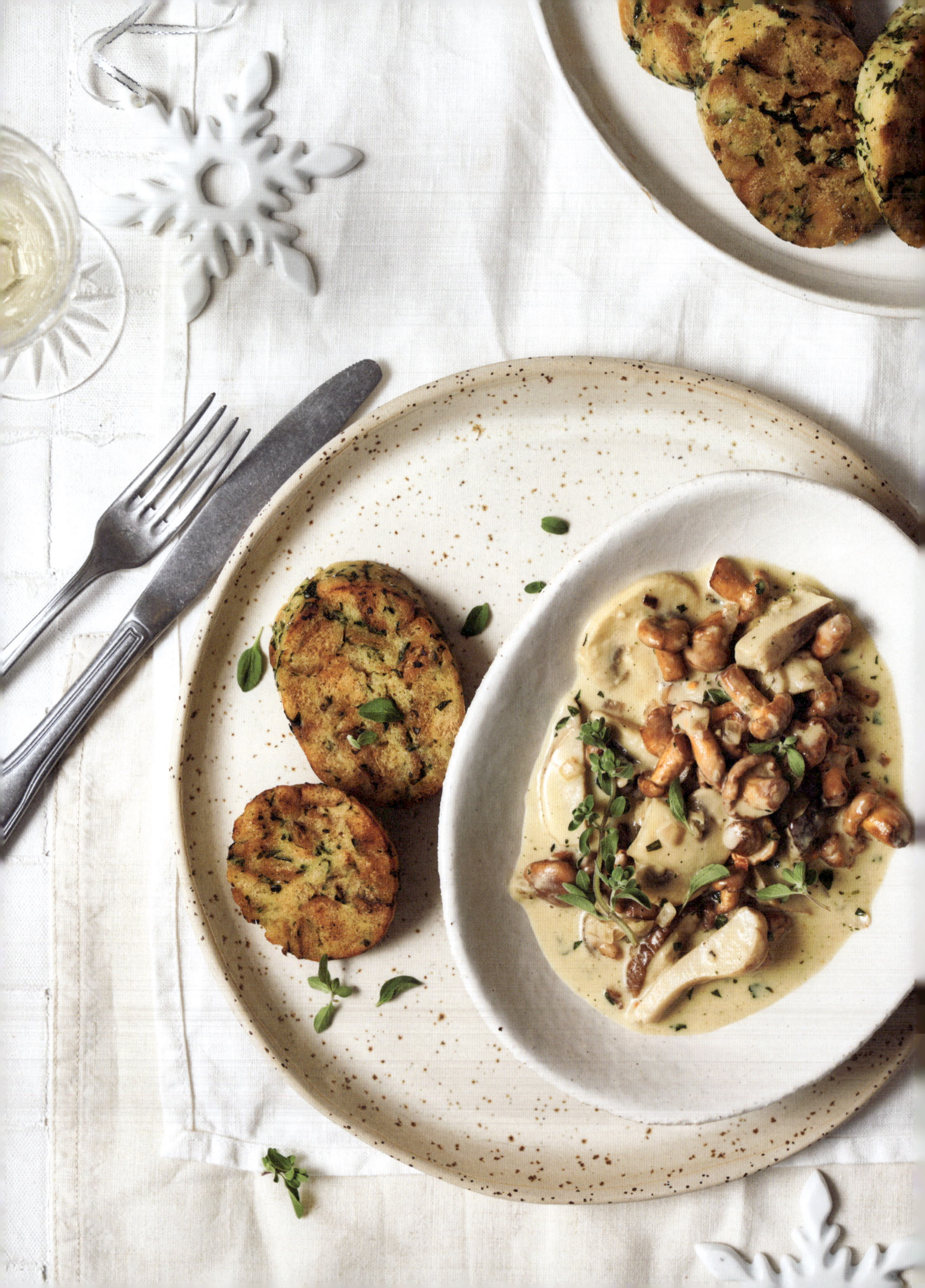

Bread dumpling with mushroom ragout

For the dumpling, cut the bread into small cubes. Melt the butter in a pan and fry the bread cubes until golden brown. Set aside to cool. Carefully separate the eggs. In a large bowl, combine the flour with the egg yolks and salt using the dough hook(s) of a hand or stand mixer. Gradually add the milk to make a pliable dough. Rinse and pat dry the parsley. Pick off and finely chop the leaves. Mix into the dough together with the toasted bread cubes. Beat the egg whites until stiff and fold in gently.

Bring a wide pot of salted water to the boil. Shape the dough into a loaf. Wrap the loaf tightly in cling film and then in a layer of aluminium foil. Simmer in the salted water over a low heat for 30 minutes.

For the ragout, gently trim the mushrooms and wipe them with kitchen paper, if necessary. Halve the smaller mushrooms and cut the larger ones into slices. Peel and finely dice the shallots. Rinse and pat dry the parsley. Pick off and chop the leaves. Grate the gouda cheese.

Heat the oil in a pan, sauté the shallots until translucent, remove and set aside. Add the mushrooms to the same pan over high heat and fry, stirring continuously, until most of the liquid has evaporated. Pour in the cream and simmer uncovered over a low heat for a few minutes. Add the gouda just before the end. Season with salt and pepper. Stir in the parsley.

Remove the dumpling and drain well. Unwrap and cut into thick slices, then serve with the ragout.

Tip: If you prefer moister dumplings, melt the butter in a small saucepan and then pour over the dumpling slices to serve. If you have leftover dumpling slices, fry them in butter the next day until crispy — delicious!

For the bread dumpling

180g (6½oz) sliced white bread
100g (3½oz) butter
2 eggs
300g (10½oz) plain (all-purpose) flour
Salt
80ml (2½fl oz) milk
1 bunch of flat-leaf parsley

For the mushroom ragout

800g (1lb 12oz) mixed mushrooms
2 French shallots
1 bunch of flat-leaf parsley
50g (1¾oz) mature gouda cheese
2 tablespoons olive oil
200ml (7fl oz) single (pure) cream
Salt
Freshly ground black pepper

Also

100g (3½oz) butter
Hand or stand mixer

Nut roast with sweet potato and chestnut mash

For the nut roast

150g (5½oz) nuts of your choice
100g (3½oz) pistachio kernels
100g (3½oz) carrots
1 onion
2 garlic cloves
200g (7oz) precooked chestnuts
2 sprigs of rosemary
2 sprigs of thyme
60g (2¼oz) Parmesan cheese
2 slices of wholemeal toast
Grated zest of ½ lemon
2 eggs
25g (1oz) mustard
2 tablespoons soy sauce
100g (3½oz) marmalade
Salt
2 tablespoons butter

For the sweet potato and chestnut mash

150g (5½oz) sweet potatoes
150g (5½oz) floury potatoes
Salt
1 cinnamon stick
75ml (2½fl oz) hot milk
100g (3½oz) precooked chestnuts
Freshly ground black pepper
3 pinches of freshly grated nutmeg

Also

Large loaf tin

For the roast, finely chop the nuts and pistachios and dry roast in a frying pan. Set aside to cool.

Peel and grate the carrots. Peel and mince the onion and garlic. Finely chop the chestnuts. Rinse the herbs and pat dry. Pick off the leaves and chop finely.

Grate the Parmesan. Cut the wholemeal toast into small cubes. Preheat the oven to 180°C (350°F/Gas 4). Line a loaf tin with baking paper.

Place all the ingredients for the roast, except the butter, in a bowl and knead well to combine. Transfer the mixture to the loaf tin, press down gently to level and cover with aluminium foil. Bake in the oven for 30 minutes.

Remove the aluminium foil, dot the roast with pats of butter and bake for a further 20 minutes.

For the mash, peel and coarsely dice the sweet potato and potato. Bring salted water to the boil in a saucepan. Add the cubed potatoes and the cinnamon stick, cover and cook for 20 minutes. Drain the potatoes, remove the cinnamon stick, add the hot milk and chestnuts and mash everything. Season with salt, pepper and nutmeg.

To serve, turn the roast out of the tin, cut into slices and divide among 4 plates together with the mash.

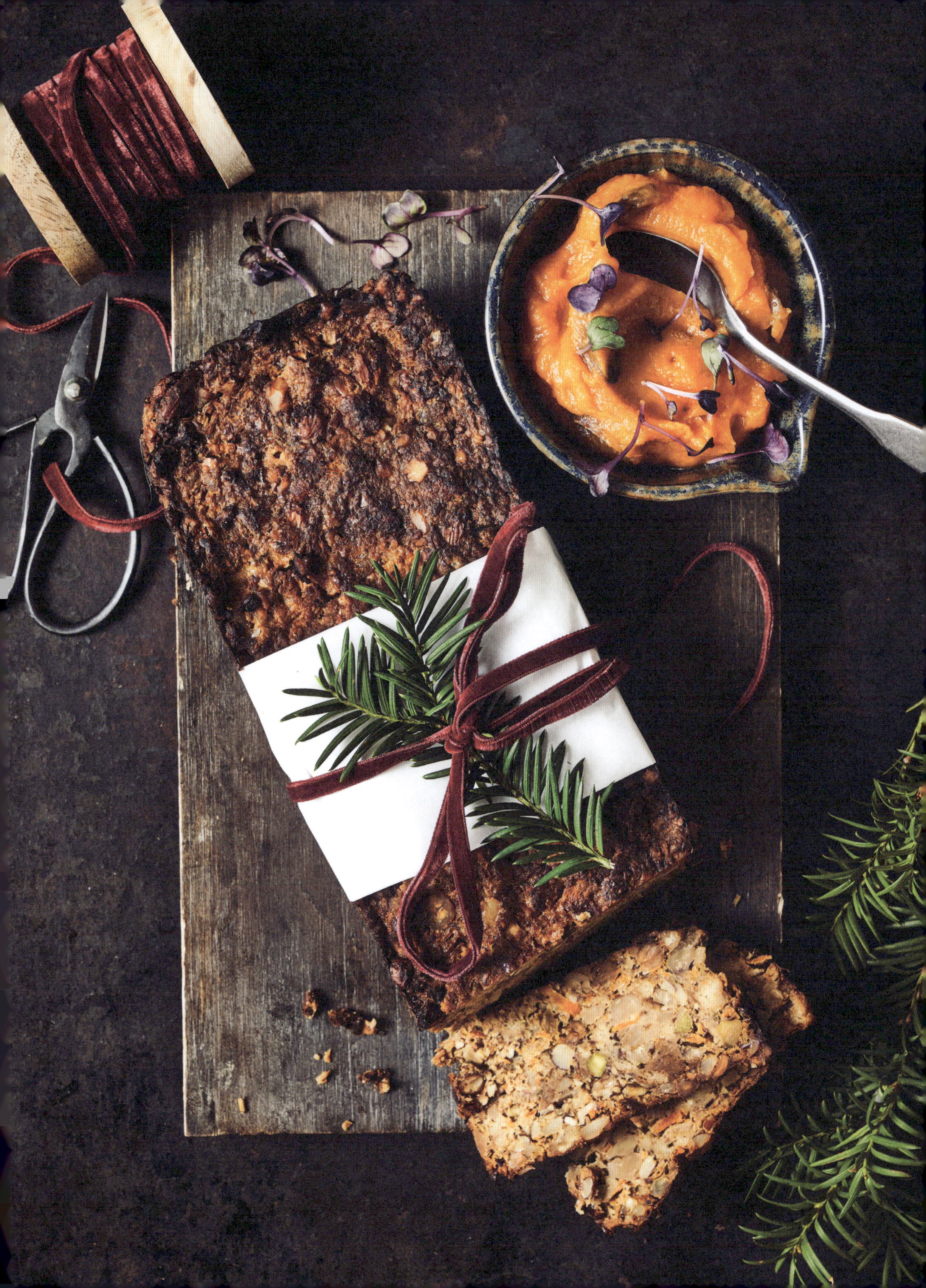

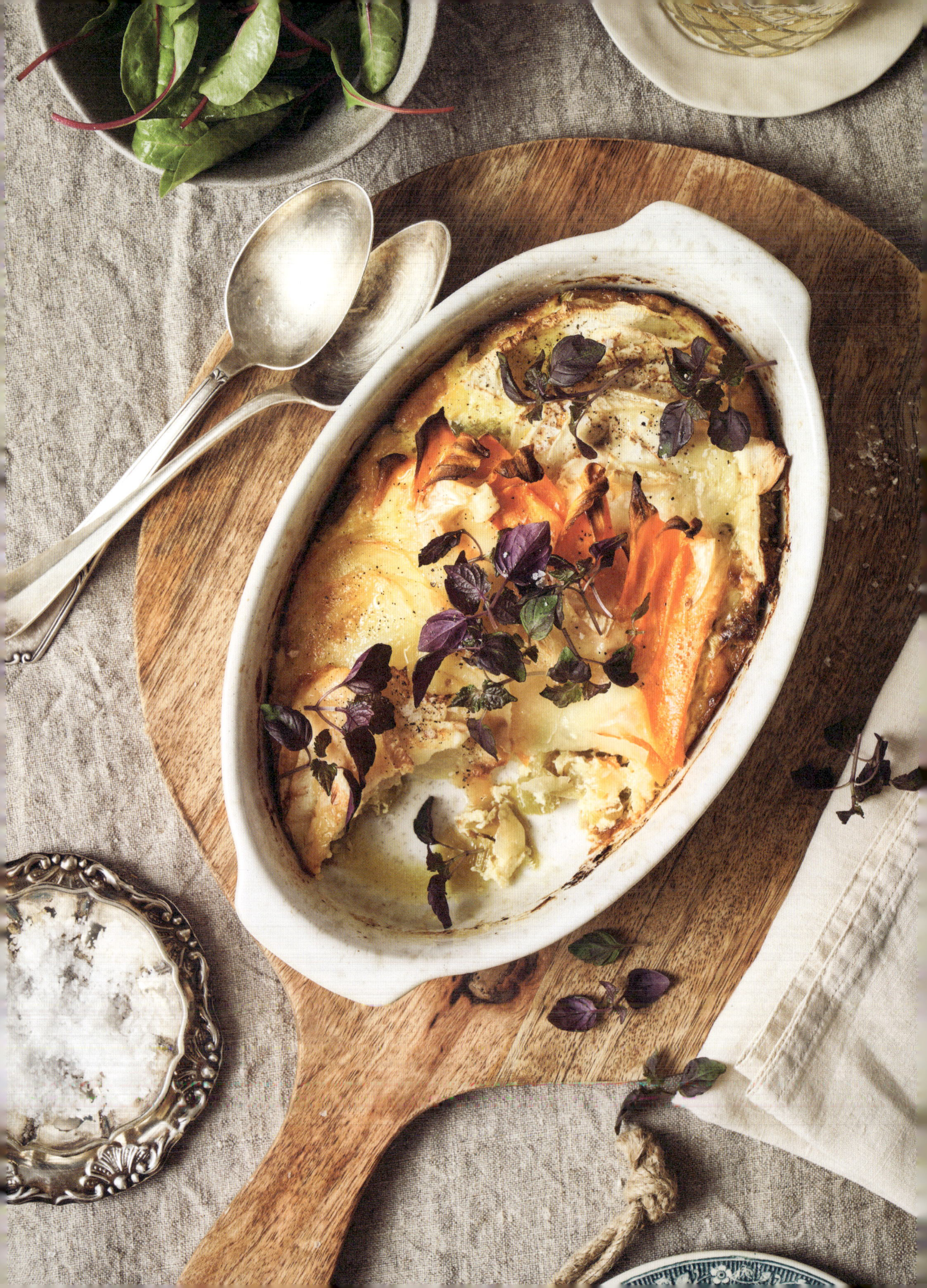

Winter vegetable gratin

Preheat the oven to 200°C (400°F/Gas 6).

Wash and trim the celery and slice thinly. Wash and trim the leeks and cut into thin rings (the light parts only).

Heat the olive oil in a large saucepan. Add the celery and leek and sweat, stirring continuously. Grease a casserole dish with butter and add the vegetables.

Peel the potatoes, celeriac and carrots. Use a mandolin to slice thinly and layer the slices on top of the vegetables in the dish. Season everything with salt and pepper.

In a bowl, whisk the egg with the cream and milk and pour the mixture over the vegetables. Remove the rind from the cheese, grate or finely slice and spread on top. Dot the butter on top.

Bake the gratin in the oven for 30-40 minutes until the cheese is nicely browned. Serve sprinkled with microgreens or cress.

Tip: Serve with a salad, for example the herb salad from page 69.

2 sticks of celery

2 leeks

1 tablespoon olive oil

1 tablespoon butter, plus a little extra for the dish

200g (7oz) potatoes (all-purpose)

150g (5½oz) celeriac

3 large carrots

Salt

Freshly ground white pepper

1 egg

200ml (7fl oz) single (pure) cream

125ml (4fl oz) milk

150g (5½oz) Reblochon or Tomme de Savoie cheese

Also

Microgreens or cress, for garnish

Mandolin

The Brothers Grimm

The Elves and the Shoemaker

A shoemaker, through no fault of his own, had become so poor that at last he had nothing left but leather for one pair of shoes. So in the evening, he cut out the shoes that he wished to begin to make the next morning, and as he had a clear conscience, he lay down quietly in his bed, commended himself to God, and fell asleep.

In the morning, after he had said his prayers, and was just going to sit down to work, the two shoes stood finished on his table. He was astounded and didn't know what to say. He took the shoes in his hands to observe them closer, and they were so neatly made that there was not one bad stitch in them, just as if they were intended as a masterpiece.

Soon after, a buyer came in, and as the shoes pleased him so well, he paid more for them than was customary, and, with the money, the shoemaker was able to purchase leather for two pairs of shoes. He cut them out at night, and the next morning was about to set to work with fresh courage; but he had no need to do so, for, when he got up, they were already made, and there was no shortage of buyers, who gave him enough money to buy leather for four pairs of shoes.

The following morning, too, he found the four pairs made; and so it went on and on. What he cut out in the evening was finished by the morning, so that he soon made a decent living from his honest trade again, and at last he became a wealthy man.

Now it happened that one evening, not long before Christmas, when the man had been cutting out the leather, he said to his wife before going to bed, 'What do you think if we were to stay up tonight to see who it is that lends us this helping hand?'

The woman liked the idea and lit a candle, and then they hid themselves in a corner of the room, behind some clothes that were hanging up there, and watched. When it was midnight, two little naked elves came, sat down by the shoemaker's table, took all the work that he had cut out earlier and began to stitch and sew and hammer so skilfully and so quickly with their little fingers that the shoemaker could not turn away his eyes for astonishment. They did not stop until all was done and stood finished on the table. Then they quickly ran away.

The next morning, the woman said, 'The little elves have made us wealthy, and we really must show that we are grateful to them. They run about like so and have nothing to wear and must be cold. I'll tell you what I'll do: I will make them little shirts and coats and vests and trousers, and knit both of them a pair of socks, and you, too, will make them two little pairs of shoes.'

The man said, 'I'll be very glad to do it,' and one night, when everything was ready, they laid their presents all together on the table instead of the cut-out work, and then they hid to see what the little elves would do.

At midnight they came bounding in and wanted to get to work straight away, but when they found no leather cut out, only the pretty little clothes, they were at first astonished and then delighted. They dressed themselves very quickly, smoothing down their pretty clothes, and sang, 'Are we not very fine young men? Why should we be shoemakers any longer?' And they danced and skipped and leapt over chairs and benches. At last they danced out of the door. From then on, they never came back, but as long as the shoemaker lived, all was well with him and he prospered in everything he did.

Salmon with potatoes and pea pesto

400g (14oz) baby potatoes
Salt
4 salmon fillets
Smoked salt
1 small lemon
8 sprigs of lemon thyme
2 tablespoons butter
180g (6½oz) peas (frozen)
50g (1¾oz) Parmesan cheese
1 garlic clove
50g (1¾oz) pine nuts
50ml (1¾fl oz) olive oil
Freshly ground black pepper

Also

Kitchen string

Bring a saucepan of salted water to the boil. Add the potatoes and cook for 20 minutes, then drain. Preheat the oven to 140°C (275°F/Gas 1).

Place each salmon fillet on a piece of baking paper and season with the smoked salt. Wash the lemon under hot water, pat dry and slice thinly. Layer the slices on top of the salmon fillets. Rinse the thyme, pat dry and add to the fillets together with dots of butter.

Fold the parcels closed and seal with kitchen string. Transfer the parcels to a heatproof dish or a baking tray and cook in the oven for 20 minutes. Add the cooked potatoes to the baking tray halfway through cooking the salmon.

Bring a saucepan of salted water to the boil. Add the peas and cook for 4-5 minutes. Drain in a colander and refresh under cold running water.

Grate the Parmesan cheese and peel the garlic.

Place the peas, garlic, pine nuts, Parmesan and olive oil in a tall beaker and blend to a creamy pesto using a stick blender. Season with salt and pepper.

Remove the salmon and potatoes from the oven and serve with the pea pesto.

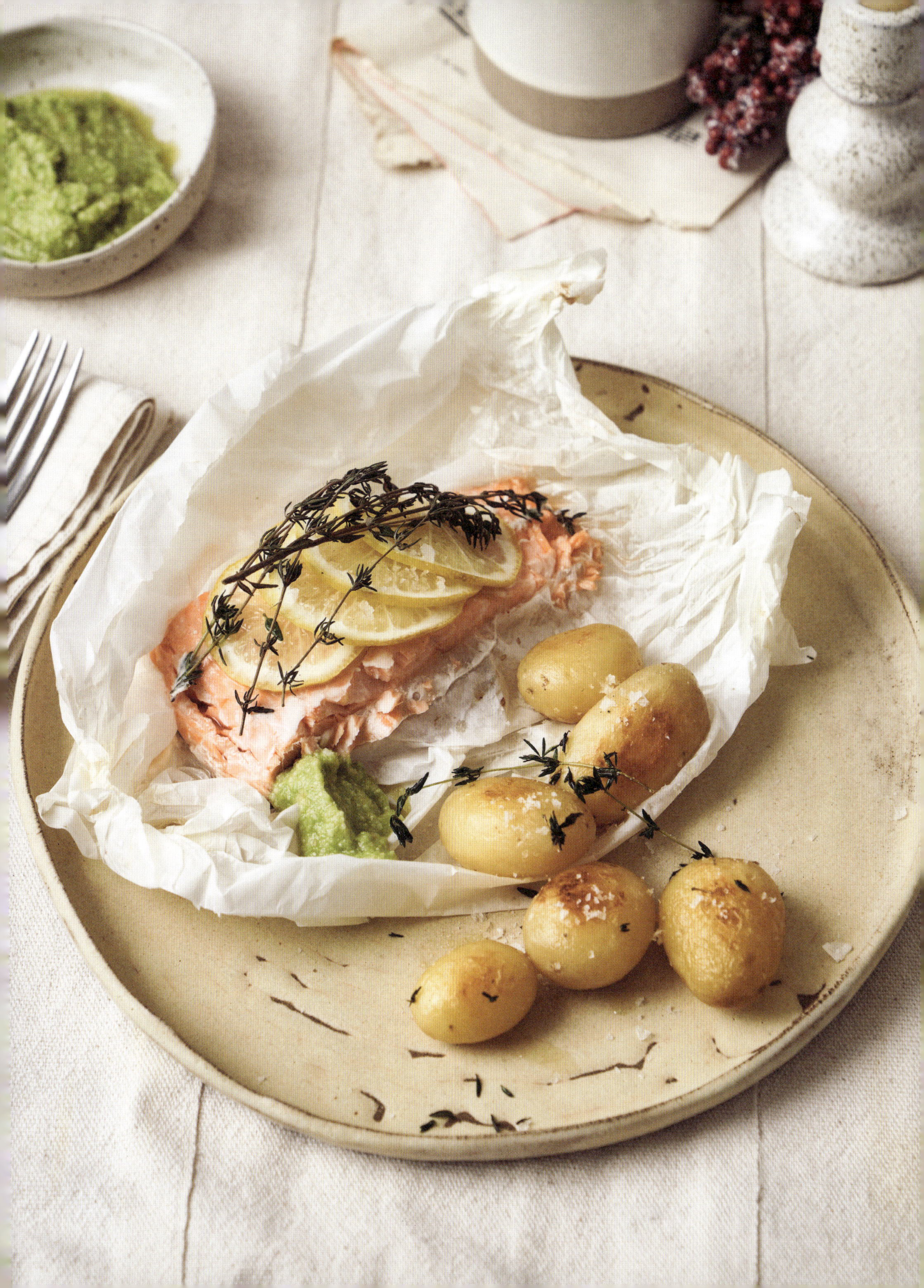

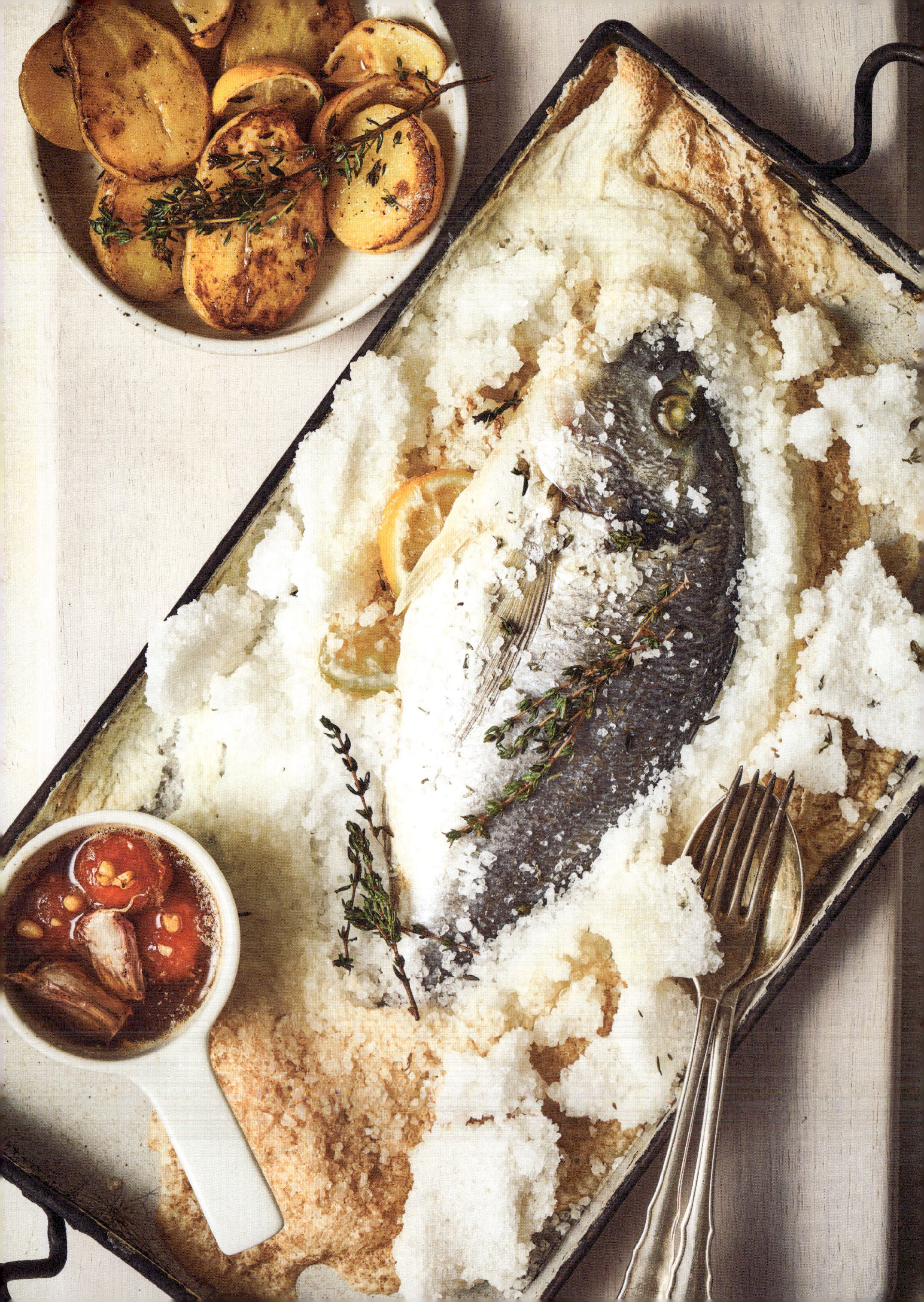

Gilthead bream in salt crust

with pine nut butter and lemon and thyme potatoes

Preheat the oven to 180°C (350°F/Gas 4).

Wash the potatoes thoroughly and halve them (no need to peel). Wash the lemons under hot water and cut into thin wedges. In a large bowl, combine the potato halves, lemon wedges, thyme and salt with plenty of olive oil and spread evenly on a baking tray.

For the fish, wash the lemon under hot water and slice thinly. Rinse the lemon thyme and pat dry. Stuff the inside of the fish with the lemon thyme and lemon.

For the salt crust, beat the egg whites in a large bowl until stiff and mix with 2 tablespoons water and the salt. Spread a 1cm (½ inch) thick layer of the salt and egg white mixture on a baking tray, slightly longer and wider than the fish. Place the fish on top, cover with the remaining salt mixture and press down firmly.

Roast the potatoes in the oven for 50-60 minutes, turning occasionally, until they are crispy and golden brown on all sides. After 10 minutes, place the tray with the fish in the oven and cook for 40-45 minutes.

In the meantime, blanch and peel the cherry tomatoes. Melt the butter in a small saucepan over medium heat, add the garlic cloves and brown the butter lightly.

Add the tomatoes and pine nuts to the butter, mix and transfer everything to a small bowl.

Remove the potatoes and fish from the oven. Tap the salt crust all around with a knife to loosen and carefully lift off. Remove the fish fillets from the bone and serve with the pine nut butter and potatoes.

For the potatoes

1kg (2lb 4oz) small waxy potatoes
2 lemons
1 tablespoon dried thyme
Sea salt
Olive oil

For the fish

1 gilthead bream or sea bass
1 lemon
1 bunch of lemon thyme
2 egg whites
2kg (4lb 8oz) rock salt

For the pine nut butter

15 cherry tomatoes
150g (5½oz) butter
2 garlic cloves
50g (1¾oz) pine nuts

Christina G. Rossetti

A Christmas Carol

In the bleak midwinter, frosty wind made moan,
Earth stood hard as iron, water like a stone;
Snow had fallen, snow on snow, snow on snow,
In the bleak midwinter, long ago.

Our God, Heaven cannot hold Him, nor earth sustain;
Heaven and earth shall flee away when He comes to reign.
In the bleak midwinter a stable place sufficed
The Lord God Almighty, Jesus Christ.

Enough for Him, whom cherubim, worship night and day,
Breastful of milk, and a mangerful of hay;
Enough for Him, whom angels fall before,
The ox and ass and camel which adore.

Angels and archangels may have gathered there,
Cherubim and seraphim thronged the air;
But His mother only, in her maiden bliss,
Worshipped the beloved with a kiss.

What can I give Him, poor as I am?
If I were a shepherd, I would bring a lamb;
If I were a Wise Man, I would do my part;
Yet what I can I give Him: give my heart.

Walter de la Mare

Mistletoe

Sitting under the mistletoe
(Pale-green, fairy mistletoe),
One last candle burning low,
All the sleepy dancers gone,
Just one candle burning on,
Shadows lurking everywhere:
Some one came, and kissed me there.

Tired I was; my head would go
Nodding under the mistletoe
(Pale-green, fairy mistletoe),
No footsteps came, no voice, but only,
Just as I sat there, sleepy, lonely,
Stooped in the still and shadowy air
Lips unseen — and kissed me there.

Fillets of lamb

with rosemary and mashed celeriac

For the lamb

4 sprigs of rosemary
2 sprigs of thyme
1½ teaspoons coarsely crushed mixed peppercorns
600g (1lb 5oz) lamb fillets
3 tablespoons olive oil

For the mash

1 celeriac (about 800g/1lb 12oz)
200g (7oz) floury potatoes
Salt
50ml (1¾fl oz) milk
50ml (1¾fl oz) single (pure) cream
20g (¾oz) butter
1 teaspoon orange zest
1 pinch of ground cinnamon
1 pinch of freshly grated nutmeg
Freshly ground black pepper

Also

Salt
200g (7oz) green and yellow French beans
Olive oil
200g (7oz) cherry tomatoes
Freshly ground black pepper

Rinse and pat dry the herbs, pick off the leaves, chop finely and mix with the pepper. Prepare the lamb by removing any skin, tendons and fat. Brush the lamb fillets with 1 tablespoon oil and coat in the pepper and herb mixture. Place in a freezer bag, seal and marinate in the fridge for at least 1 hour.

Preheat the oven to 180°C (350°F/Gas 4).

Fill a bowl with cold water. Peel and dice the celeriac and add it to the bowl to prevent it from discolouring. Peel and dice the potatoes. Cook both in plenty of salted water for 20 minutes. Drain and keep warm.

Heat the remaining oil in a frying pan. Sear the lamb fillets for 90 seconds on each side. Transfer the fillets to an ovenproof dish and cook in the oven for a further 7 minutes. Remove from the oven, transfer onto a carving board, cover with aluminium foil and leave to rest briefly.

Mash the potatoes and celeriac, gradually adding the milk and cream. Whisk in the butter. Season with the orange zest, cinnamon, nutmeg, salt and pepper.

Bring a pot of salted water to the boil on the stove.

Wash and trim the French beans and blanch in the boiling water for 1 minute, then drain. Heat the olive oil in a frying pan and sauté the French beans with the cherry tomatoes, salt and pepper over a low heat, turning frequently.

Slice the meat and serve with the mashed celeriac and sautéed vegetables.

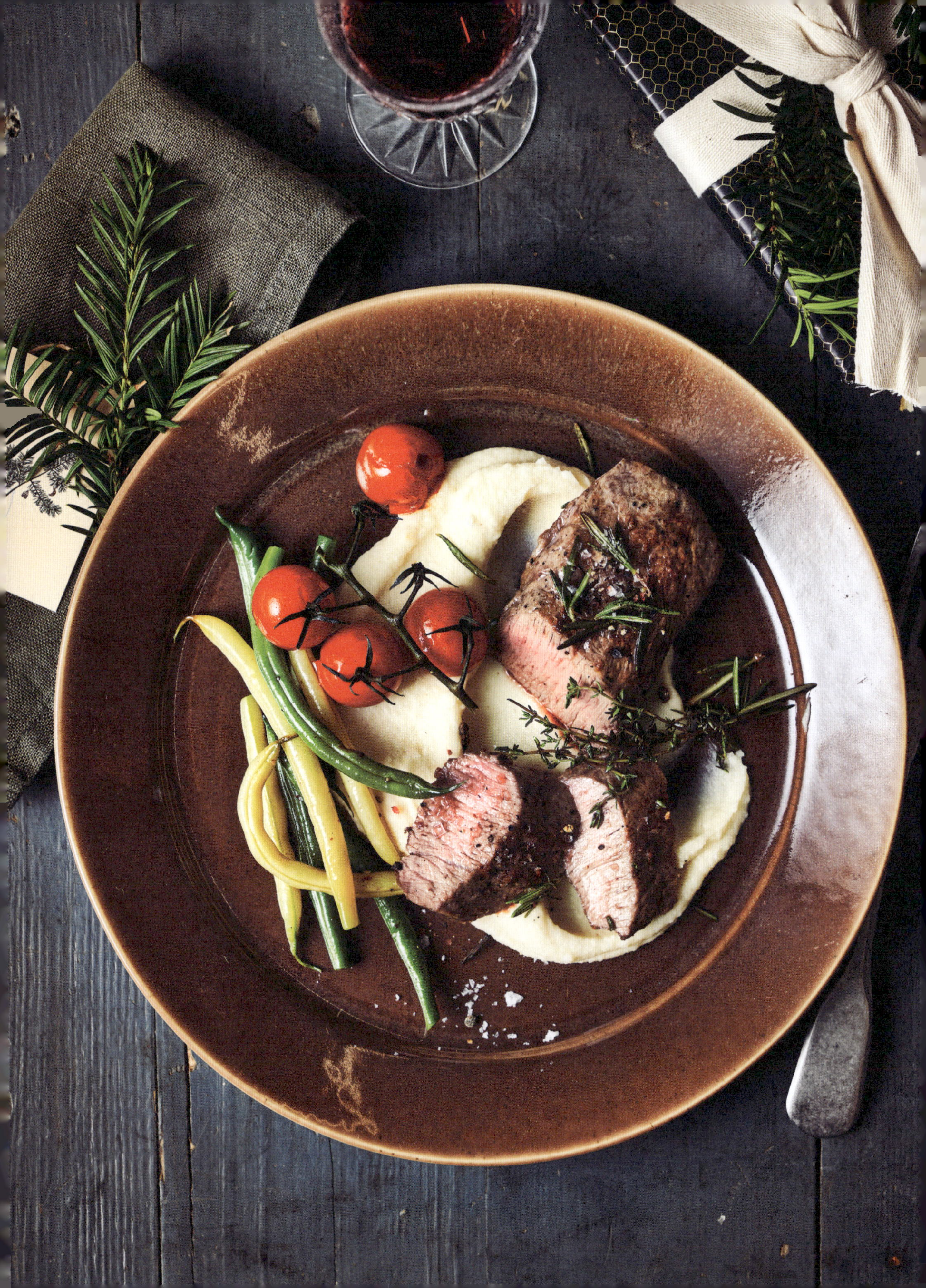

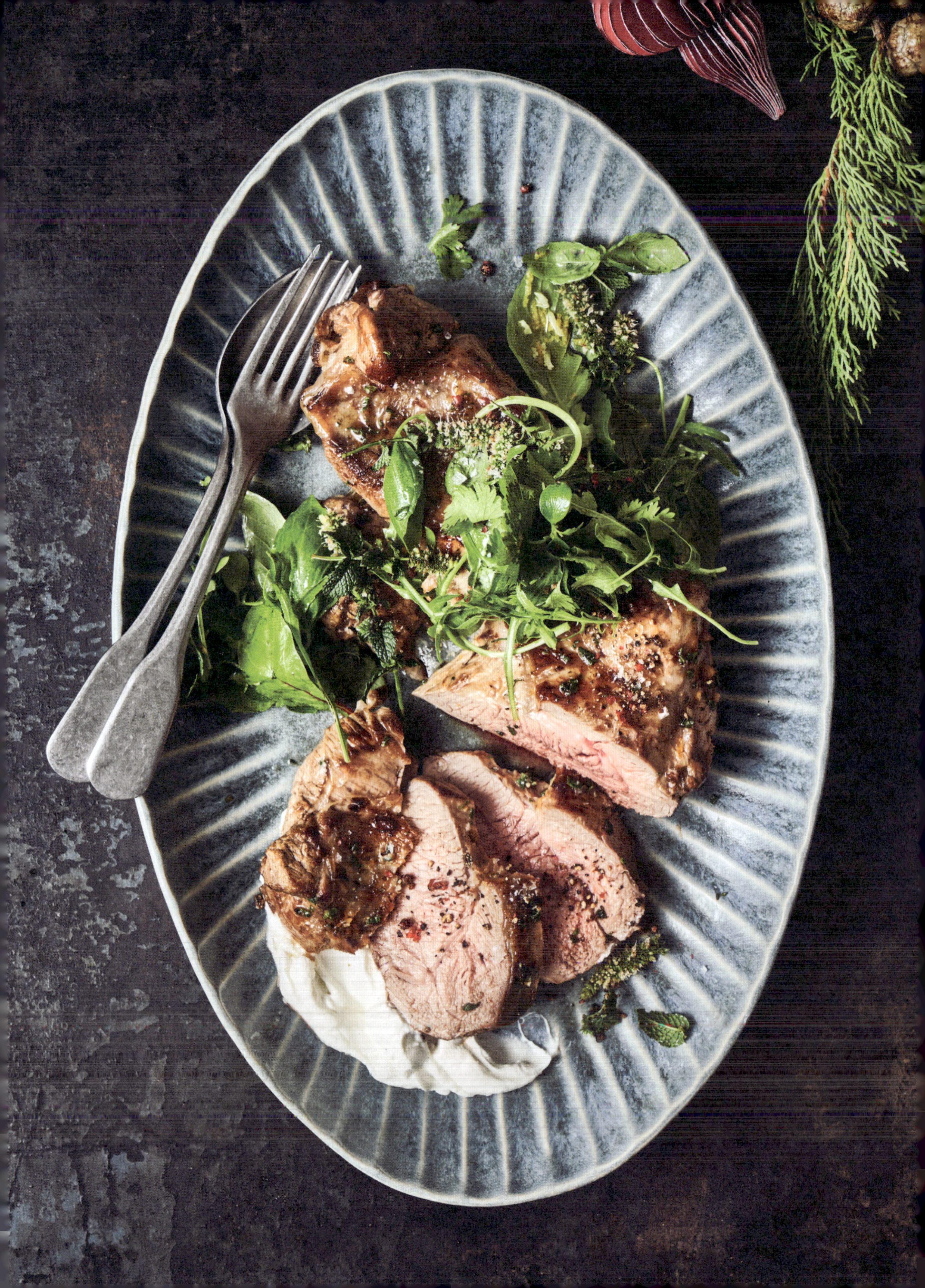

Leg of lamb

with goat's cheese and herb salad

For the leg of lamb, peel the garlic, rinse the oregano, pat dry and pick off the leaves. Transfer both to a mortar and pestle and combine with the lemon zest, sea salt and 1 tablespoon olive oil to make a paste. Add the remaining olive oil and mix well.

Prick the leg of lamb all over with a sharp knife and rub thoroughly with the herb paste. Place in an airtight freezer bag and marinate in the fridge for at least 3 hours or overnight, turning occasionally so that the meat absorbs the seasoning evenly on all sides.

Remove the leg of lamb from the fridge and allow to warm to room temperature for 2–3 hours. Preheat the oven grill to its highest setting (240°C/475°F).

Grill the marinated meat for 15 minutes on each side. Remove from the oven and set aside to rest for 10 minutes.

While the meat is resting, prepare the salad. Rinse the herbs and rocket, shake dry, chop coarsely and toss in a bowl with the olive oil and lemon juice. Season the salad with salt and pepper.

Cut the grilled meat into thick slices on a wooden board. Arrange on a serving platter together with the herb salad and goat's or cream cheese. Serve and enjoy.

Tip: This goes particularly well with honeyed balsamic carrots (see page 26) and lemon and thyme potatoes (see page 63).

For the leg of lamb

5 garlic cloves
1 bunch of oregano
Zest of 2 lemons, grated
1 teaspoon sea salt
6 tablespoons olive oil
½ leg of lamb (deboned and butterflied)

For the salad

2 bunches of herbs of your choice (e.g. basil, mint, coriander (cilantro), parsley or tarragon)
50g (1¾oz) rocket (arugula)
3 tablespoons olive oil
Juice of 1 lemon
Salt
Freshly ground black pepper

Also

200g (7oz) soft goat's cheese or cream cheese

Kenneth Grahame

Carol

Villagers all, this frosty tide,
Let your doors swing open wide,
Though wind may follow, and snow beside,
Yet draw us in by your fire to bide;
Joy shall be yours in the morning!

Here we stand in the cold and the sleet,
Blowing fingers and stamping feet,
Come from far away you to greet —
You by the fire and we in the street —
Bidding you joy in the morning!

For ere one half of the night was gone,
Sudden a star has led us on,
Raining bliss and benison —
Bliss to-morrow and more anon,
Joy for every morning!

Goodman Joseph toiled through the snow —
Saw the star o'er a stable low;
Mary she might not further go —
Welcome thatch, and litter below!
Joy was hers in the morning!

And then they heard the angels tell
'Who were the first to cry NOWELL?
Animals all, as it befell,
In the stable where they did dwell!
Joy shall be theirs in the morning!'

Ernst Anschütz

O Christmas Tree

O Christmas tree, O Christmas tree,
How lovely are your branches!
Not only green in summer's heat,
But also winter's snow and sleet.
O Christmas tree, O Christmas tree,
How lovely are your branches!

O Christmas tree, O Christmas tree,
Of all the trees most lovely;
Each year you bring to us delight
With brightly shining Christmas light!
O Christmas tree, O Christmas tree,
Of all the trees most lovely.

Crispy pork belly
with vegetables and potatoes

Serves 6

5 carrots
6 garlic cloves
4 onions
¼ celeriac
1 leek
3 sprigs of rosemary
A few bay leaves
Salt
Freshly ground black pepper
2 tablespoons vegetable oil
2kg (4lb 8oz) pork belly
500ml (17fl oz) vegetable stock
1kg (2lb 4oz) baby potatoes
100ml (3½fl oz) single (pure) cream
2 tablespoons plain (all-purpose) flour

Preheat the oven to 175°C fan (375°F/Gas 5).

Peel, trim and roughly chop the carrots, garlic, onions and celeriac. Wash and trim the leek, discard the dark green parts, wash well and slice into rings. Rinse the rosemary and pat dry. Pick off the leaves.

Place the bay leaves in a roasting tin, season with salt and pepper and drizzle the oil on top.

Use a sharp knife to score the pork belly rind. Rub the meat with salt and pepper and place between the bay leaves in the roasting tin.

Roast in the preheated oven for about 2 hours 45 minutes. After about 1 hour, deglaze the roasting tin with the vegetable stock and add the vegetables and potatoes.

Towards the end of the roasting time, increase the oven temperature to 220°C fan (475°F/Gas 8) top heat and continue to roast for a further 6-10 minutes until crispy. Remove the roast from the oven and keep warm. Transfer the vegetables and gravy to a sieve and collect the gravy in a saucepan.

Reheat the gravy, stir in the cream and season to taste. Mix the flour with a little cold water and add to the gravy to thicken.

Carve the roast and serve with the vegetables and gravy.

Tip: A herb salad (see page 69) makes a perfect accompaniment to this roast.

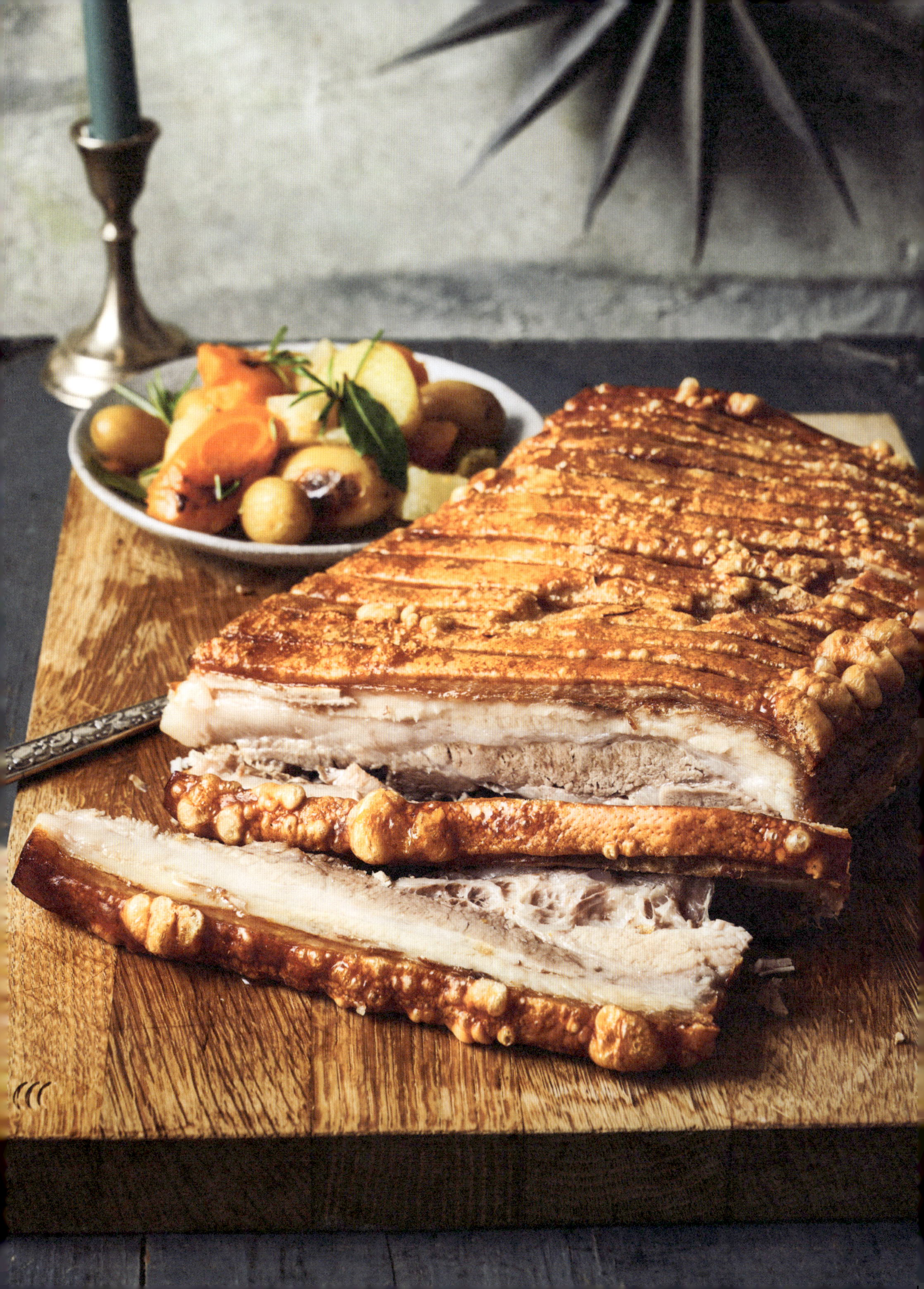

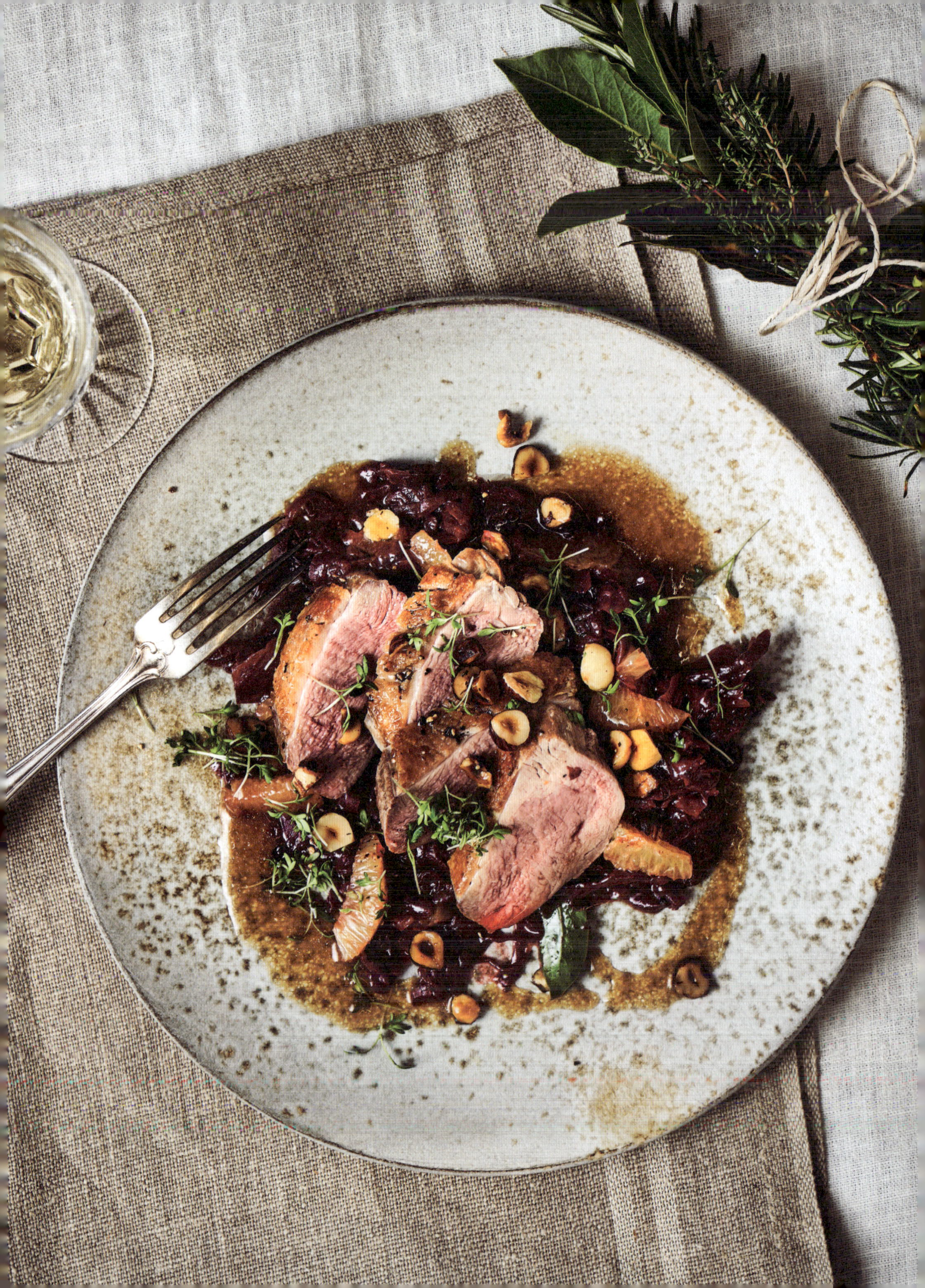

Duck breast
with spiced orange red cabbage

Trim the red cabbage, remove the stalk and slice thinly with a mandolin, if you have one. Juice 1 orange, peel and segment the other. Peel and dice 3 shallots. Press the cloves into the remaining shallot. Set half of the diced shallots aside.

Melt the butter in a saucepan. Add the remaining half of the shallots and fry gently. Add the red cabbage and sauté for 3 minutes. Deglaze with the wine, vinegar and orange juice. Add the bay leaf, salt, pepper and the clove-studded shallot. Cook the red cabbage for 20-30 minutes over medium heat. Stir in the honey and orange segments. Remove from the heat.

Preheat the oven to 200°C (400°F/Gas 6).

Score the skins of the duck breasts in a diamond pattern. Season the meat with salt and pepper on both sides. Dry roast in a hot frying pan, skin side down, over medium heat for 2 minutes. Turn and fry on the other side for a further 2 minutes. Transfer the duck breasts to an ovenproof dish, reserving the juices in the frying pan. Cook the meat in the oven for 10-15 minutes.

Meanwhile, caramelise the remaining diced shallots with the sugar in the roasting juices over medium heat. Add the wine and stock and simmer until reduced to a sauce. Season with salt and pepper. Remove the duck breasts from the oven, wrap in aluminium foil and set aside to rest for 2-3 minutes.

Dry roast the hazelnuts evenly in a frying pan.

Heat the red cabbage briefly before serving. Remove the bay leaf and shallot from the cabbage. Slice the duck breasts and serve with the sauce and red cabbage, garnished with cress and roasted hazelnuts.

Tip: The red cabbage also goes very well with Christmas goose or turkey.

For the red cabbage

1 head of red cabbage (about 700g/1lb 9oz)
2 oranges
4 French shallots
3 cloves
3 tablespoons butter
75 ml (2½fl oz) dry red wine
1 tablespoon apple cider vinegar
1 bay leaf
Salt
Freshly ground black pepper
3 tablespoons honey

For the duck

4 duck breasts
Salt
Freshly ground black pepper
2 teaspoons brown sugar
45ml (1½fl oz) dry red wine
200ml (7fl oz) duck stock

Also

1 handful of chopped hazelnuts
1 handful of cress

Roast goose

with potato dumplings and red cabbage

For the roast goose

1 goose, kitchen-ready (about 4kg/9lb)
Salt
Freshly ground black pepper
2 tart apples
3 onions
1 sprig of marjoram
100g (3½oz) raisins

For the red cabbage

1.5kg (3lb 5oz) red cabbage
4 French shallots
7 cloves
4 apples
3 tablespoons butter
150ml (5fl oz) apple juice
375ml (13fl oz) dry red wine
6 tablespoons apple cider vinegar
400g (14oz) cranberries (from a jar)
1 cinnamon stick
3 bay leaves
Freshly ground black pepper

For the potato dumplings

Salt
1kg (2lb 4oz) floury potatoes
2 eggs
100g (3½oz) plain (all purpose) flour

Also

Kitchen string
Chives, for garnish

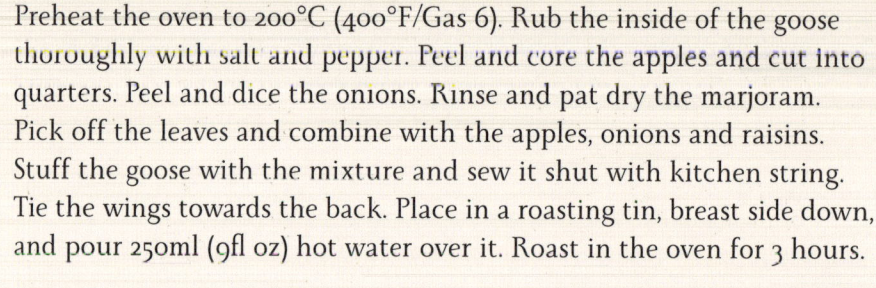

Preheat the oven to 200°C (400°F/Gas 6). Rub the inside of the goose thoroughly with salt and pepper. Peel and core the apples and cut into quarters. Peel and dice the onions. Rinse and pat dry the marjoram. Pick off the leaves and combine with the apples, onions and raisins. Stuff the goose with the mixture and sew it shut with kitchen string. Tie the wings towards the back. Place in a roasting tin, breast side down, and pour 250ml (9fl oz) hot water over it. Roast in the oven for 3 hours.

After 30 minutes, reduce the temperature to 180°C (350°F/Gas 4). Baste the goose regularly with the salt water and turn over when the back is browned. Pierce occasionally during roasting to allow the fat to drain.

Trim the red cabbage, remove the stalk and slice thinly with a mandolin, if you have one. Peel and dice 3 shallots. Press the cloves into 1 shallot. Peel, core and dice the apples. Melt the butter in a saucepan. Add the diced apples and shallots and fry gently. Add the red cabbage and sauté for 3 minutes, stirring continuously. Deglaze with the apple juice, wine and cider vinegar. Add the cranberries, cinnamon, bay leaves, pepper and the clove-studded shallot. Cook the red cabbage for 30 minutes over medium heat, stirring repeatedly. Cover and simmer over low heat for a further 1½ hours, stirring regularly.

Bring a pan of salted water to the boil. Add half the potatoes and cook for 20 minutes. Drain, refresh under cold water and peel. Peel and finely grate the remaining potatoes. Transfer to a clean tea towel and squeeze out as much liquid as you can, collecting the liquid in a bowl. Press the cooked potatoes through a potato ricer and add to the grated potatoes. Drain the reserved liquid and add about 2 tablespoons of the starchy liquid from the bottom of the bowl to the potatoes with 1 teaspoon salt. Add the eggs and flour and knead well. Refrigerate for 30 minutes.

Remove the cooked roast from the oven and keep warm. Allow the gravy to cool slightly, skim off and discard the fat. Bring the rest to the boil and season with salt and pepper.

With moistened hands, shape the potato mixture into 8–10 dumplings. Cook in plenty of simmering (not boiling!) salted water for 20 minutes. Remove from the pot and drain. Remove the bay leaves and the clove-studded shallot from the red cabbage. Season with salt and pepper.

Carve the goose and serve with the gravy, dumplings and red cabbage. Add chopped chives to garnish.

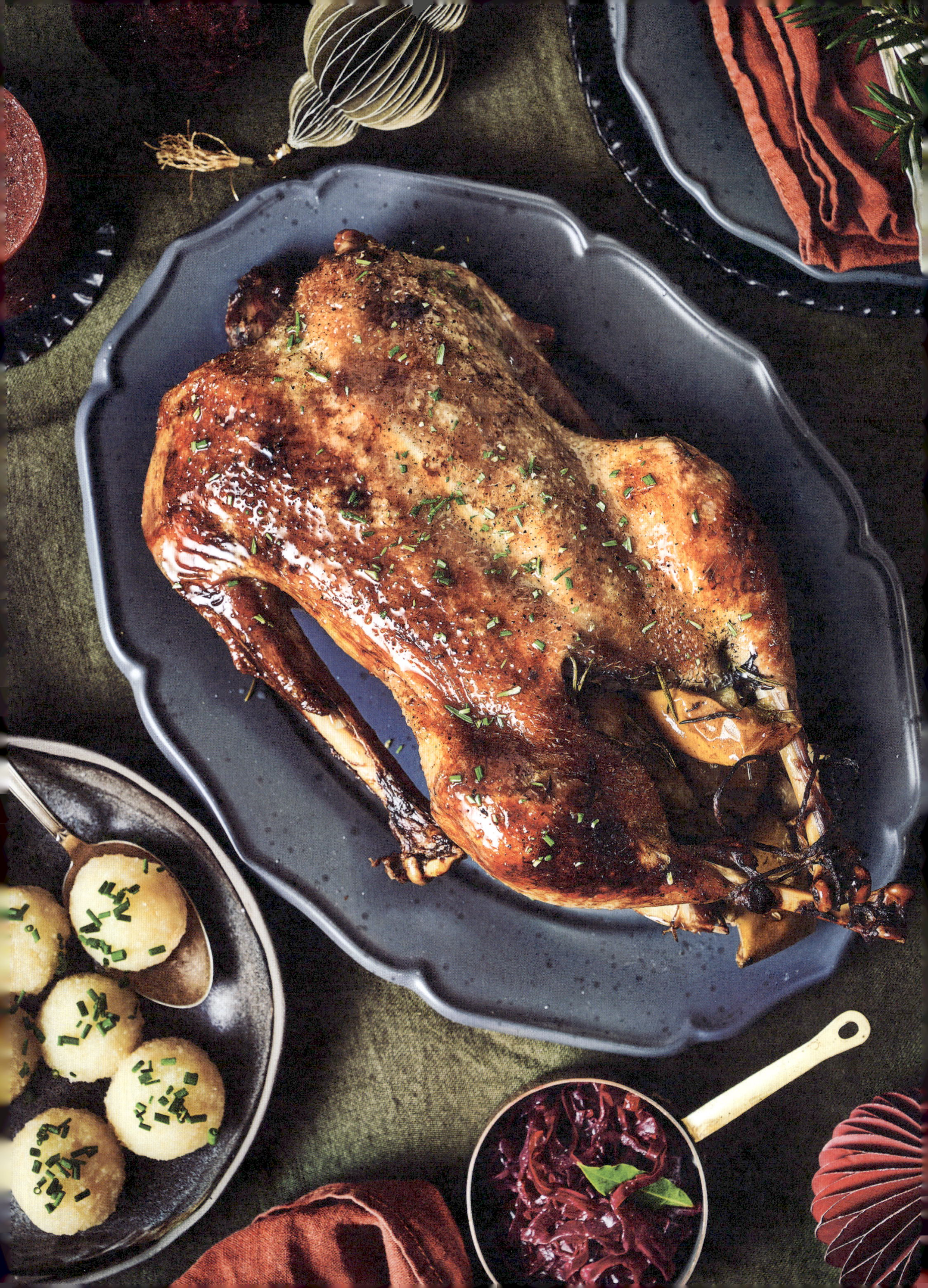

Charles Dickens

A Christmas Carol (extract)

'What's to-day!' cried Scrooge, calling downward to a boy in Sunday clothes, who perhaps had loitered in to look about him.

'Eh?' returned the boy, with all his might of wonder.

'What's to-day, my fine fellow?' said Scrooge.

'To-day!' replied the boy. 'Why, Christmas Day.'

'It's Christmas Day!' said Scrooge to himself. 'I haven't missed it. The Spirits have done it all in one night. They can do anything they like. Of course they can. Of course they can. Hallo, my fine fellow!'

'Hallo!' returned the boy.

'Do you know the Poulterer's, in the next street but one, at the corner?' Scrooge inquired.

'I should hope I did,' replied the lad.

'An intelligent boy!' said Scrooge. 'A remarkable boy! Do you know whether they've sold the prize Turkey that was hanging up there? Not the little prize Turkey: the big one?'

'What, the one as big as me?' returned the boy.

'What a delightful boy!' said Scrooge. 'It's a pleasure to talk to him. Yes, my buck!'

'It's hanging there now,' replied the boy.

'Is it?' said Scrooge. 'Go and buy it.'

'Walk-er!' exclaimed the boy.

'No, no,' said Scrooge, 'I am in earnest. Go and buy it, and tell 'em to bring it here, that I may give them the direction where to take it. Come back with the man, and I'll give you a shilling. Come back with him in less than five minutes and I'll give you half-a-crown!'

The boy was off like a shot. He must have had a steady hand at a trigger who could have got a shot off half so fast.

'I'll send it to Bob Cratchit's!' whispered Scrooge, rubbing his hands, and splitting with a laugh. 'He sha'n't know who sent it. It's twice the size of Tiny Tim. Joe Miller never made such a joke as sending it to Bob's will be!'

'Here's the Turkey! Hallo! Whoop! How are you! Merry Christmas!'

It was a Turkey! He never could have stood upon his legs, that bird. He would have snapped 'em short off in a minute, like sticks of sealing-wax.

'Why, it's impossible to carry that to Camden Town,' said Scrooge. 'You must have a cab.'

The chuckle with which he said this, and the chuckle with which he paid for the Turkey, and the chuckle with which he paid for the cab, and the chuckle with which he recompensed the boy, were only to be exceeded by the chuckle with which he sat down breathless in his chair again, and chuckled till he cried.

In the afternoon he turned his steps towards his nephew's house.

He passed the door a dozen times, before he had the courage to go up and knock. But he made a dash, and did it:

'Is your master at home, my dear?' said Scrooge to the girl. Nice girl! Very.

'Yes, sir.'

'Where is he, my love?' said Scrooge.

'He's in the dining-room, sir, along with mistress. I'll show you up-stairs, if you please.'

'Thank'ee. He knows me,' said Scrooge, with his hand already on the dining-room lock. 'I'll go in here, my dear.'

He turned it gently, and sidled his face in, round the door. They were looking at the table (which was spread out in great array); for these young housekeepers are always nervous on such points, and like to see that everything is right.

'Fred!' said Scrooge.

Dear heart alive, how his niece by marriage started! Scrooge had forgotten, for the moment, about her sitting in the corner with the footstool, or he wouldn't have done it, on any account.

'Why bless my soul!' cried Fred, 'Who's that?'

'It's I. Your uncle Scrooge. I have come to dinner. Will you let me in, Fred?'

Let him in! It is a mercy he didn't shake his arm off. He was at home in five minutes. Nothing could be heartier. His niece looked just the same. So did Topper when he came. So did the plump sister when she came. So did every one when they came. Wonderful party, wonderful games, wonderful unanimity, won-der-ful happiness!

Italian roast goose
Parma-style

1 goose, kitchen-ready (about 3kg/6lb 12oz)
Salt
300g (10½oz) Parma ham
8 onions
3 tablespoons olive oil
Freshly ground black pepper
3 tablespoons granulated (white) sugar
100ml (3½fl oz) balsamic vinegar
5 spiced biscuits (e.g. speculaas/Biscoff)
½ bunch of parsley
40g (1½oz) Parmesan cheese
150g (5½oz) breadcrumbs
1 egg
80ml (2½fl oz) milk

Also

Kitchen string

Preheat the oven to 180°C (350°F/Gas 4). Place a roasting tin on the lowest rack and preheat. Rub the goose with salt.

Finely dice the ham. Peel and quarter the onions. Heat the olive oil in a frying pan and sauté the onions. Add the ham, sprinkle with salt, pepper and sugar and allow to caramelise briefly. Deglaze with the balsamic vinegar, simmer for 1 minute and remove from the heat. Stuff the goose with the ham mixture and sew it shut with kitchen string.

Place the goose in the roasting tin, breast side down, add 350ml (12fl oz) boiling water and place the roast in the oven. Baste regularly with the juices. After 45 minutes, skim off the fat and continue to roast for a further 2-2½ hours, turning the bird once.

Chop the biscuits for the breading. Rinse and pat dry the parsley. Pick off and chop the leaves. Grate the Parmesan. Add the biscuit crumbs and parsley to a bowl together with the breadcrumbs, Parmesan, egg and milk. Combine well and season with salt and pepper.

About 10 minutes before the end of the roasting time, remove the roasting tin from the oven and switch the oven to grill. Spread the breading on the goose breast and press down gently. Return the goose roast to the oven, breast side up, and grill for 10-15 minutes until the crust is golden brown.

Tip: A fresh herb salad (see page 69) makes an excellent accompaniment to this roast.

German roast goose
with gingerbread sauce

Preheat the oven to 200°C (400°F/Gas 6). Rub the goose with salt, pepper and marjoram.

Peel and dice the onions. Peel, core and dice the apples. Dice the chestnuts and crumble the gingerbread. Add everything to a bowl and combine well. Stir in the thyme. Stuff the goose with the mixture and sew it shut with kitchen string.

Transfer the goose to a roasting tin and pour in 150ml (5fl oz) water. Roast in the oven for 1 hour, basting occasionally with the juices. Reduce the temperature to 120°C (250°F/Gas 1) and roast for a further 4 hours, turning once and continuing to baste regularly with the juices.

Meanwhile, for the sauce, peel the celeriac, carrots and onion. Trim and wash the leek. Dice the vegetables. Heat half the butter in a saucepan. Add the goose giblets and fry. Add the vegetables and sauté for 3 minutes. Deglaze with the chicken stock or roast juices and simmer for 15 minutes.

Finely chop the chestnuts and gingerbread. Heat the remaining butter in another saucepan. Add the chopped chestnuts and gingerbread and fry. Deglaze with the beer, then pour in the simmering stock through a sieve and reduce considerably while the goose continues to roast. Finally, season with thyme, sugar, salt and pepper.

Serve the goose with the stuffing and the sauce.

Tip: Serve with spiced orange red cabbage (see page 75) and potato dumplings (see page 76).

For the roast

1 goose, kitchen-ready (about 5kg/11lb)
Salt
Freshly ground black pepper
2 tablespoons dried marjoram
2 onions
4 tart apples
500g (1lb 2oz) precooked chestnuts
400g (14oz) gingerbread (without chocolate)
2 tablespoons thyme, chopped

For the sauce

½ celeriac
2 carrots
1 onion
1 leek
100g (3½oz) butter
1 goose liver, heart and neck (giblets)
600ml (21fl oz) chicken stock or juices from the goose roast, fat skimmed off
150g (5½oz) precooked chestnuts
200g (7oz) gingerbread (without chocolate)
1.5 litres (52fl oz) dark beer
2 tablespoons thyme, chopped
1 tablespoon granulated (white) sugar
Salt
Freshly ground black pepper

Also

Kitchen string

The Wassail Song

Here we come a-wassailing
Among the leaves so green,
Here we come a-wandering
So fair to be seen.

Love and joy come to you
And to your wassail too,
And God bless you, and send you
A happy New Year.

We are not daily beggars
That beg from door to door,
But we are neighbours' children
That you have seen before.

Good Master and good Mistress,
As you sit by the fire,
Pray think of us poor children
Who are wandering in the mire.

Bring us out a table
And spread it with a cloth;
Bring us out a mouldy cheese
And some of your Christmas loaf.

God bless the master of this house,
Likewise the mistress too;
And all the little children
That round the table go.

Karl Enslin

Ring, Little Bells

Ring bells, go ting-a-ling-a-ling,
ring little bells!
Oh, how cold the winter,
will you let me enter?
Do not bar the doorway
on my blessed birthday!

Ring bells, go ting-a-ling-a-ling,
ring little bells!
Maid and Infant tender,
will you let us enter?
To us shelter giving,
And the Father praising?

Ring bells, go ting-a-ling-a-ling,
ring little bells!
In our hearts now stealing,
'mid the bells all pealing,
joy and blessing holy
from the Child so lowly.
Ring bells go ting-a-ling-a-ling,
ring little bells!

Pepper-crusted fillet of beef
with sweet potato rosti

For the beef fillet

600g (1lb 5oz) beef fillet
3 tablespoons olive oil
3 tablespoons pink or black peppercorns
1 teaspoon coarse sea salt

For the sweet potato rosti

500g (1lb 2oz) sweet potatoes
1 garlic clove
40g (1½oz) Parmesan cheese
2 tablespoons olive oil, plus some extra for frying
1 egg yolk

Preheat the oven to 200°C (400°F/Gas 6). Rub the meat with the oil. Coarsely crush the peppercorns and sea salt in a mortar and sprinkle over the meat.

Peel the sweet potatoes and finely grate into a bowl. Squeeze out as much liquid as you can and drain. Peel and crush the garlic and add to the sweet potatoes. Grate the Parmesan. Add to the mixture together with the olive oil and egg yolk and combine everything well.

Sear the fillets in a frying pan for 2 minutes on each side. Transfer them to a baking tray lined with baking paper and continue to cook in the oven for a further 10–15 minutes.

Heat a generous amount of oil in another frying pan. Add the sweet potato mixture, shaped into portion-sized patties, and press flat. Fry over medium heat for 10–12 minutes on each side.

Serve the beef fillets with the rosti.

Tip: Steamed broccolini and a fresh salad make excellent accompaniments to this dish.

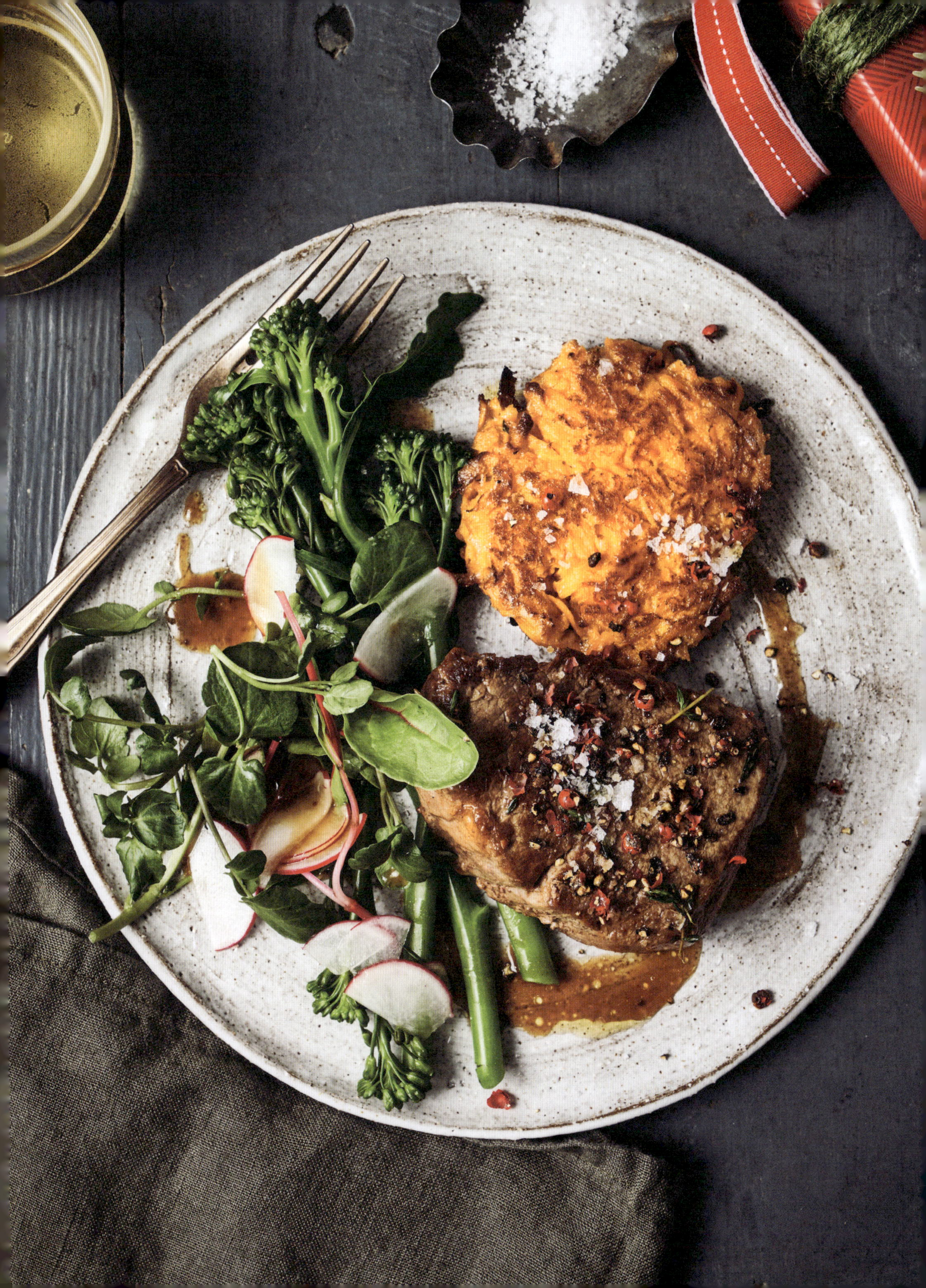

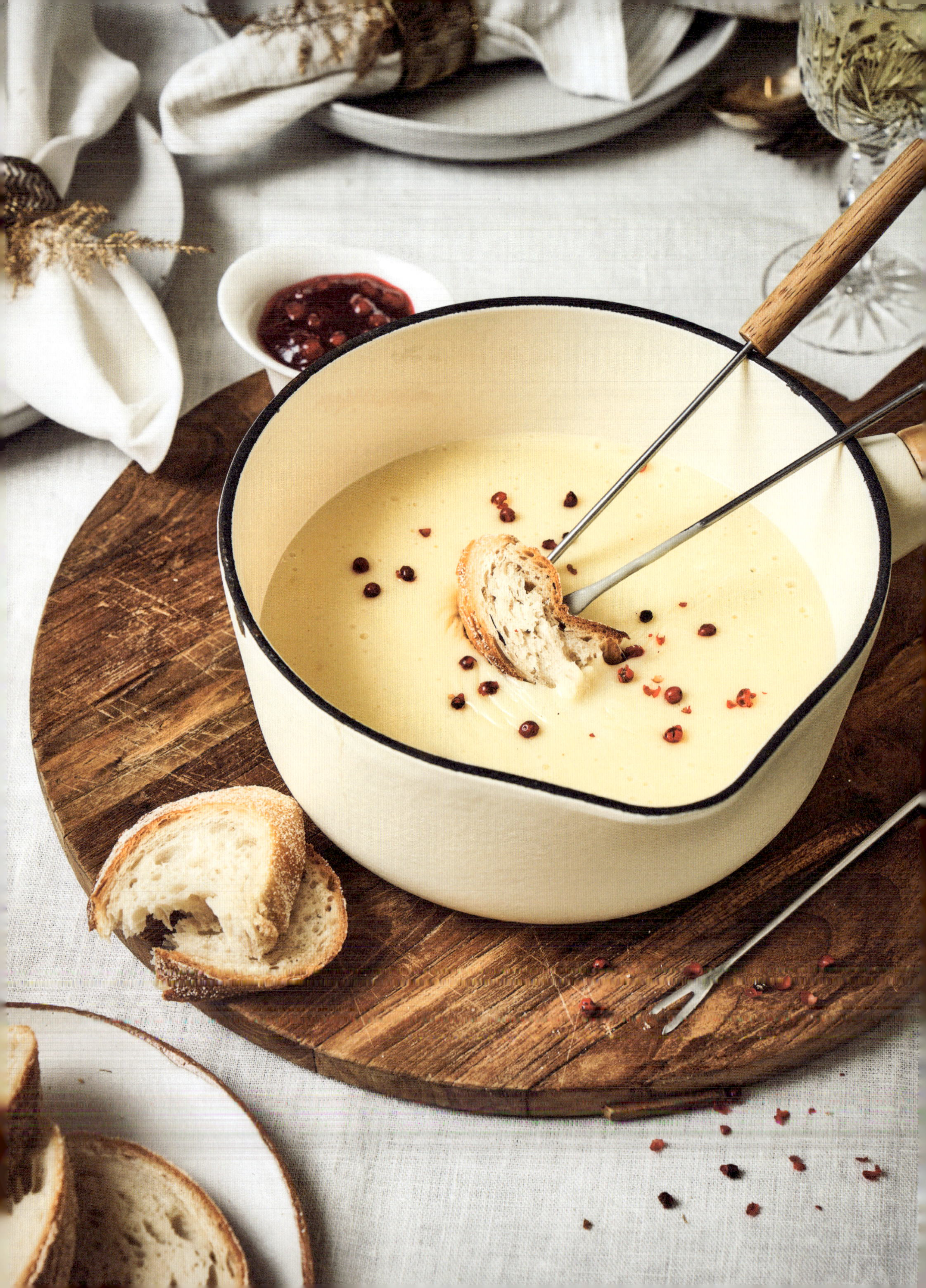

Swiss cheese fondue

Peel and halve the garlic clove. Rub the fondue pot thoroughly with the garlic. Cut the cheese into small cubes and add to the pot together with the wine.

Heat, stirring continuously, until the cheese is completely dissolved. Whisk the potato starch with the Kirsch and stir into the cheese mixture. Briefly return everything to the boil, season with pepper and nutmeg and serve topped with pink peppercorns.

While enjoying your meal, continue to simmer the fondue on a fondue burner with an adjustable flame. Make sure that you pull the skewered bread pieces through the cheese mixture close to the bottom of the pot so that it remains creamy and does not burn.

Tip: The Swiss enjoy their fondue cooked in a shallow saucepan made of glazed ceramic or heavy cast iron called a fondue pot or *caquelon*.

1 garlic clove
1kg (2lb 4oz) Swiss fondue cheese
350-400ml (12-14fl oz) dry white wine
1 teaspoon potato starch
20-30ml (½-1fl oz) Kirsch
Freshly ground white pepper
Freshly grated nutmeg
Pink peppercorns

Also

Plenty of rustic white bread or baguette, cut into pieces
Fondue pot
Fondue burner

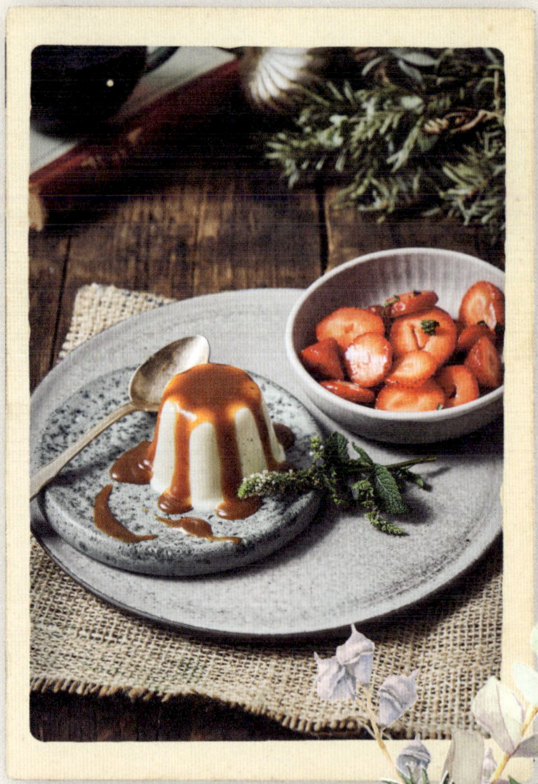

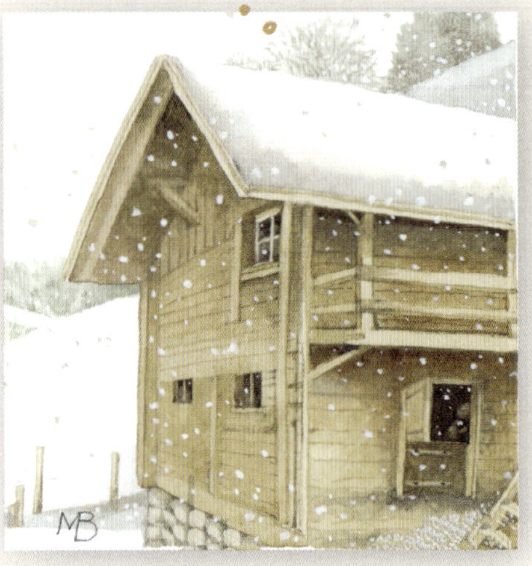

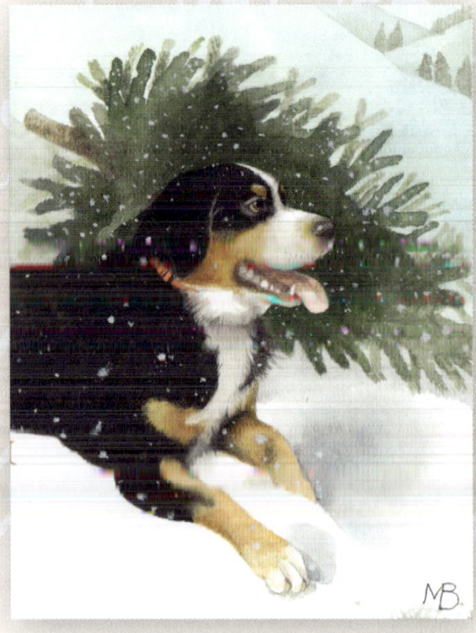

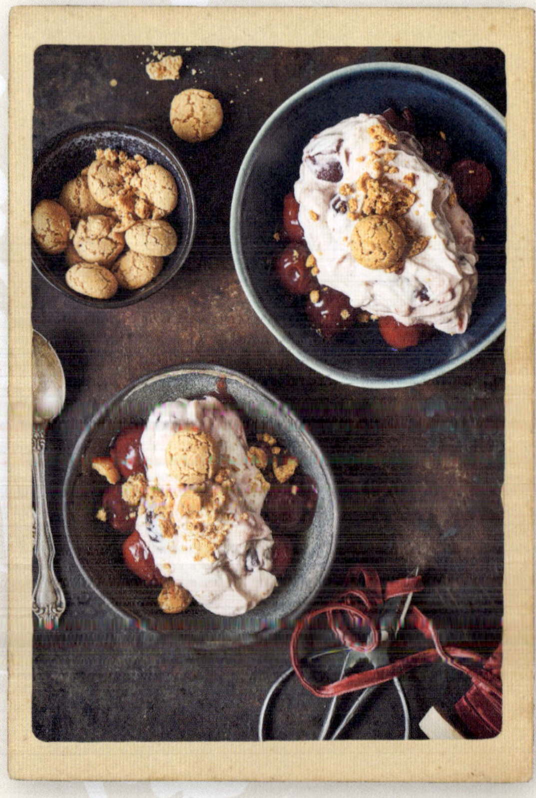

Enticing

desserts

Clement Clarke Moore

A Visit from St. Nicholas

'Twas the night before Christmas, when all through the house
Not a creature was stirring, not even a mouse;
The stockings were hung by the chimney with care,
In hopes that St. Nicholas soon would be there;
The children were nestled all snug in their beds;
While visions of sugar-plums danced in their heads;
And mamma in her 'kerchief, and I in my cap,
Had just settled our brains for a long winter's nap,
When out on the lawn there arose such a clatter,
I sprang from my bed to see what was the matter.
Away to the window I flew like a flash,
Tore open the shutters and threw up the sash.
The moon on the breast of the new-fallen snow,
Gave a lustre of midday to objects below,
When what to my wondering eyes did appear,
But a miniature sleigh and eight tiny rein-deer,
With a little old driver so lively and quick,
I knew in a moment he must be St. Nick.
More rapid than eagles his coursers they came,
And he whistled, and shouted, and called them by name:
'Now, Dasher! Now, Dancer! Now, Prancer and Vixen!
On, Comet! On, Cupid! On, Donder and Blitzen!
To the top of the porch! To the top of the wall!
Now dash away! Dash away! Dash away all!'
As leaves that before the wild hurricane fly,
When they meet with an obstacle, mount to the sky;
So up to the housetop the coursers they flew

With the sleigh full of toys, and St. Nicholas too —
And then, in a twinkling, I heard on the roof
The prancing and pawing of each little hoof.
As I drew in my head, and was turning around,
Down the chimney St. Nicholas came with a bound.
He was dressed all in fur, from his head to his foot,
And his clothes were all tarnished with ashes and soot;
A bundle of toys he had flung on his back,
And he looked like a pedler just opening his pack.
His eyes — how they twinkled! His dimples, how merry!
His cheeks were like roses, his nose like a cherry!
His droll little mouth was drawn up like a bow,
And the beard on his chin was as white as the snow;
The stump of a pipe he held tight in his teeth,
And the smoke, it encircled his head like a wreath;
He had a broad face and a little round belly
That shook when he laughed, like a bowl full of jelly.
He was chubby and plump, a right jolly old elf,
And I laughed when I saw him, in spite of myself;
A wink of his eye and a twist of his head
Soon gave me to know I had nothing to dread;
He spoke not a word, but went straight to his work,
And filled all the stockings; then turned with a jerk,
And laying his finger aside of his nose,
And giving a nod, up the chimney he rose;
He sprang to his sleigh, to his team gave a whistle,
And away they all flew like the down of a thistle.
But I heard him exclaim, ere he drove out of sight —
'Happy Christmas to all, and to all a good night!'

Chestnut ice cream

with vanilla and Amarena cherries

1 vanilla pod
500ml (17fl oz) milk
50g (1¾oz) granulated (white) sugar
300g (10½oz) precooked chestnuts
50g (1¾oz) dark chocolate, plus a little extra for garnish
Amarena cherries

Also

Potato ricer

Slice the vanilla pod open lengthways and scrape out the seeds. Add the milk, sugar, vanilla pod and seeds to a small saucepan and bring to a boil. Add the chestnuts and simmer over medium heat for about 20 minutes. Remove the vanilla pod and purée the chestnut mixture thoroughly.

Coarsely chop the chocolate and melt it in the chestnut mixture. When cool enough, cover with cling film and chill for at least 1 hour.

Make chocolate curls or shavings for the garnish. Press the chestnut mixture through a potato ricer into serving bowls and serve garnished with chocolate and Amarena cherries.

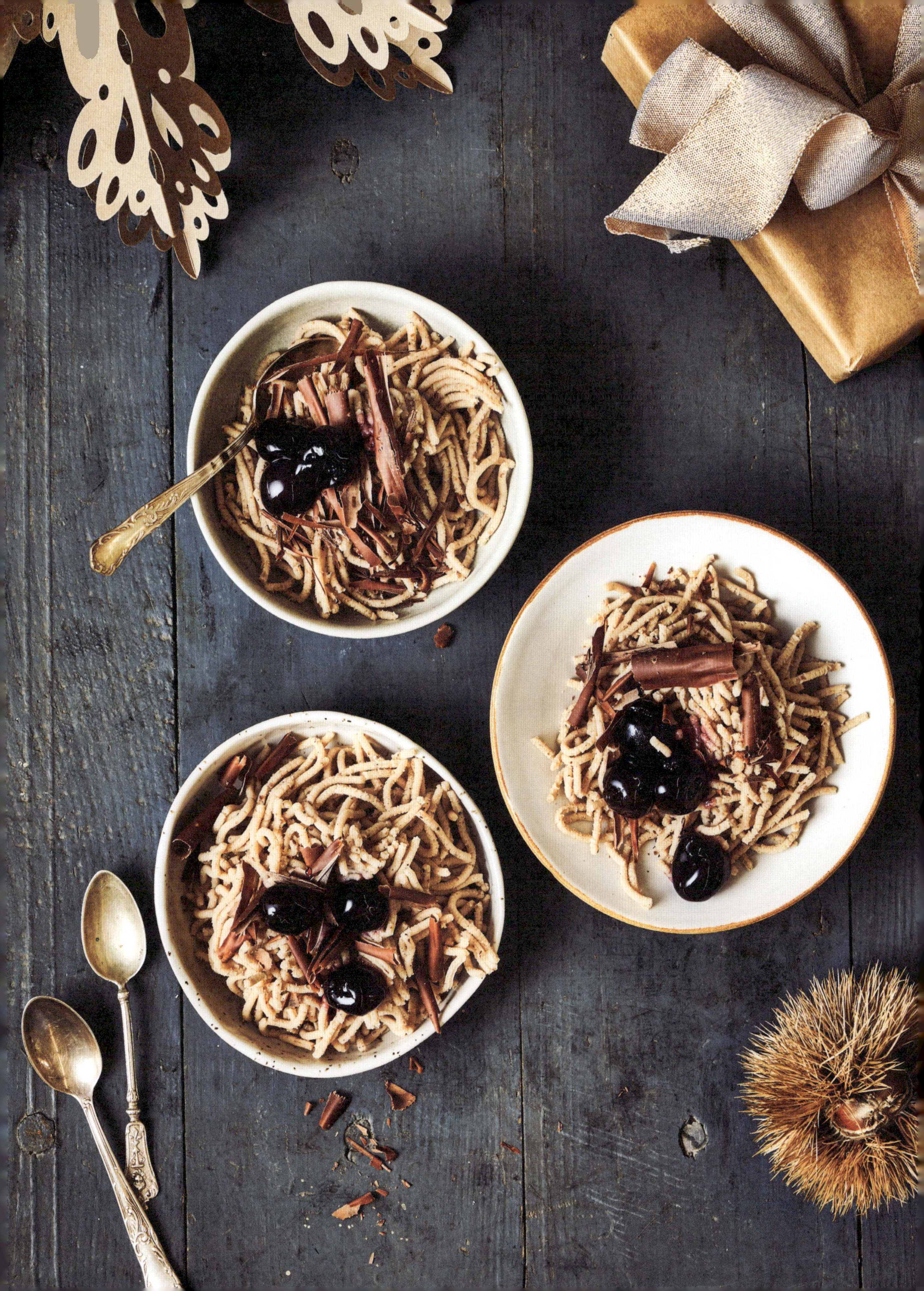

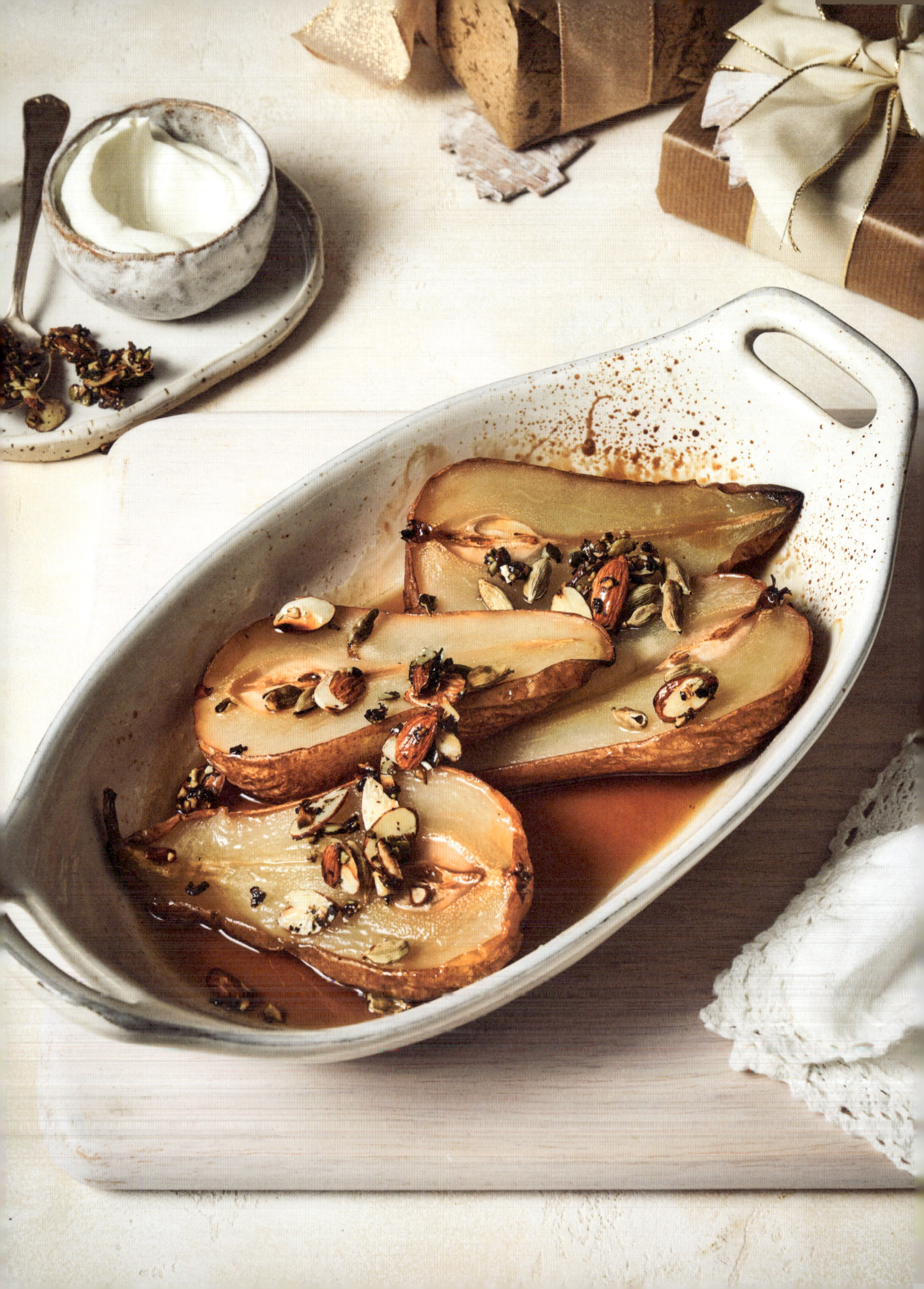

Roasted maple pears

with almond praline and yoghurt

Preheat the oven to 200°C (400°F/Gas 6) and grease a baking dish with butter. For the maple pears, peel the pears and halve them lengthways.

Mix the maple syrup and cardamom in a bowl, turn the pear halves in the mixture and place the pears, cut side up, in the baking dish. Drizzle the remaining maple syrup and cardamom mixture over the pears and bake in the oven for 20 minutes. When the pears are soft and lightly browned, remove from the oven, cover and keep warm.

For the almond praline, coarsely chop the pumpkin seeds and slice the almonds and dry roast over medium heat. Be careful, they burn easily! Add the maple syrup and salt and allow to caramelise briefly. Spread the mixture on a sheet of baking paper, leave to cool and break into small pieces.

To serve, divide the yogurt and pears among 4 small plates. Drizzle a little maple syrup on top and finish with the almond praline.

For the pears

4 ripe pears
4 tablespoons maple syrup
1 teaspoon ground cardamom

For the almond praline

70g (2½oz) pumpkin seeds (pepitas)
150g (5½oz) almonds
2 tablespoons maple syrup, plus a little extra for drizzling
1 pinch of salt

Also

Butter, for the dish
300g (10½oz) Greek yoghurt

Honey parfait

with mulled wine plums

For the parfait

90g (3¼oz) blossom honey
4 eggs yolks
1 pinch of salt
300ml (10½fl oz) single (pure) cream
1 teaspoon orange liqueur

For the mulled wine plums

500g (1lb 2oz) sugar plums
2 tablespoons honey, plus extra for drizzling
1 cinnamon stick
100ml (3½fl oz) dry red wine

Also

Oil, for the tin
Loaf tin

For the parfait, heat the honey in a pan over medium heat, bring to the boil briefly, then set aside.

Whisk the egg yolks and salt in a bowl for about 10 minutes until the mixture is quite firm. Stir in the honey.

In a separate bowl, whip the cream until stiff. Fold in the orange liqueur and egg yolk mixture. Grease a loaf tin with oil, pour in the mixture, cover with cling film and chill in the freezer for 24 hours.

For the mulled wine plums, pit and halve the plums. Place in a pan with the remaining ingredients and simmer for about 10 minutes to reduce a little. Remove the cinnamon stick.

Arrange the plums on top of the parfait and drizzle honey over both to taste. Cut into slices to serve.

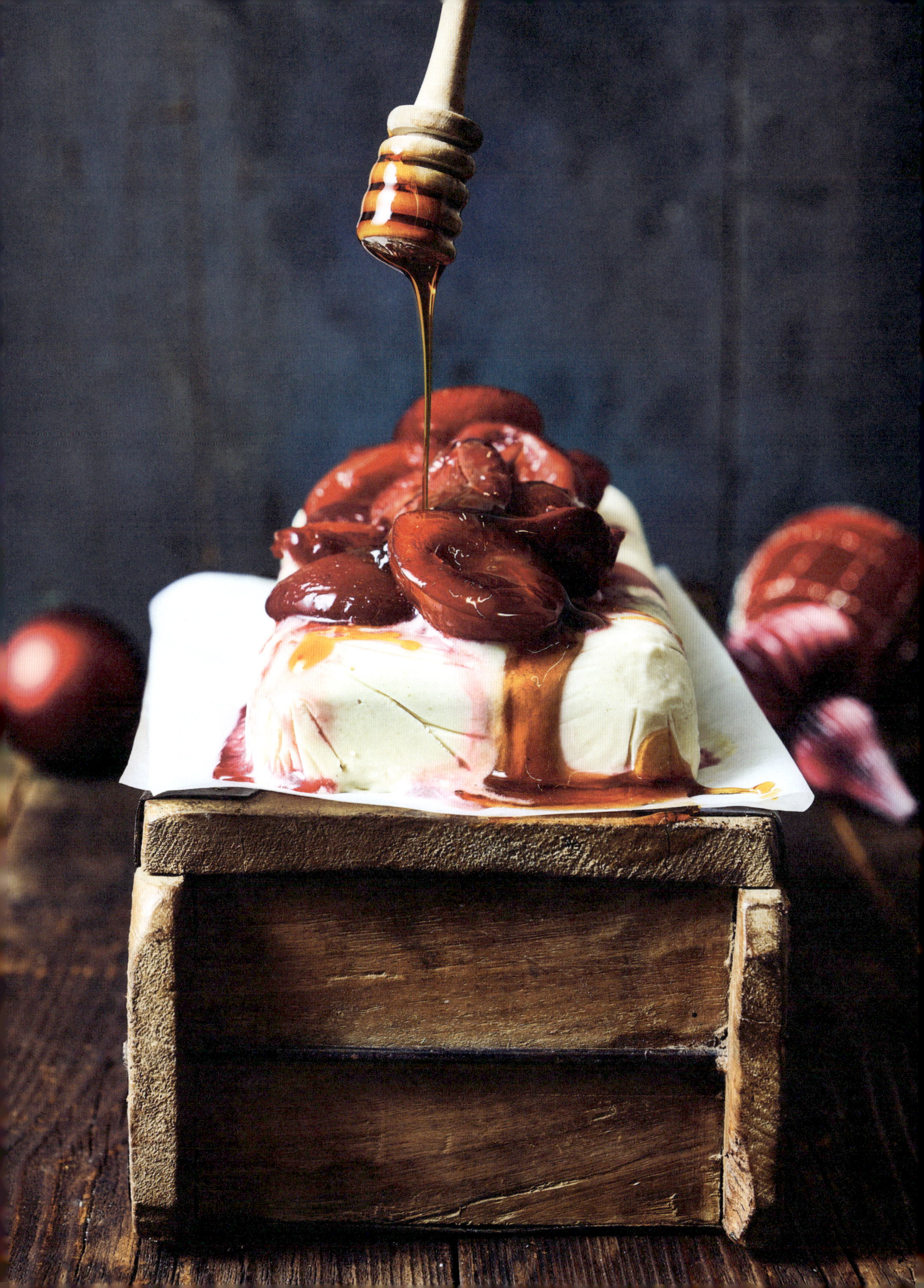

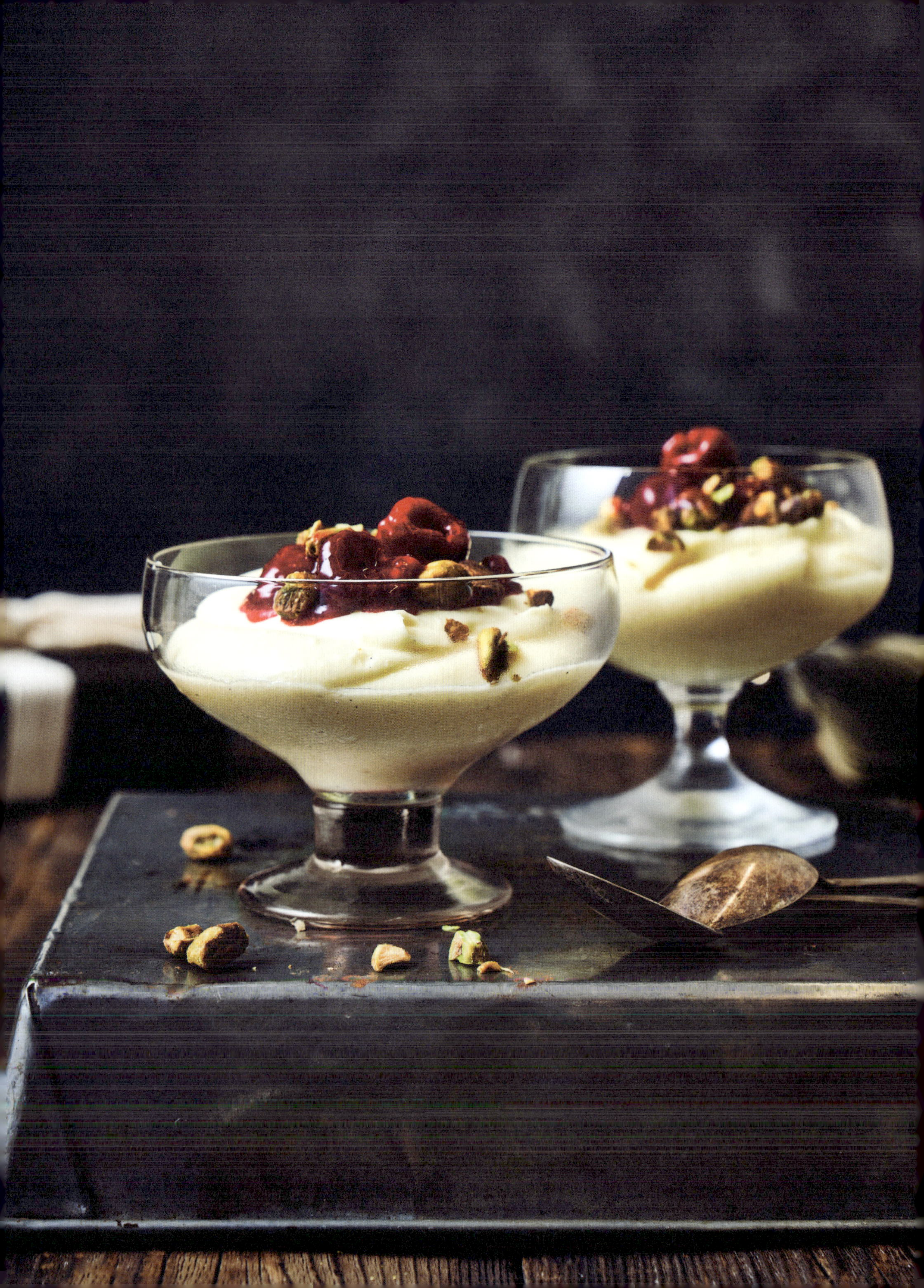

White chocolate cream

with raspberries

In a small stainless steel bowl, gently melt the chocolate in a double boiler over low heat. Remove from the heat and set aside to cool a little.

Slice the vanilla pod open lengthways and scrape out the seeds. Stir the mascarpone, vanilla seeds and yoghurt into the melted chocolate. Transfer the cream to 4 serving glasses or bowls, cover with cling film and refrigerate.

For the raspberry sauce, allow the raspberries to defrost a little. Set a handful aside and purée the rest with the icing sugar, lemon juice and zest. Pass through a fine sieve into a bowl. Stir in the remaining whole raspberries. Spoon the raspberry sauce over the cream, sprinkle with the pistachios and serve.

For the cream

200g (7oz) white chocolate
½ vanilla pod
250g (9oz) mascarpone
100g (3½oz) yoghurt

For the sauce

300g (10½oz) raspberries (frozen)
2 tablespoons icing (confectioners') sugar
Juice and grated zest of ½ lemon

Also

A handful of green pistachio nuts
Double boiler

Maurice Reinhold von Stern

Winter Prayer

On this snowy winter's night
The new moon coldly shines
Silver shards of frosted light
Flicker in the forest pines
O you beautiful world!

The enchanted moon shivers
In the frozen lake's mirror
The eternal stars shimmer
So far yet so much nearer
O you beautiful world!

Softly glides the moon's shadow
Over village and valley and dell
And lovingly through ice and snow
Floats the silver sound of a bell
O you beautiful world!

Emily and Fritz Koegel

The Baked Apple

Guess children, come,
Which treat is almost done!
Hear it sizzle and hiss!
Soon ready for your dish!
The pipple, the papple,
The tipple, the tapple,
The yellow-red apple.

Children make haste;
Pick up a plate;
Forks at your side;
Make your mouth wide
For the pipple, the papple,
The tipple, the tapple,
The golden-brown apple.

They go at it, blow at it,
They greet it and eat it,
Their lips are smacking,
Their tongues are lapping
The pipple, the papple,
The tipple, the tapple,
The delectable apple.

Pannacotta
with caramel sauce

1 vanilla pod
100ml (3½fl oz) milk
200ml (7fl oz) single (pure) cream
80g (2¾oz) granulated (white) sugar
3 leaves gelatine

Also

4 small ramekins

Rinse the ramekins with water. Slice the vanilla pod open lengthways and scrape out the seeds. Set aside the pod.

Add the milk, cream, vanilla pod and seeds and 30g (1oz) sugar to a small saucepan. Bring to a boil and simmer over low heat for 15 minutes. Remove the saucepan from the heat.

In another small saucepan, caramelise the remaining sugar over medium heat. Once the sugar has turned golden brown, deglaze with 2 tablespoons water and whisk until the mixture comes away from the sides of the pan. Divide the caramel mixture among the ramekins.

Soak the gelatine leaves in cold water for about 5 minutes, then squeeze out. Remove the vanilla pod from the cream mixture. Dissolve the gelatine in the mixture and divide it evenly among the ramekins.

Leave to cool to room temperature, then refrigerate until set, at least 3 hours, but preferably overnight.

To serve, briefly place the ramekins in hot water so that the pannacotta comes away from the edges. If necessary, slide a sharp knife around the edges. Turn the pannacotta out onto dessert plates and serve.

Tip: Serve with fresh strawberries and mint leaves.

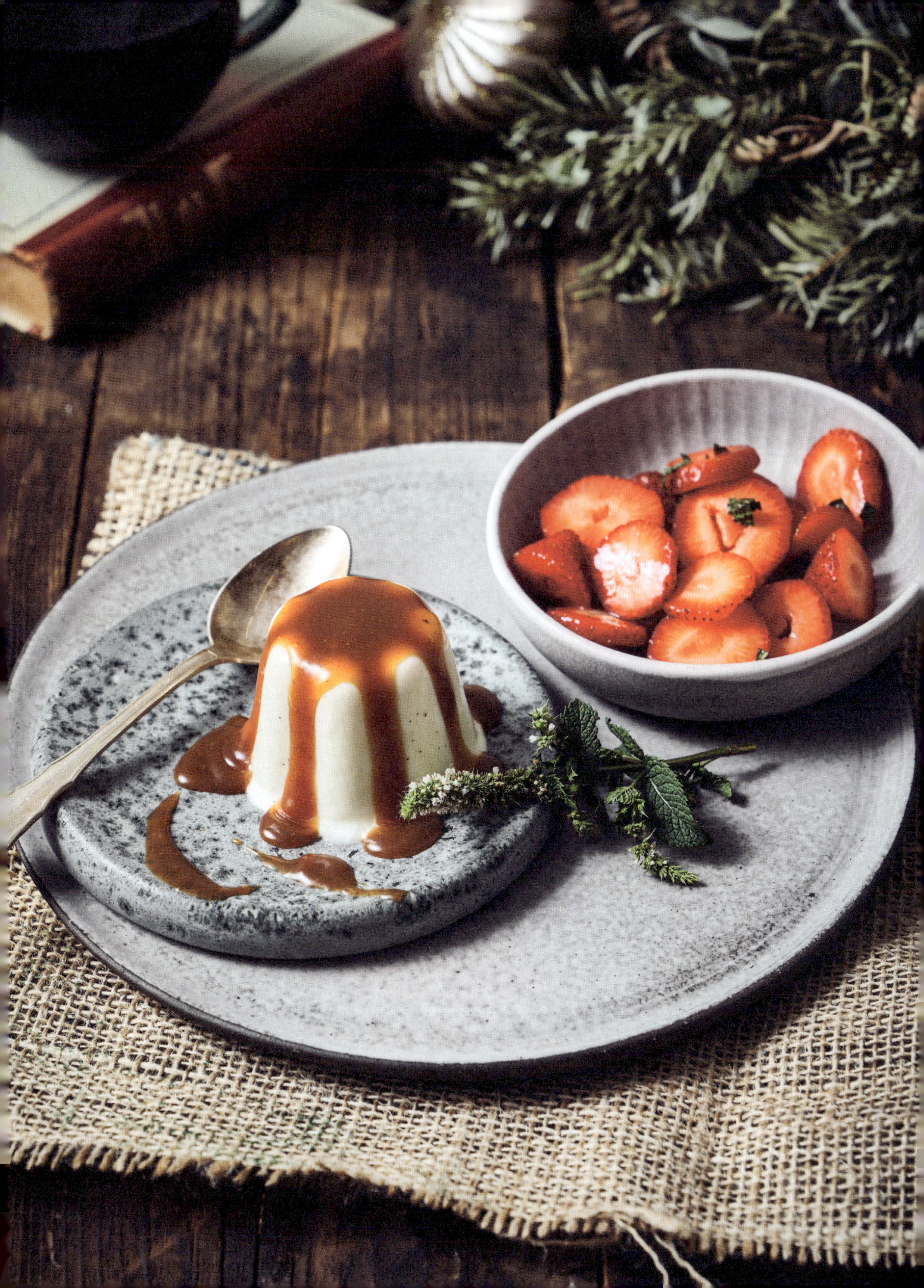

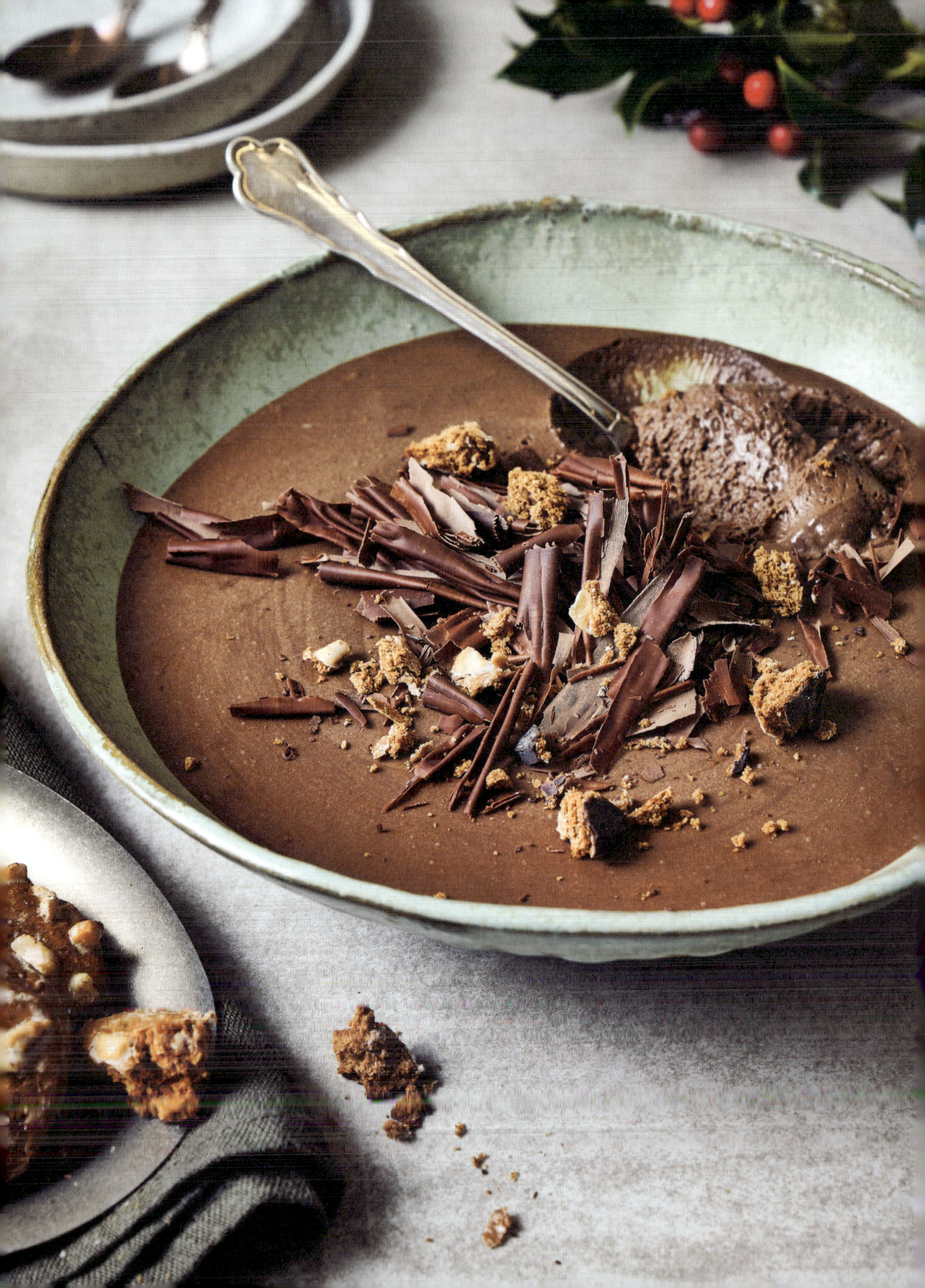

Mousse au chocolat

Coarsely chop the chocolate and transfer to a saucepan together with the milk. Heat both gently to melt the chocolate. Add the butter, sugar, cinnamon and espresso and heat through. Remove the saucepan from the heat, add orange liqueur to taste and leave everything to cool to room temperature.

Whip the cream in a bowl until stiff and fold it into the chocolate mixture, adding more sugar to your taste.

Divide the mousse among 4 dessert glasses or transfer it to a bowl. Cover with cling film and chill for at least 4 hours. It should be nice and firm for serving.

Make chocolate curls or shavings for the garnish. Crumble the gingerbread biscuits and garnish the mousse to taste with chocolate, gingerbread and cinnamon.

200g (7oz) dark chocolate (minimum 70% cocoa)
90ml (3fl oz) milk
20g (¾oz) butter
50g (1¾oz) caster (superfine) sugar, plus a little more for the cream
½ teaspoon ground cinnamon
2 tablespoons cold espresso
Orange liqueur, to taste
250ml (9fl oz) single (pure) cream

Also

Dark chocolate, for garnish
3 gingerbread biscuits (lebkuchen)
Ground cinnamon

Christmas cookie custard

Serves 6

1 (37g/1⅓oz) sachet of vanilla custard powder

500ml (17fl oz) milk

40g (1½oz) granulated (white) sugar

200ml (7fl oz) single (pure) cream

300 g (10½oz) speculaas (Biscoff) biscuits

50g (1¾oz) ground hazelnuts

3 tablespoons amaretto

4 tablespoons strawberry jam

Also

A handful of speculaas (Biscoff) biscuits, for garnish

A little mint

6 fresh figs

In a cup, whisk the custard powder with 5 tablespoons milk and the sugar until smooth. Bring the remaining milk to a boil in a small saucepan. Add the custard powder mixture, whisking continuously. Bring to the boil briefly and then remove the saucepan from the heat. When cool enough, cover the custard with cling film and leave to cool completely.

Whip the cream in a bowl until stiff and fold into the custard. Place the biscuits in a large bowl and crush roughly. Sprinkle the hazelnuts on top and drizzle with the amaretto and jam.

Transfer the custard to the bowl. Leave the cookie custard to infuse for at least 6 hours, best overnight.

Serve with crumbled biscuits, finely chopped mint and halved figs.

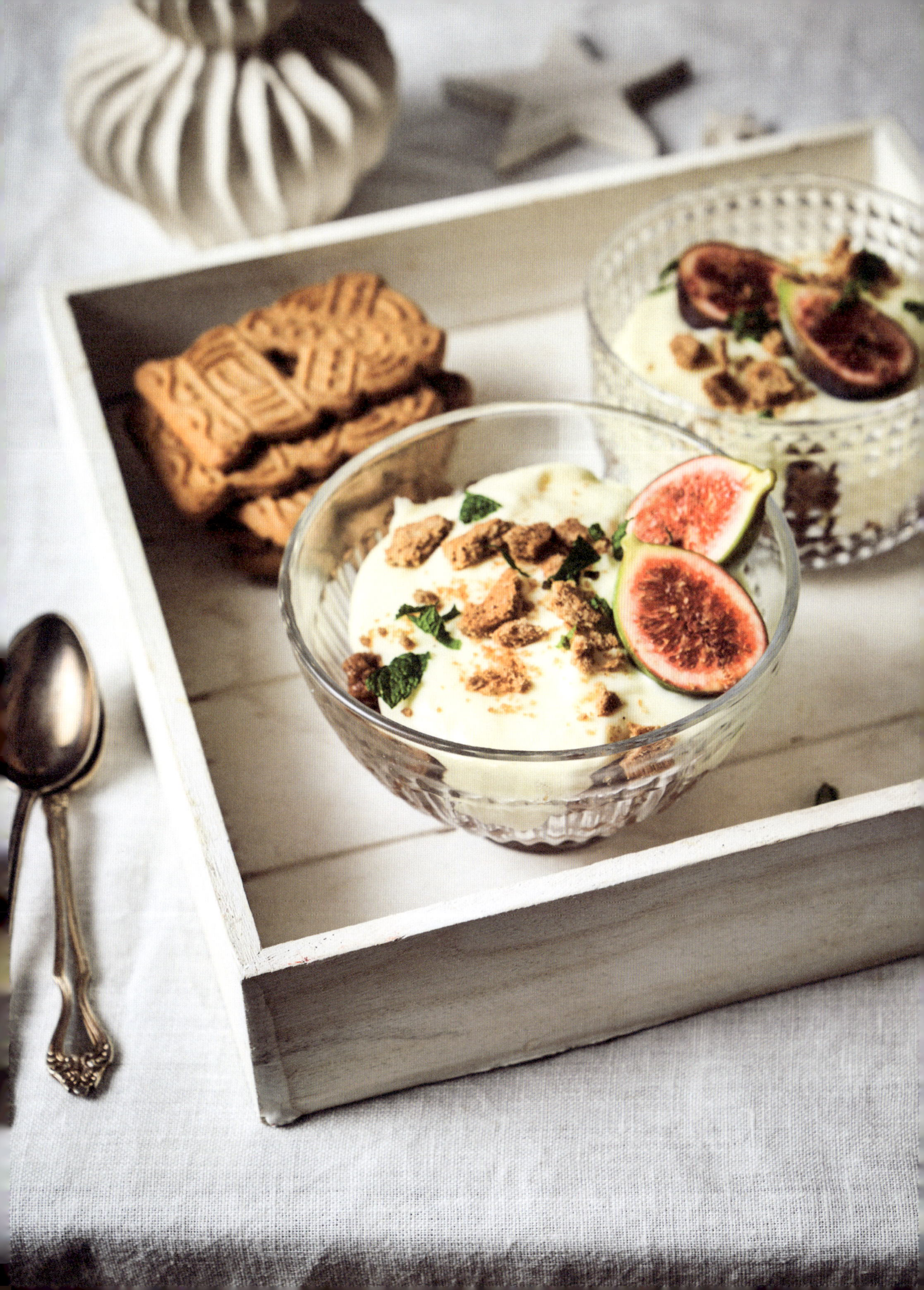

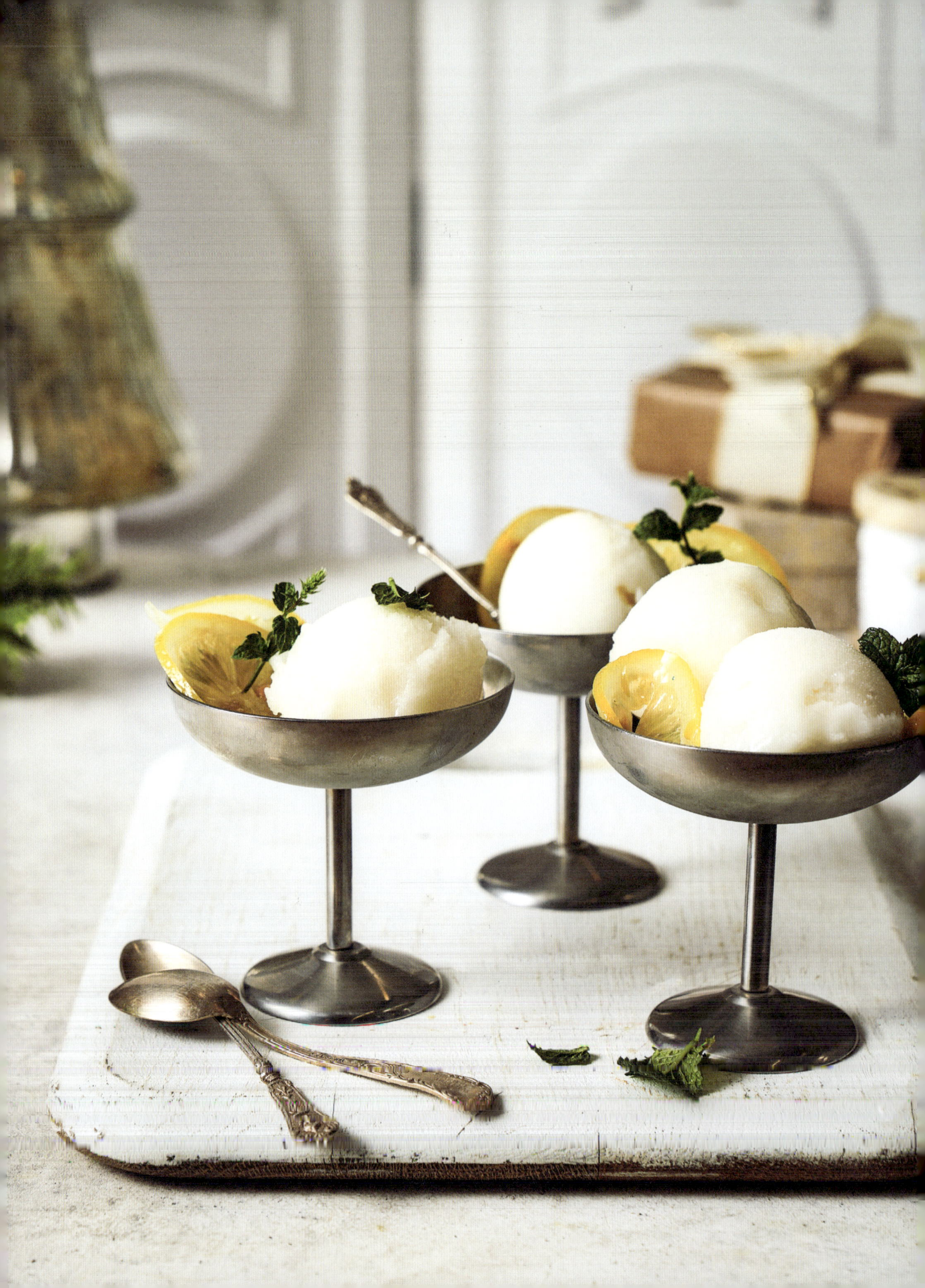

Lemon sorbet

Heat the sugar with 200ml (7fl oz) water in a small saucepan, stirring constantly until the sugar has dissolved. Boil for about 1 minute to make a syrup and remove from the heat.

Mix the lemon juice and orange juice in a bowl. In another bowl, beat the egg white until very stiff, fold into the juice and then fold in the cooled syrup and lemon zest. Cover the mixture with cling film and chill for at least 20 minutes.

Mix well with a hand or stand mixer, transfer to an ice cream maker and leave to churn for 30-45 minutes. Meanwhile, wash the lemon and cut into thin slices. Bring the remaining sugar and 50ml (1¾fl oz) water to the boil in a small saucepan. Add the lemon slices and simmer over a low heat for 2 minutes. Remove from the heat and leave to cool completely.

Place 2 lemon slices in each serving bowl, add the sorbet and garnish with mint leaves. Serve immediately, as the sorbet will melt quickly.

Makes about 800ml (28fl oz)

200g (7oz) caster (superfine) sugar, plus 50g (1¾oz) extra
Juice of 7 lemons
Juice of ½ orange
1 egg white
Grated zest of 1 lemon

*****Also*****

Hand or stand mixer
Ice cream maker
1 lemon
Mint leaves, for garnish

Orange mascarpone cream
with slivered almonds

Serves 2

2 oranges

1 vanilla pod

150g (5½oz) mascarpone

50g (1¾oz) quark

2 tablespoons granulated (white) sugar

3 tablespoons single (pure) cream

1 tablespoon butter

50g (1¾oz) slivered or flaked almonds

3 teaspoons cinnamon sugar

Also

Fresh mint and ground cinnamon, for garnish

Peel and segment the oranges and remove any pith. Divide between 2 dessert bowls, keeping aside a few to garnish. Slice the vanilla pod open lengthways and scrape out the seeds. In a bowl, whisk the mascarpone and quark with the vanilla seeds, sugar and cream. Spread the mixture over the orange segments.

Melt the butter in a pan. Add the slivered almonds. Sprinkle with the cinnamon sugar and toast the almonds until golden. Leave to cool and garnish the mascarpone cream with the remaining orange slices, toasted almonds, mint leaves and cinnamon.

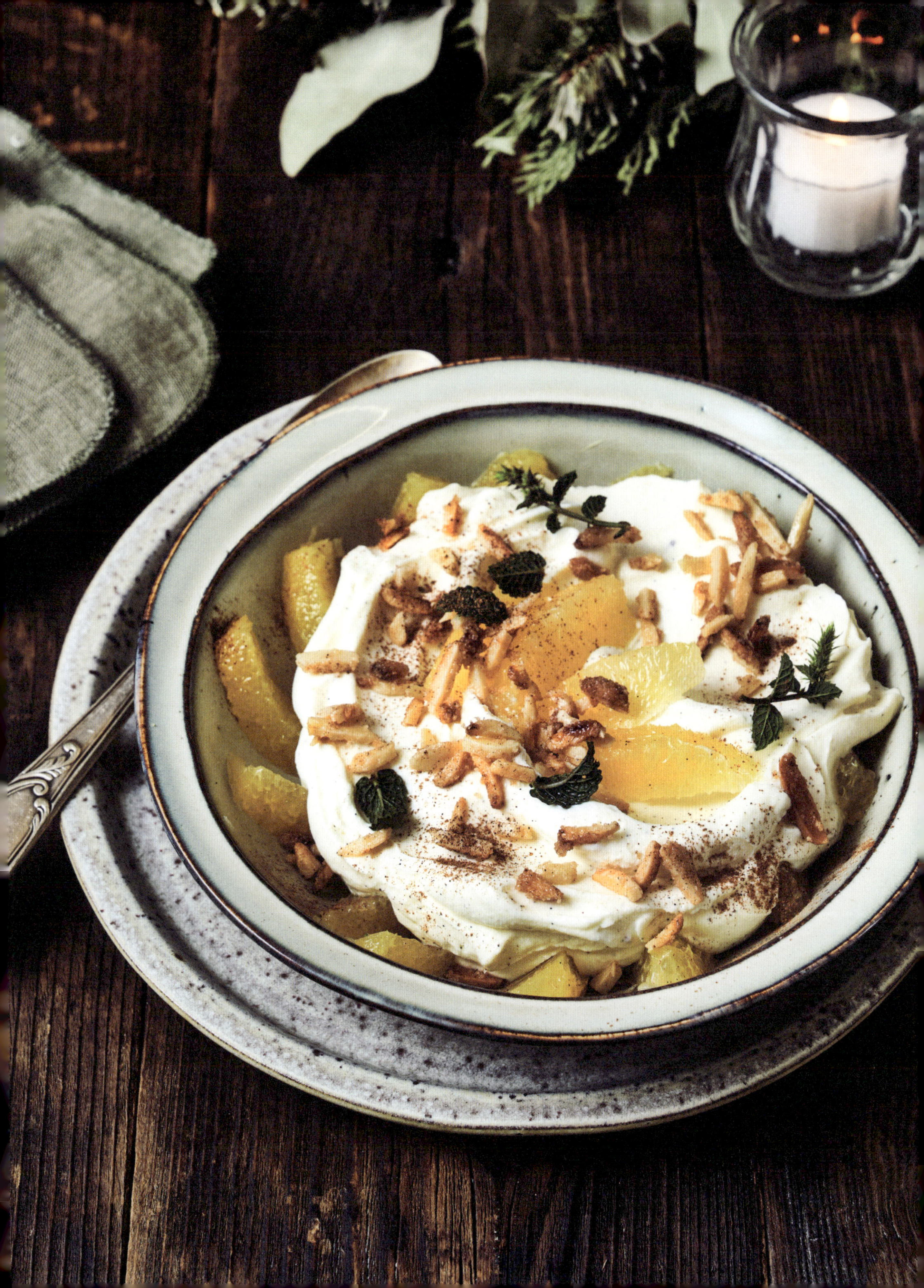

E.T.A. Hoffmann

The Nutcracker (extract)

The Nutcracker led Marie to the closet in the hallway. The closet door was open and Marie could see her father's coat. The nutcracker nimbly climbed into the closet, and in an instant, a delicate staircase came down through the coat sleeve.

'You go ahead,' said the Nutcracker. When Marie reached the top of the collar, she suddenly found herself in a wonderfully fragrant meadow, from which millions of sparks shone like flashing gemstones.

'We're at Candy Meadow,' said the Nutcracker. 'That way!'

Marie noticed a beautiful gate in front of her, as if made of the finest marble. But as they got closer, she saw that it was made of sugared almonds and raisins.

Marie and the Nutcracker went through the gate and soon the sweetest smells wafted around them from a small forest. Golden and silver fruits hung from brightly coloured stems and bathed the forest in a mysterious light.

'We're in the Christmas Forest,' the Nutcracker explained, clapping his hands several times, summoning little shepherds and shepherdesses, huntsmen and huntswomen, who came and did a delightful dance.

Then the two of them followed a sweetly babbling, whispering stream, the Orange Brook. Beyond it was the Almond Milk Lake and immediately after that they came to the Lemonade River, which radiated a pleasant freshness. Not much further on, they came to a dark yellow river, rolling through its bed, with wonderfully sweet scents emanating from it.

Not far from there was a little village, where the houses, the church, the presbytery, in short, everything, was dark brown, but richly decorated with almonds and candied lemon peel, and shining with golden roofs. 'That's Marzipan Hamlet,' said the Nutcracker. 'The people here are always grumpy because they suffer from constant toothaches.'

Beyond it was a small town of colourful, transparent houses. 'That's Candy Town,' said the Nutcracker. 'But we don't have time to visit every village and town in the country. Come on, to the capital!'

The Nutcracker strode ahead briskly. Soon they were standing in front of rose-red shimmering water, rippled with pink-silver waves, from which wafted a wonderful scent of roses. 'This is the lake that Uncle Drosselmeier was going to make for me,' Marie exclaimed with delight.

The Nutcracker smiled mockingly and said, 'Your uncle could never do such a thing, it's you who is much more likely to achieve that.' Then the Nutcracker clapped his hands and a seashell carriage, pulled by two golden-scaled dolphins, came to the shore. From it, twelve servants jumped ashore to carry Marie and the Nutcracker to the carriage. Marie gazed dreamily at the waves, from which a pretty girl's face smiled at her. 'Look!' she exclaimed in surprise. 'There's Princess Pirlipat down there!'

The Nutcracker sighed and said, 'That's not Princess Pirlipat, that's you, and always only you, always only your own face smiling from every passing rose-coloured wave.' Marie shrank back and felt very embarrassed.

Shortly afterwards, they were carried ashore by servants. 'There's the capital,' said the Nutcracker, taking Marie by the hand.

Oh, the sights Marie saw there! The beauty and splendour of the capital was almost beyond words! Its walls and towers were resplendent in the most vivid colours. The roofs were crowned with fine braids and the towers were decorated with delicate colourful leaves. Silver soldiers presented their rifles to the Nutcracker and Marie, and an elegantly dressed man called out: 'Welcome to Marmaladeburg!'

They had barely taken a few steps when they came to a large market square. All the houses around it were made of pure sugar. At the centre of the square stood a tall pillar of colourful sweets, surrounded by fountains of bubbling lemonade. But even more delightful than all that were the thousands of little people in the square, strolling arm in arm, laughing and singing.

Enchanted, Marie watched the hustle and bustle around her as she and the Nutcracker made their way through the crowd. Suddenly they came to a palace bathed in a rosy light, with a hundred turrets reaching high into the sky. The vast dome at the centre of the magnificent palace, and the pyramid-shaped roofs of the towers, were covered with a thousand ornaments, shining in all colours.

'This is the Palace of the Marzipans,' said the Nutcracker, not without pride. The palace gates opened and twelve little pageboys emerged, carrying clove stalks lit up like torches. They were followed by four ladies, who were almost as tall as Marie's doll Clara, but dressed so splendidly that they could only be princesses. The Nutcracker took Marie's hand and introduced her to his sisters: 'This is Miss Marie Stahlbaum, who has saved my life!'

The princesses escorted Marie and the Nutcracker to the dining room through a hall whose walls were covered with crystals sparkling in all colours. They brought in a large number of tiny pots and bowls, spoons, knives and other kitchen utensils made of gold and silver. Then they brought in the most beautiful fruit and cakes Marie had ever seen.

The Nutcracker told of the terrible battle between his army and that of the Mouse King. Marie heard the Nutcracker's voice as if from afar. There was a soft singing and humming in the air, and she felt as if thin clouds of mist were rising, on which the princesses, the Nutcracker and she herself were floating. Up she went, higher and higher and higher...

Then suddenly there was a prrr – paff, and Marie felt as if she were falling from a great height. She opened her eyes and found herself in her bed. It was broad daylight and her mother was standing in front of her. 'How can you sleep for so long?' she said with a smile.

'You cannot imagine the wonders that the Nutcracker showed me last night!' Marie exclaimed and began to tell all that she had seen.

Mother looked at Marie in amazement. Then she said quietly: 'You had a long and very beautiful dream, my child.' But Marie stubbornly insisted that she had not dreamed it, that she had seen it all.

Amaretto dessert

1 jar of sour cherries (about 350g/12oz drained weight)

80g (2¾oz) amarettini biscuits, plus 4 whole biscuits for garnish

1 sachet of vanilla custard powder

80g (2¾oz) icing (confectioners') sugar

200ml (7fl oz) single (pure) cream

250g (9oz) mascarpone

60ml (2fl oz) amaretto

Transfer the cherries and their juice to a saucepan, setting aside 4 tablespoons of the juice. Heat the cherries through. Coarsely crush the amarettini biscuits. Whisk the custard powder with the reserved 4 tablespoons cherry juice until smooth. Bring the cherries to the boil and stir in the custard powder mixture. Add 20g (¾oz) icing sugar and simmer to reduce slightly. Remove the saucepan from the heat and leave the cherry mixture to cool.

Divide the mixture among 4 dessert glasses or bowls. In a bowl, whip the cream until stiff. Fold in the mascarpone and remaining icing sugar and stir in the amaretto. Divide the cream among the dessert bowls.

Cover with cling film and chill for at least 20 minutes.

Sprinkle with the amarettini crumbs and garnish with a whole amarettini biscuit each to serve.

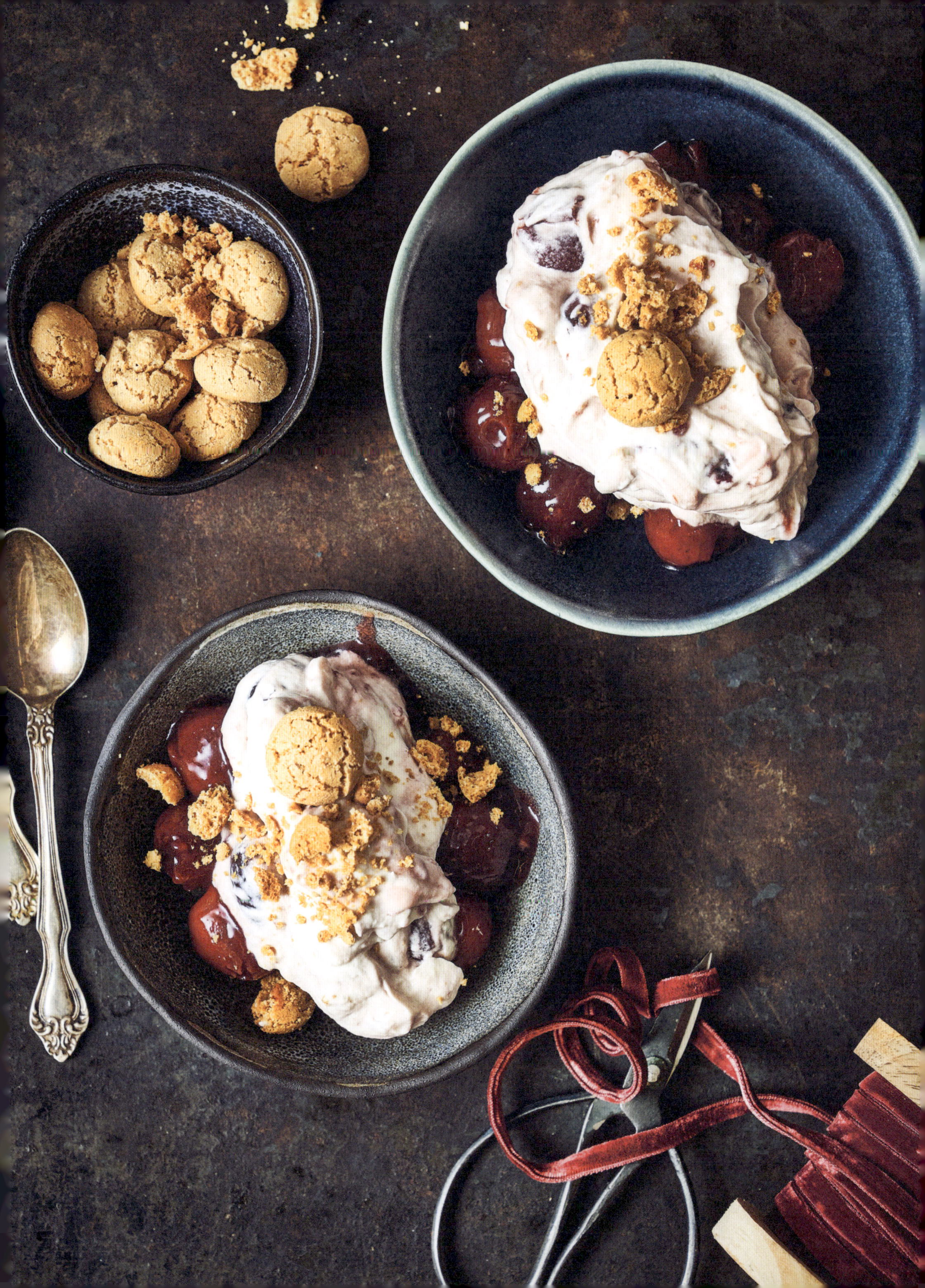

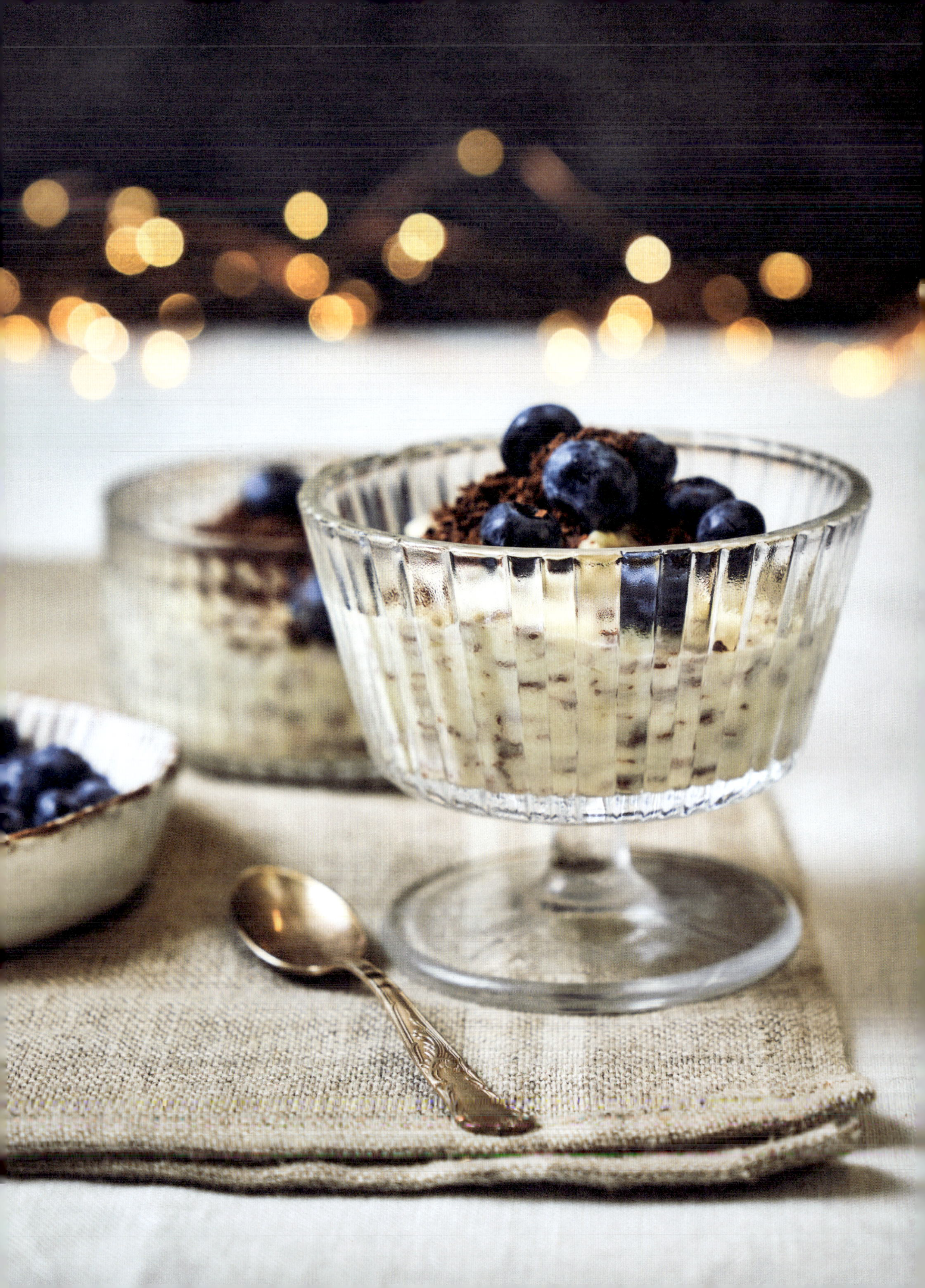

Gentleman's pudding

In a small bowl, mix the custard powder with 40g (1½oz) sugar and stir in 3 tablespoons of the milk. Heat the remaining milk in a small saucepan. Remove from the heat and whisk in the custard powder mixture. Return the pan to the heat and briefly bring the custard to the boil. Set aside to cool, stirring often to prevent a skin from forming.

In another bowl, whip the cream and the remaining sugar until stiff. Grate the chocolate. When the custard has cooled, stir in the Kirsch and 100g (3½oz) of the chocolate. Fold the cream into the custard.

Transfer the custard to glass bowls and garnish with the blueberries and the remaining grated chocolate.

30g (1oz) vanilla custard powder

50g (1¾oz) granulated (white) sugar

500ml (17fl oz) milk

250ml (9fl oz) single (pure) cream

150g (5½oz) dark chocolate

1 tablespoon Kirsch

1 handful of fresh blueberries

White chocolate and coconut parfait
with red fruit jelly

For the parfait

20g (¾oz) desiccated or finely shredded coconut
150g (5½oz) white chocolate
125ml (4fl oz) whipping cream
1 vanilla pod
50ml (1¾fl oz) coconut milk
Juice and grated zest of ½ lime
1 pinch of salt

For the red fruit jelly

1 teaspoon cornflour (cornstarch)
2 tablespoons orange juice
100ml (3½fl oz) red wine
20g (¾oz) granulated (white) sugar
1 cinnamon stick
2 cloves
250g (9oz) mixed berries (frozen)

Also

Double boiler
1 round tin (500ml/17fl oz capacity)

Lightly dry roast the coconut in a pan. Remove and set aside to cool. Coarsely chop the chocolate. Melt in a stainless steel bowl over a double boiler and set aside to cool a little. In another bowl, whip the cream until stiff and gently fold it into the chocolate.

Slice the vanilla pod open lengthways and scrape out the seeds. Add the seeds to the chocolate cream. Add the coconut milk, lime juice and zest and salt and mix to combine.

Finally, fold in half of the coconut. Line the tin with cling film.

Pour the mixture into the tin and freeze overnight.

For the red fruit jelly, dissolve the cornflour in the orange juice. Bring the red wine to the boil with the sugar, cinnamon stick and cloves. Reduce for 1 minute, then whisk in the cornflour mixture to thicken.

Immediately stir the frozen berries into the hot red wine mixture. Remove the cinnamon stick and cloves and set aside.

The next day, turn the parfait out onto a plate. Garnish with the remaining coconut and serve with the red fruit jelly.

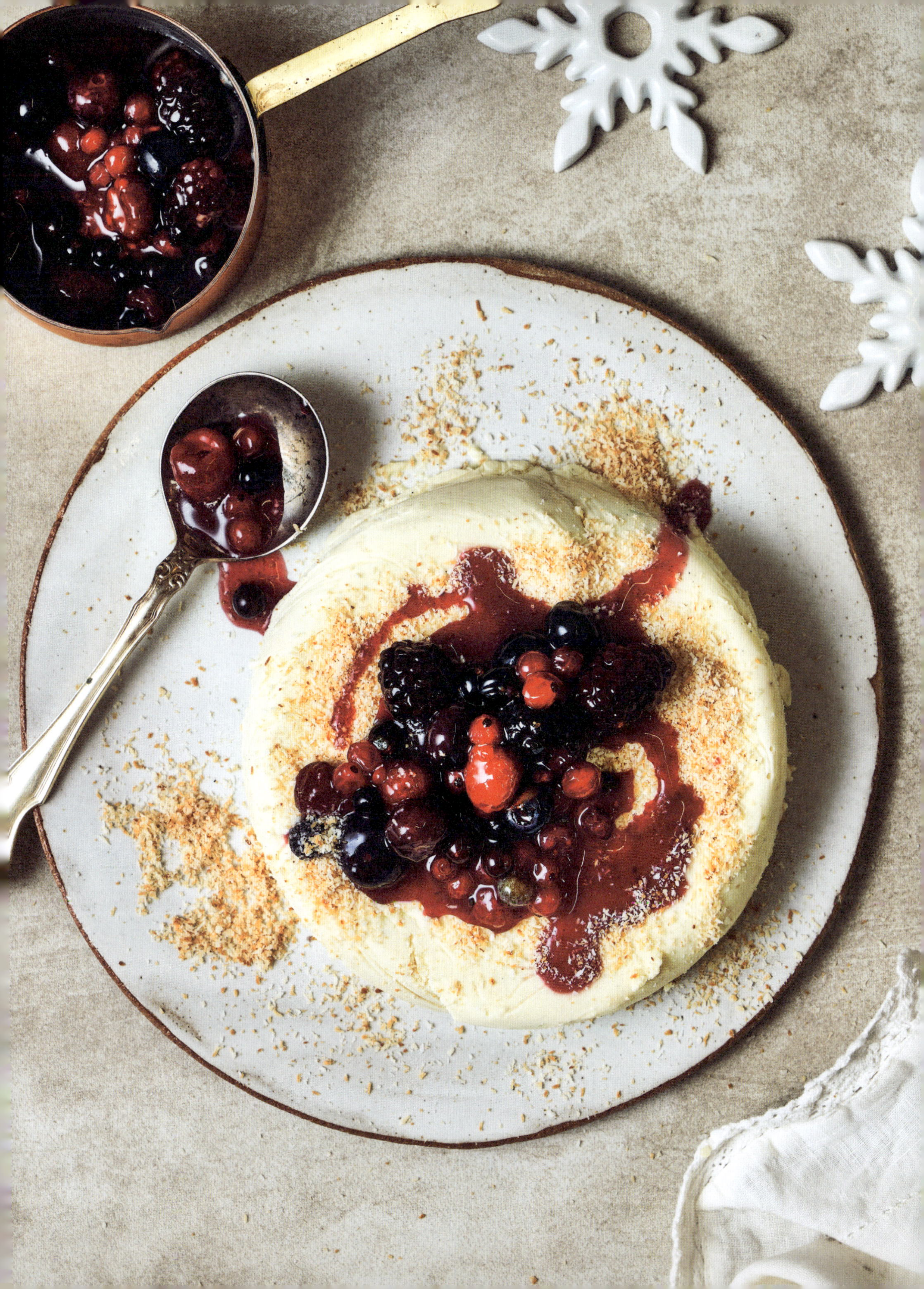

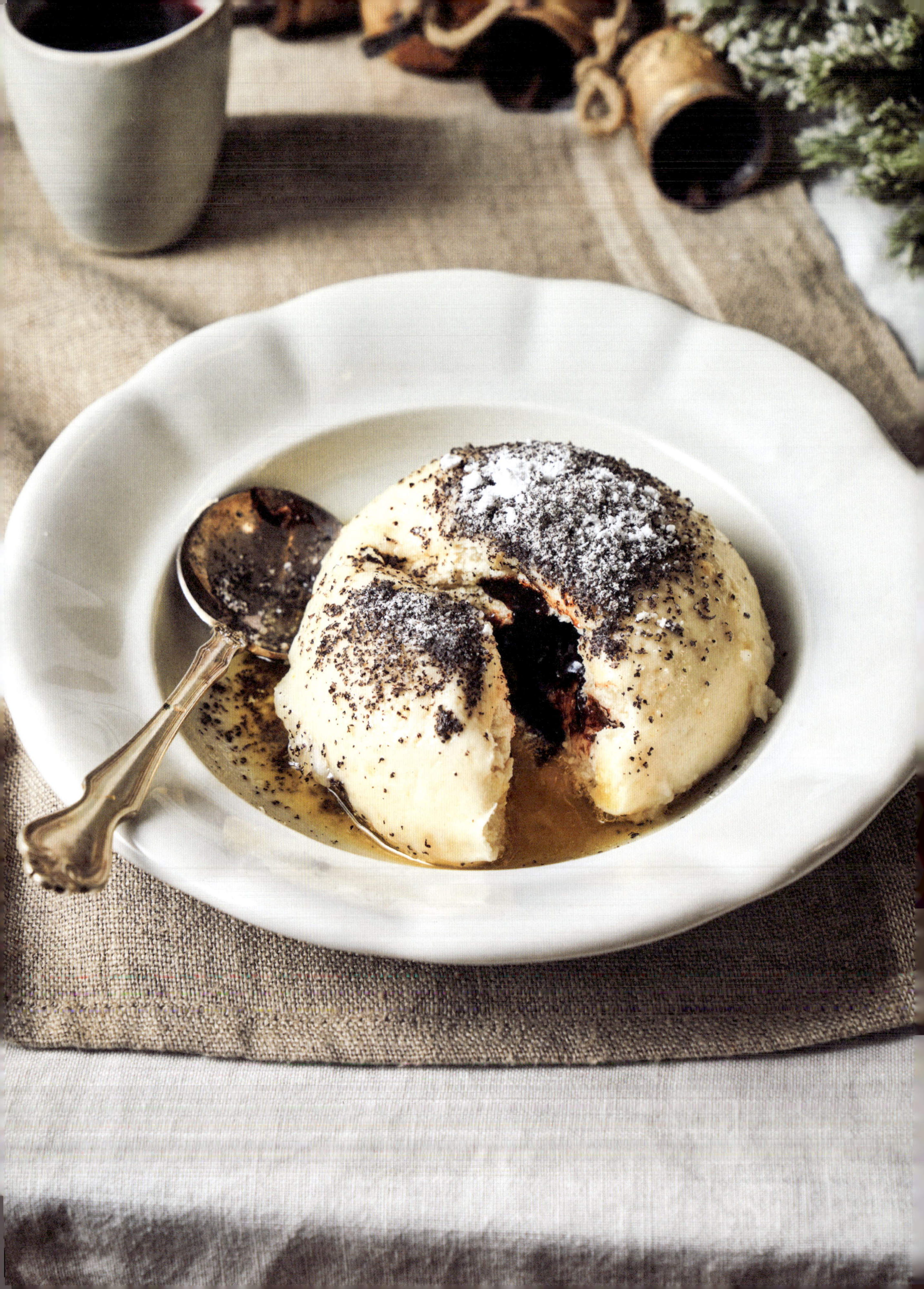

Sweet fluffy dumplings
with poppy seed butter

For the dumplings, crumble the yeast into a mixing bowl. Mix with 50ml (1¾fl oz) lukewarm milk and 1 teaspoon vanilla sugar. Leave to rise for about 15 minutes. Using the dough hook(s) of a hand or stand mixer, combine the remaining milk, the remaining sugar, the flour, the egg yolk and the yeast mixture. Finally, add the butter and salt. Dust the dough lightly with flour, cover with a clean tea towel and leave to rise for 45 minutes until doubled in volume.

Transfer the dough onto a floured work surface. Knead well and divide into 4 portions. Flatten each portion into 1.5cm (⅝ inch) thick rounds. Place 1 tablespoon of plum jam in the centre of each round, fold the dough over on all sides and gently shape into a dumpling. Place on a baking tray lined with baking paper with the folded side down. Cover with a tea towel and leave to rise for a further 20 minutes.

Fill a wide saucepan with water to a depth of 2–3cm (¾–1¼ inches) and bring to the boil. Line a steamer tray with a clean tea towel and place in the saucepan. Place the dumplings on the steamer tray, leaving a little space between them. Cover and cook over medium heat for about 15 minutes. Remove from the heat and leave for a further 2 minutes.

In the meantime, heat the butter in a pan until lightly browned, then stir in the poppy seeds and icing sugar. Remove the dumplings from the saucepan and arrange on plates. Drizzle the poppy seed butter over the dumplings, then sprinkle more icing sugar on top to finish.

Tip: Serve with a warm vanilla sauce if you like.

For the dumplings

20g (¾oz) fresh yeast
125ml (4fl oz) milk
40g (1½oz) vanilla sugar
250g (9oz) plain (all-purpose) flour, plus some extra
1 egg yolk
50g (1¾oz) butter, at room temperature
1 pinch of salt
4 tablespoons plum jam

For the poppy seed butter

40g (1½oz) butter
1 tablespoon poppy seeds
1 tablespoon icing (confectioners') sugar, plus more for garnish

Also

Hand or stand mixer
Steamer tray

Joseph von Eichendorff

Christmas

The market and streets stand still and ghostly,
Each house in all the silence glows,
Along the lanes my thoughts come with me,
As the festive spirit ever grows.

In every window a housewife places
A toy with colours of faith a-gleam
A thousand children's enchanted faces
Silently wonder their happy dream.

Now away I wander beyond the wall
Out to where the fields are free,
To towering beauty, to holy awe,
To the grand and silent world I see!

The stars weave round and all the spheres
And in that solitude of snow
Are songs such as an angel hears —
And oh, the time of grace I know!

Wilhelm Lobsien

Winter Night

Twilight bliss and fields of fog.
Snowed-in solitude and quiet
And a wondrous soft and mellow
Christmas peace both far and wide.

Yet now and then, lost in the wind
There comes a rustling sound.
And the faintest peal of bells
Roams across the ground.

And your eyes illuminate
The dark of sleep wakes up to light ...
And so you wander in the silent,
Soft and gentle winter night.

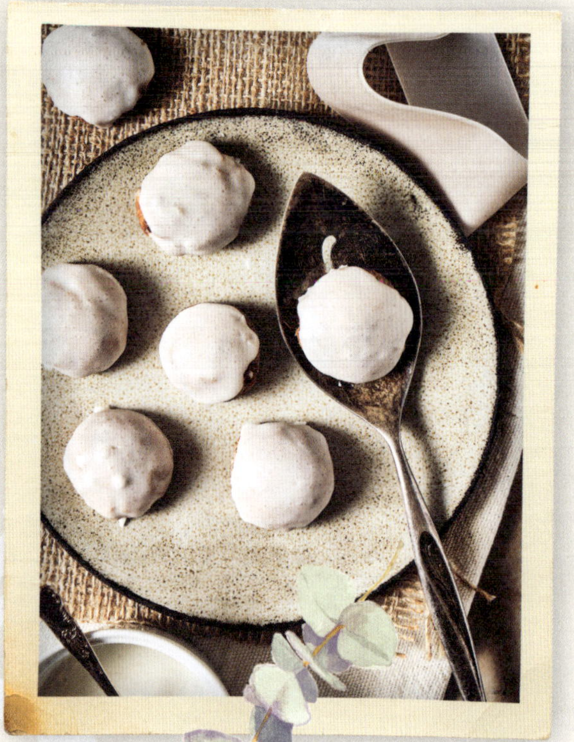

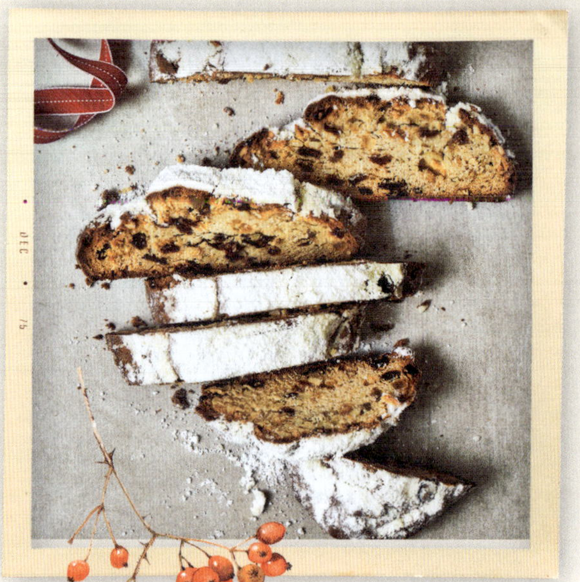

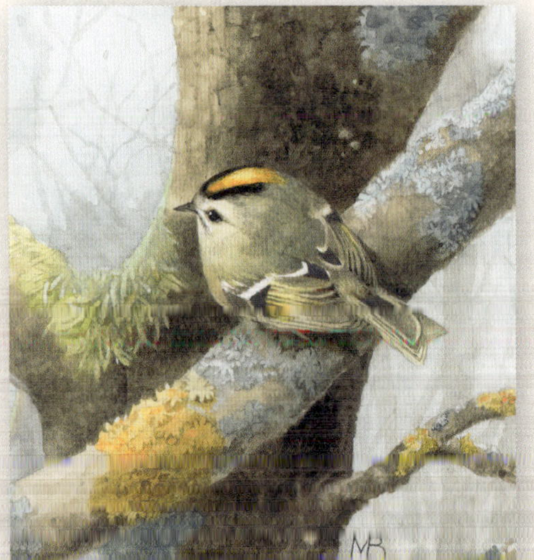

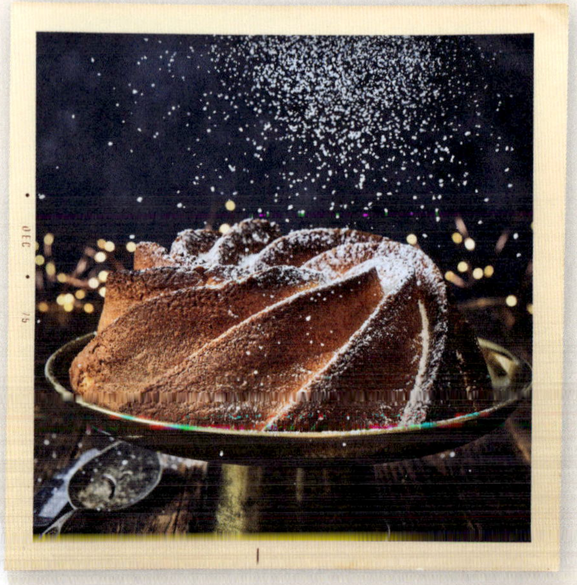

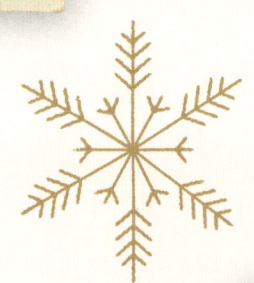

Sweet
Christmas baking

Vanilla crescents

Makes 2 trays of biscuits

For the dough

200g (7oz) butter, at room temperature
250g (9oz) plain (all-purpose) flour
100g (3½oz) ground almonds
70g (2½oz) granulated (white) sugar
1 pinch of salt

For rolling

100g (3½oz) icing (confectioners') sugar
90g (3¼oz) granulated (white) sugar
10g (¼oz) vanilla sugar

Cut the butter into cubes in a large bowl and mix with the remaining dough ingredients. Knead into a smooth dough. Shape into a 5cm (2 inch) thick log, wrap in cling film and refrigerate for 2 hours.

Preheat the oven to 180°C (350°F/Gas 4) and line 2 baking trays with baking paper. Cut the dough log into finger-thick slices. Shape into crescents, place on the baking trays and bake for about 12 minutes until lightly golden.

Meanwhile, mix the icing sugar, granulated sugar and vanilla sugar in a flat bowl. Gently roll the hot crescents in the sugar mixture using 2 forks. Be careful, they are very fragile when hot!

Cinnamon stars

Line 2 baking trays with baking paper. In a large bowl, beat the egg whites until stiff. Gradually whisk in the icing sugar. Set aside just under 100g (3½oz) of this mixture.

Fold 300g (10½oz) ground almonds and the cinnamon into the remaining egg white mixture. You should be able to roll out the mixture. If the dough is too sticky, add a little more ground almonds.

Sprinkle the remaining ground almonds onto a work surface and roll the dough out to 1cm (½ inch) thick. Cut out star shapes and carefully transfer onto the baking paper. Brush with the remaining egg white mixture and leave to dry overnight.

The next day, preheat the oven to 180°C (350°F/Gas 4) and bake the cinnamon stars for about 8 minutes.

Makes 2 trays of biscuits

3 egg whites
250g (9oz) icing (confectioners') sugar
400g (14oz) ground almonds
2 teaspoons ground cinnamon

Butter biscuits

Makes 2 trays of biscuits

250g (9oz) plain (all-purpose) flour, plus some extra for dusting
100g (3½oz) icing (confectioners') sugar
10g (¼oz) vanilla sugar
1 pinch of salt
125g (4½oz) butter, at room temperature
1 egg yolk
Grated zest of ½ lemon

Sift the flour and icing sugar into a large bowl. Stir in the vanilla sugar and salt. Dice the butter and add to the mixture, followed by the egg yolk and lemon zest. Knead well until there are no lumps. Wrap the dough in cling film and refrigerate for 30 minutes.

Preheat the oven to 180°C (350°F/Gas 4) and line 2 baking trays with baking paper. Lightly dust your work surface with flour and roll out the dough to 3mm (⅛ inch) thick. Use cookie cutters to cut out shapes as desired. Dust your fingers with flour and carefully place the biscuits on the trays. Bake for about 10 minutes until golden brown.

Tip: For a spicier version, you can substitute the vanilla sugar with 1 tablespoon Licor 43.

Almond shortbread nests

In a large bowl, beat the butter, icing sugar, vanilla sugar, salt, egg and egg yolk until foamy. Stir in the flour and baking powder, then incorporate the ground almonds. Shape the dough into a ball, cover with cling film and chill for 30 minutes.

Preheat the oven to 180°C (350°F/Gas 4). Line a baking tray with baking paper. Transfer the dough to a piping bag with a star nozzle and pipe nests and rosettes onto the baking tray. Bake in the oven for about 15 minutes until golden brown.

Makes 1 tray of biscuits

125g (4½oz) butter, at room temperature
120g (4¼oz) icing (confectioners') sugar
10g (¼oz) vanilla sugar
1 pinch of salt
1 egg
1 egg yolk
250g (9oz) plain (all-purpose) flour
1 teaspoon baking powder
100g (3½oz) ground almonds

Also

Piping bag with star nozzle

Clockwise from top left: Butter biscuits, Cinnamon stars, Almond shortbread nests, Vanilla crescents, Hazelnut rounds, Coconut macaroons

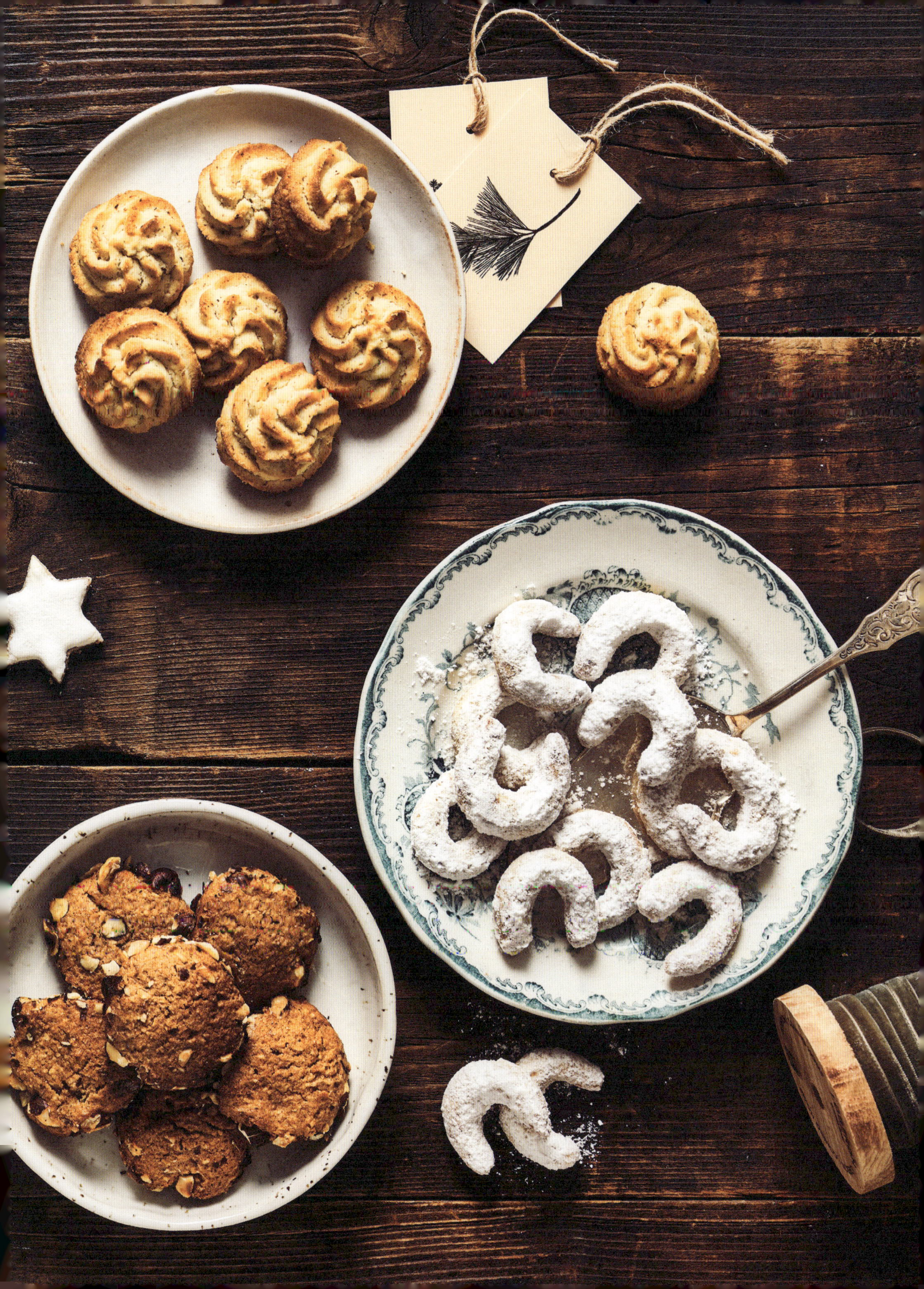

Coconut macaroons

Makes 2 trays of biscuits

2 egg whites

1 pinch of salt

75g (2½oz) raw cane sugar

75g (2½oz) caster (superfine) sugar

170g (6oz) desiccated or finely shredded coconut

In a bowl, lightly whisk the egg whites with the salt. Add the raw cane sugar and continue to beat until stiff. Gradually add the caster sugar and continue to beat for a further 2 minutes. Carefully fold in 150g (5½oz) coconut.

Preheat the oven to 150°C (300°F/Gas 2) and line 2 baking trays with baking paper. Using 2 teaspoons, place the egg white mixture on the trays in small mounds. Sprinkle the macaroons with the remaining coconut. Bake the macaroons in the oven, a tray at a time, until they just start to colour, about 14 minutes. Leave to cool.

Hazelnut rounds

Beat the butter in a bowl until foamy, gradually adding the honey. Whisk in the egg and continue to mix for 1 minute. Stir in the tea, cocoa powder, cinnamon, vanilla sugar, salt and ground hazelnuts. Sift in the flour and baking powder and fold in gently.

Transfer everything to a lightly floured work surface, knead to combine well and shape into logs (3–4cm/1¼–1½ inches diameter). Wrap the dough logs in cling film and refrigerate overnight.

The next day, preheat the oven to 180°C (350°F/Gas 4) and line a baking tray with baking paper. Place the chopped hazelnuts on a flat plate. Whisk the egg white and brush the dough logs with the egg white on all sides. Then turn them in the nuts until they are completely covered. Cut the dough logs into 3mm (⅛ inch) slices and transfer the rounds to the baking tray, leaving a little space between them.

Place in the oven and bake for 15 minutes until light brown. Pull the biscuits off the trays with the baking paper and set aside to cool on a wire rack.

Makes 1 tray of biscuits

80g (2¾oz) butter, at room temperature

200g (7oz) liquid honey

1 egg

4 tablespoons strong black tea

½ teaspoon cocoa powder

1 teaspoon ground cinnamon

½ teaspoon vanilla sugar

1 pinch of salt

80g (2¾oz) ground hazelnuts

200g (7oz) wholemeal flour, plus some extra for dusting

1 teaspoon baking powder

Also

60g (2¼oz) hazelnuts, chopped

1 egg white

Spiced biscuits

Makes 2 trays of biscuits

2 eggs
250g (9oz) granulated (white) sugar
30g (1oz) candied lemon peel
½ teaspoon ground cinnamon
½ teaspoon ground allspice
1 pinch ground cardamom
1 pinch of ground aniseed
1 pinch of freshly ground white pepper
250g (9oz) plain (all-purpose) flour
1 teaspoon baking powder

Beat the eggs and sugar in a bowl until foamy. Mince the candied lemon peel. Combine the minced candied lemon peel with the cinnamon, allspice, cardamom, aniseed, pepper, flour and baking powder. Add the egg and sugar mixture and knead to form a smooth dough. Do not overmix. Wrap the dough in cling film and chill for 30 minutes. Line 2 baking trays with baking paper. Shape the dough into walnut-sized balls and place on the trays. Leave to dry overnight.

The next day, preheat the oven to 180°C (350°F/Gas 4) and bake the biscuits for about 18 minutes, one tray at a time. Pull the biscuits off the trays with the baking paper and set aside to cool.

Tip: If you like, glaze these spiced biscuits with an icing made of 250g (9oz) icing (confectioners') sugar, 1 egg white and 3 drops lemon juice. Whisk until smooth and brush on the cooled biscuits.

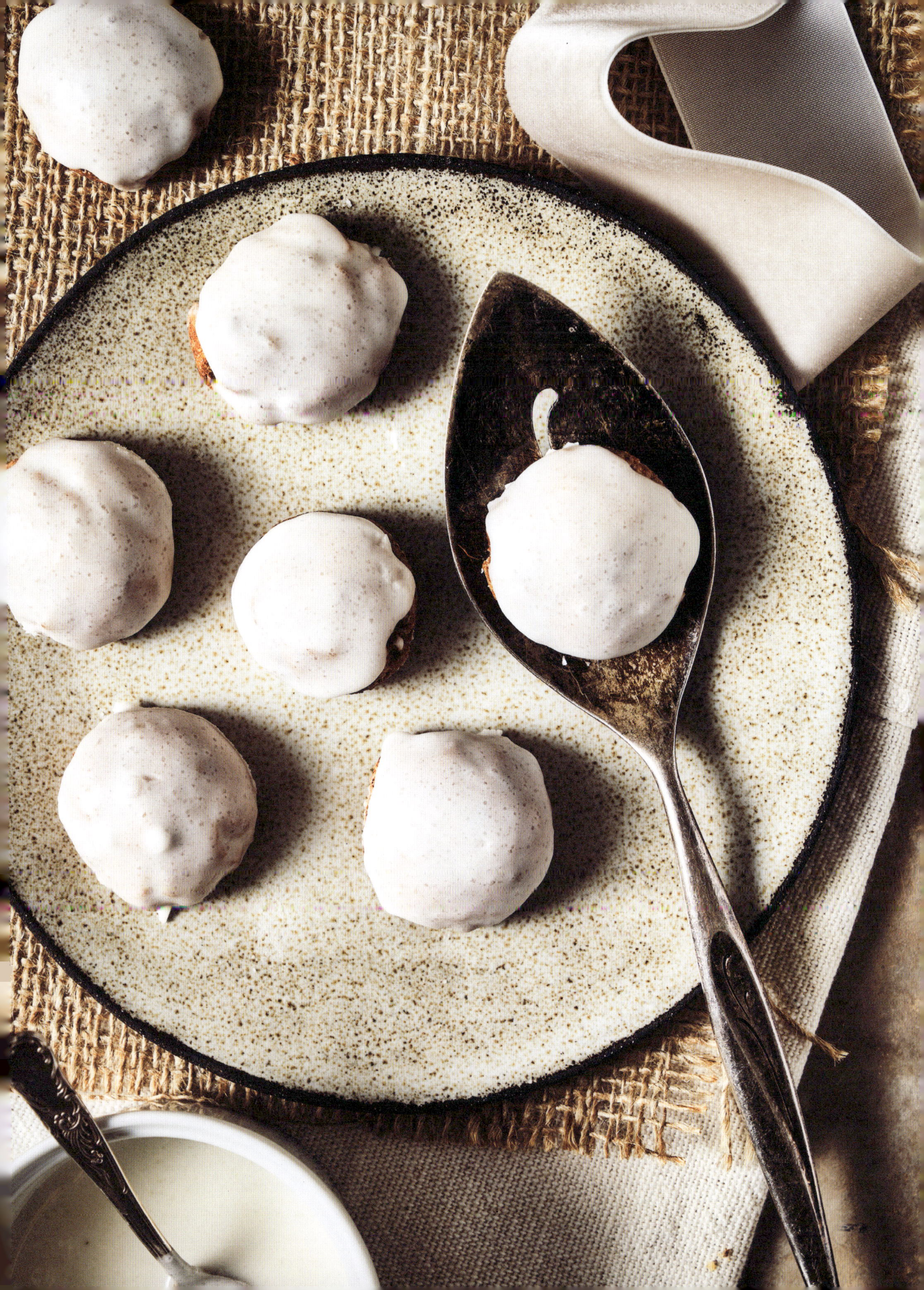

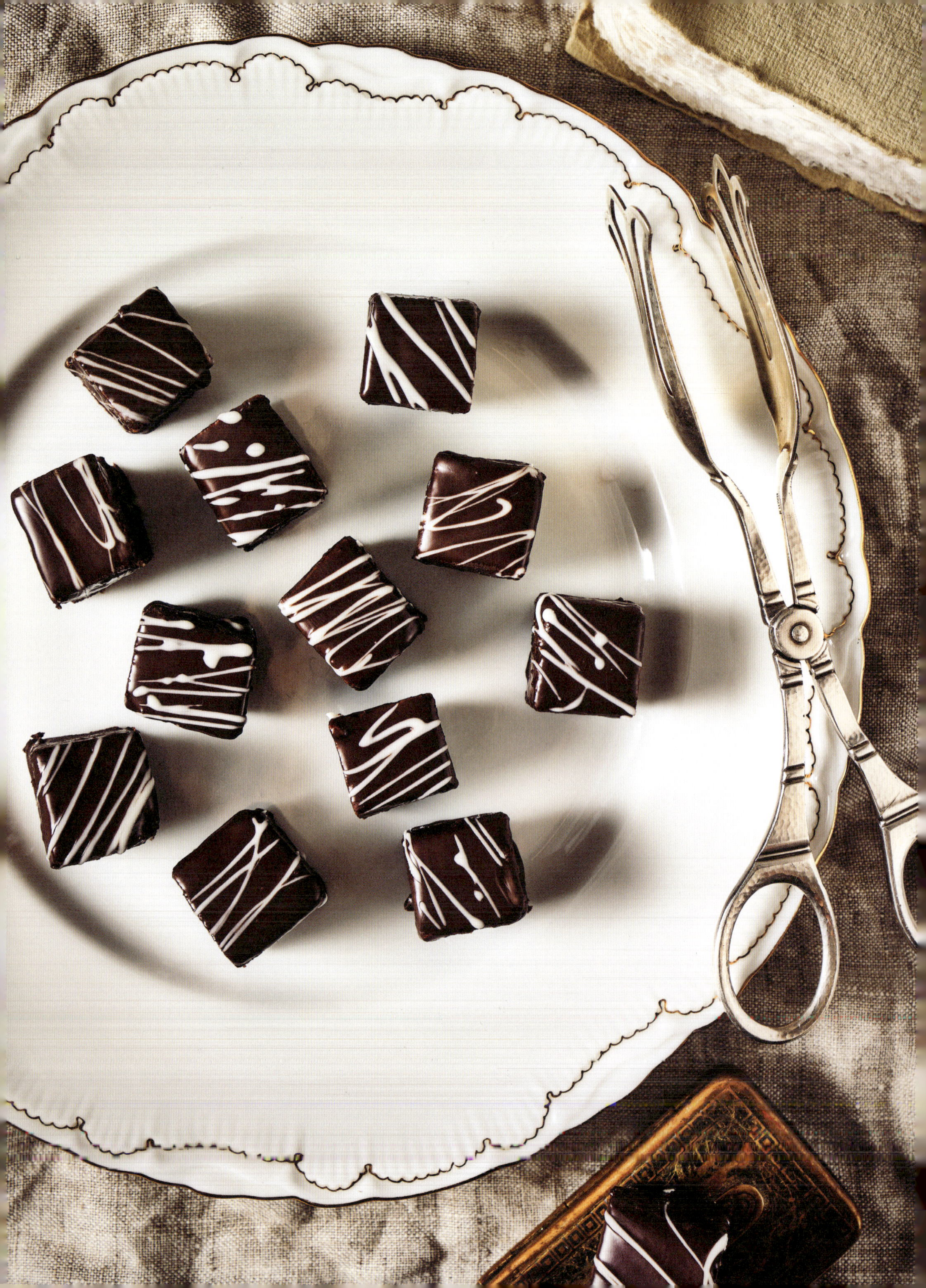

Layered domino biscuits

Preheat the oven to 200°C (400°F/Gas 6) and grease a baking tray. For the dough, combine the flour, baking powder, cinnamon and ground cloves in a mixing bowl. Add the honey, sugar and butter to a small saucepan and heat. Leave to cool briefly, then add to the flour mixture together with the egg. Knead everything into a loose dough.

Roll out the dough on the baking tray to a thickness of 1cm (½ inch). Bake in the oven for 15 minutes. Remove from the oven and cut horizontally into two equal pieces while still hot.

For the filling, heat the jelly and stir until smooth. Spread half thinly on one of the cake layers. Finely chop the marzipan and knead in the rum. Roll the marzipan out between 2 sheets of baking paper to the size of the cake layers. Remove the baking paper, place the marzipan sheet on top of the jelly layer and cover with the remaining jelly. Carefully top with the second cake layer and cut everything into cubes.

Melt the dark cooking chocolate in a small stainless steel bowl over a double boiler. Glaze the domino biscuits evenly with the chocolate. Finely chop the white cooking chocolate, melt over a double boiler and use a small spoon to drizzle delicate lines on top of the dark glaze. Leave to cool.

Makes ½ tray of biscuits

For the dough

500g (1lb 2oz) plain (all-purpose) flour
15g (½oz) baking powder
½ teaspoon ground cinnamon
1 pinch of ground cloves
200g (7oz) honey
100g (3½oz) brown sugar
50g (1¾oz) butter
1 egg

For the filling

200g (7oz) redcurrant jelly
200g (7oz) marzipan paste
1 tablespoon rum

Also

Butter or oil, for the tray
300g (10½oz) dark cooking chocolate
50g (1¾oz) white cooking chocolate
Double boiler

Black-and-white biscuits

Makes 1 of tray of biscuits

290g (10¼oz) plain (all-purpose) flour, plus some extra for dusting

125g (4½oz) icing (confectioners') sugar

1 teaspoon baking powder

1 pinch of salt

150g (5½oz) cold butter

1 egg yolk

3 teaspoons cocoa powder

Also

Milk, for brushing

Mix the flour, icing sugar, baking powder and salt on a clean work surface. Dice the butter and rub into the flour mixture until the mixture resembles coarse breadcrumbs. Add the egg yolk and knead everything into a smooth dough. Divide the dough into 2 equal portions. Add the cocoa to one half and knead in thoroughly. Wrap the portioned dough in cling film and chill for at least 2 hours.

On a lightly floured work surface, roll out the 2 pieces of dough into 1cm (½ inch) thick squares. Cut into 1cm (½ inch) wide strips. Place 3 strips of dough on your work surface, alternating light and dark strips. Brush the edges with a little milk and gently press the strips together. Next, top a light strip with a dark one and vice versa, again brushing the edges with milk and gently pressing together. Repeat this process until you have several square sticks of dough, each with 9 strips joined together. Wrap the sticks in cling film and place in the freezer for 10 minutes. This will make them easier to cut.

Preheat the oven to 180°C (350°F/Gas 4) and line a baking tray with baking paper. Cut the dough sticks into 3mm (⅛ inch) slices with a very sharp knife. Transfer to the baking tray and bake in the oven for 12 minutes until light golden. Remove from the oven and leave to cool on a wire rack.

Tip: If you're pressed for time, simply roll out the light and dark dough to a thickness of 3mm (⅛ inch). Shape into 2 equal rectangles and brush one side with milk. Place the 2 layers of dough on top of each other and roll up tightly. Freeze the roll as above, cut into 3mm (⅛ inch) slices and bake in the same way as the squares.

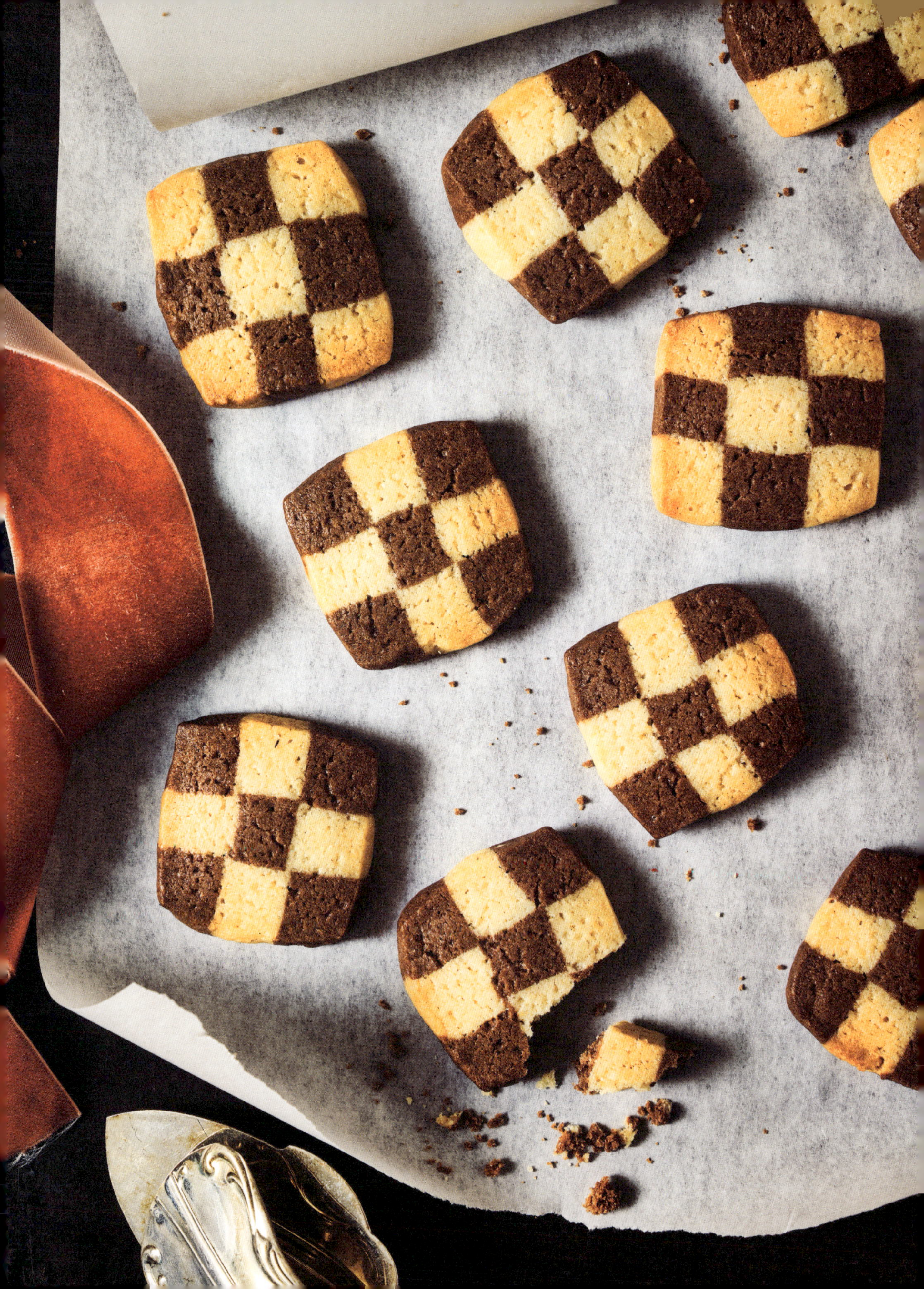

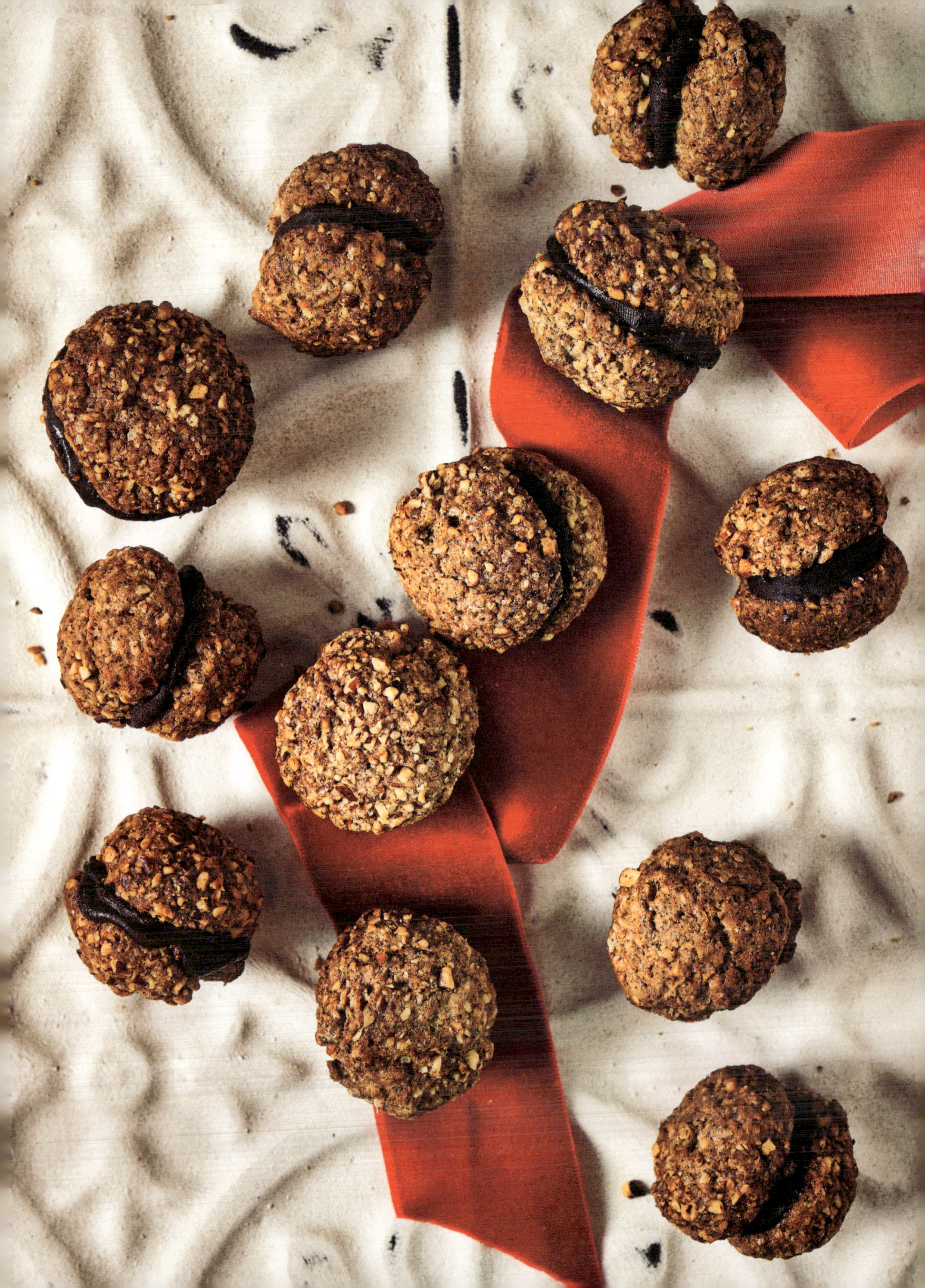

Pecan biscuits

with chocolate filling

Finely chop the pecan nuts and set a third of them aside on a flat plate. In a large bowl, beat the butter and sugar until light and foamy. Combine the flour with the baking powder and espresso powder in a bowl and add to the butter mixture. Add the egg and mix well. Fold in the nuts.

Preheat the oven to 180°C (350°F/Gas 4).

Shape the mixture into about 30 small balls. Roll in the chopped pecan nuts and place on a baking sheet lined with baking paper, leaving a little space as they will spread. Bake in the oven for 10 minutes.

Spread half of the rounds with the chocolate spread and top with a second round. Press gently together.

Makes 15

60g (2¼oz) pecan nuts

100g (3½oz) butter, at room temperature

70g (2½oz) raw cane sugar

110g (3¾oz) plain (all-purpose) flour

1 teaspoon baking powder

2 teaspoons instant espresso powder

1 small egg

100g (3½oz) dark chocolate spread

Helen Maria Williams

To Mrs K____, on Her Sending Me an English Christmas Plum-Cake, at Paris

What crowding thoughts around me wake,
What marvels in a Christmas-cake!
Ah say, what strange enchantment dwells
Enclosed within its odorous cells?
Is there no small magician bound
Encrusted in its snowy round?
For magic surely lurks in this,
A cake that tells of vanished bliss;
A cake that conjures up to view
The early scenes, when life was new;
When memory knew no sorrows past,
And hope believed in joys that last! —
Mysterious cake, whose folds contain

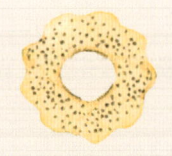

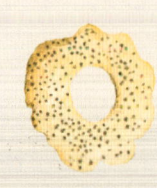

Life's calendar of bliss and pain;
That speaks of friends for ever fled,
And wakes the tears I love to shed.
Oft shall I breathe her cherished name
From whose fair hand the offering came:
For she recalls the artless smile
Of nymphs that deck my native isle;
Of beauty that we love to trace,
Allied with tender, modest grace;
Of those who, while abroad they roam,
Retain each charm that gladdens home,
And whose dear friendships can impart
A Christmas banquet for the heart!

Cranberry shortbread

Makes 2 trays of biscuits

100g (3½oz) dried cranberries
300g (10½oz) plain (all-purpose) flour
200g (7oz) cold salted butter
100g (3½oz) granulated (white) sugar
2 teaspoons vanilla extract

Preheat the oven to 180°C (350°F/Gas 4) and line 2 baking trays with baking paper. Finely chop the cranberries.

Sift the flour into a bowl. Dice the butter and rub into the flour until the mixture resembles breadcrumbs. Stir in the sugar, chopped cranberries and vanilla extract and form the mixture into a ball. Wrap in cling film and refrigerate for 15 minutes.

Roll out the dough, cut out cookie shapes and bake for about 15 minutes until lightly golden.

Carefully remove from the baking paper and leave to cool on a wire rack.

Tip: Don't overmix the dough — the lighter your touch, the crumblier this deliciously buttery shortbread will be!

Apricot crumble gingerbread

Preheat the oven to 180°C (350°F/Gas 4). Line a baking tray with baking paper. Finely chop the candied ginger.

Combine the flour and baking powder and sift into a large bowl. Dice the butter and rub into the flour with your fingertips until a crumbly mixture is formed. Stir in the granulated sugar, vanilla sugar, orange zest and ground ginger and mix well.

Knead half of the mixture into a smooth dough and roll out on the baking tray. Spread with the apricot jam and sprinkle with the chopped ginger and the remaining crumble mixture.

Bake for 20 minutes. Remove from the oven and leave to cool, then cut into rectangles of about 2 × 4cm (¾ × 1½ inches).

Makes 1 tray of biscuits

75g (2½oz) candied ginger

250g (9oz) plain (all-purpose) flour

¼ teaspoon baking powder

170g (6oz) butter, at room temperature

120g (4¼oz) granulated (white) sugar

10g (¼oz) vanilla sugar

Zest of 1 orange

1 teaspoon ground ginger

75g (2½oz) apricot jam

German gingerbread biscuits

Makes 2 trays of biscuits

250g (9oz) golden syrup

1 level teaspoon potash or baking powder

50g (1¾oz) brown sugar

75g (2½oz) white sugar crystals

300g (10½oz) plain (all-purpose) flour

1 teaspoon each ground cinnamon, aniseed and ginger

¼ teaspoon each ground cloves, cardamom, coriander and allspice

Also

Milk, for brushing

100g (3½oz) blanched almonds

Two to three days before baking, bring the syrup and 2 tablespoons water to a boil. Whisk the potash with 1 tablespoon water and stir in. Stir in both types of sugar and leave to cool, stirring frequently. Mix in the flour and spices and knead to form a dough. Cover and leave to rest at room temperature.

If using baking powder, the dough does not need to be made in advance. Sift the baking powder into a bowl with the flour and spices. Bring the syrup and 2 tablespoons water to a boil, then stir in both types of sugar and leave to cool, stirring frequently. Mix in to the flour and knead to form a dough. Cover and leave to rest at room temperature until you're ready to bake.

On the day you want to bake, preheat the oven to 180°C (350°F/Gas 4) and line 2 baking trays with baking paper. Knead the dough again and roll out to 5mm (¼ inch) thick. Cut into rectangles of about 3 × 8cm (1¼ × 3¼ inches). Brush with milk and decorate with almonds. Bake for about 15 minutes. Remove from the paper before setting aside to cool.

Flourless chocolate gingerbread

Preheat the oven to 160°C (325°F/Gas 2-3) and line 2 baking trays with baking paper.

In a bowl, beat the eggs with the icing sugar, salt and lemon juice until thick and foamy. Mix in the lemon zest, ground almonds and hazelnuts and gingerbread spice. Use 2 teaspoons to scoop the mixture onto the wafers. Place on the baking trays. Bake in the oven for 15 minutes, then set aside to cool.

Melt the cooking chocolate in a bowl over a double boiler and use to glaze the gingerbread.

Tip: If you prefer, glaze with icing instead of cooking chocolate. Whisk 250g (9oz) icing (confectioners') sugar, 1 egg white and 3 drops lemon juice until smooth and brush on the gingerbread.

Makes approx. 48 biscuits

4 eggs
150g (5½oz) icing (confectioners') sugar
1 pinch of salt
1 teaspoon juice and zest from 1 lemon
200g (7oz) ground almonds
200g (7oz) ground hazelnuts
1½ teaspoons gingerbread spice

Also

48 baking wafers (5cm/2 inch diameter)
200g (7oz) dark cooking chocolate
Double boiler

Clockwise from far left: Apricot crumble gingerbread, Flourless chocolate gingerbread (unglazed), German gingerbread biscuits, Cranberry shortbread

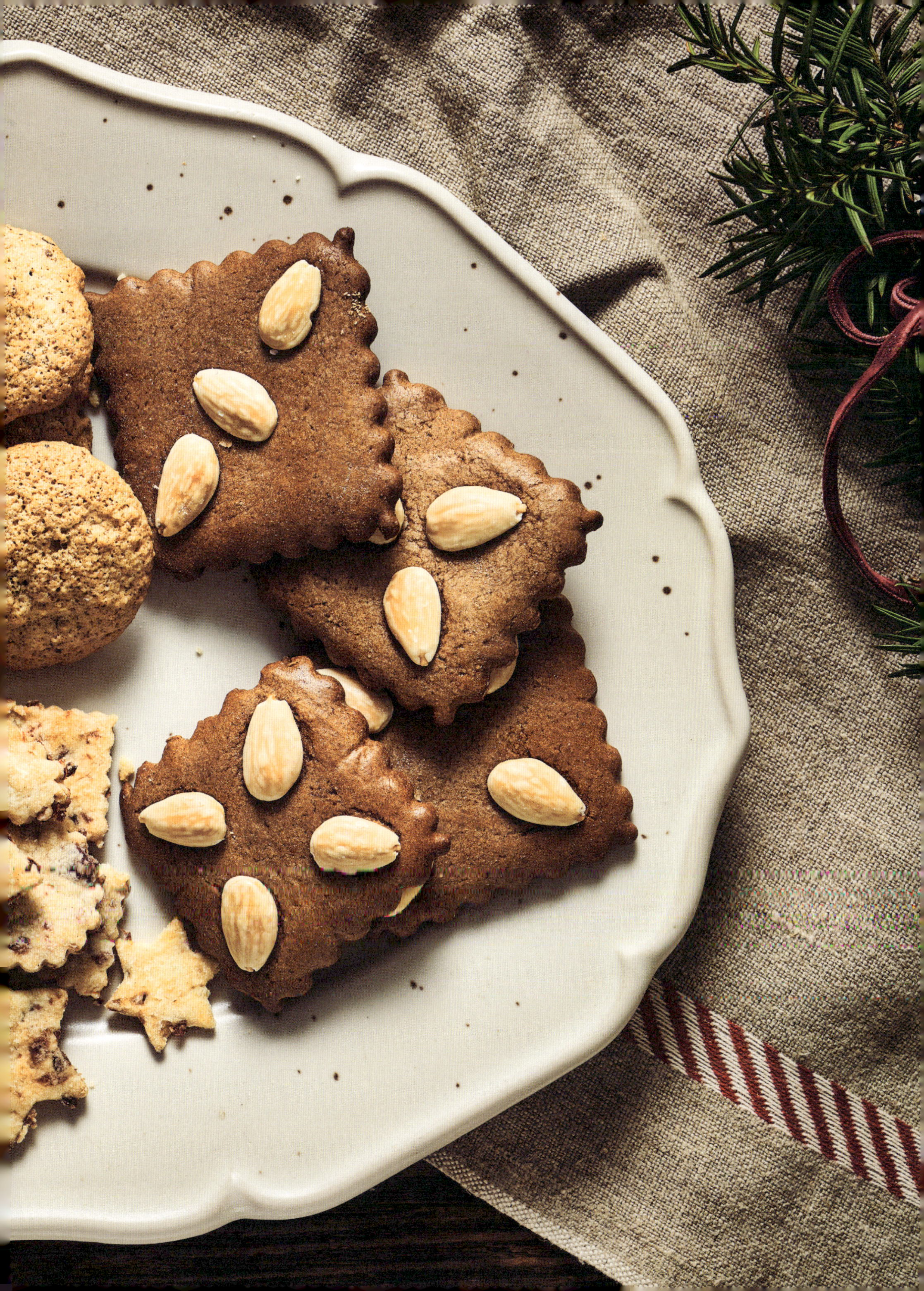

Nut triangles

Makes 1 tray of biscuits

250g (9oz) butter, at room temperature
100g (3½oz) golden syrup
100g (3½oz) brown sugar
10g (¼oz) vanilla sugar
2 eggs
350g (12oz) rolled oats
3 teaspoons baking powder
100g (3½oz) ground hazelnuts
100g (3½oz) hazelnuts, chopped

Also

250g (9oz) milk cooking chocolate
Double boiler

Preheat the oven to 160°C (325°F/Gas 2–3) and line a baking tray with baking paper. Whisk the butter in a bowl until foamy, about 5 minutes. Add the golden syrup, brown sugar and vanilla sugar and beat for a further 3 minutes. Whisk in the eggs. Mix the rolled oats and baking powder in another bowl and gradually fold into the butter and sugar mixture. Fold in the ground and chopped hazelnuts.

Spread the mixture evenly on the baking tray to a thickness of 1cm (½ inch). Bake until golden brown, about 30 minutes. Leave to cool. Melt the cooking chocolate in a double boiler. Cut the nut cake into small triangles and dip 2 ends of each triangle into the melted chocolate glaze. Leave to cool on a cooling rack.

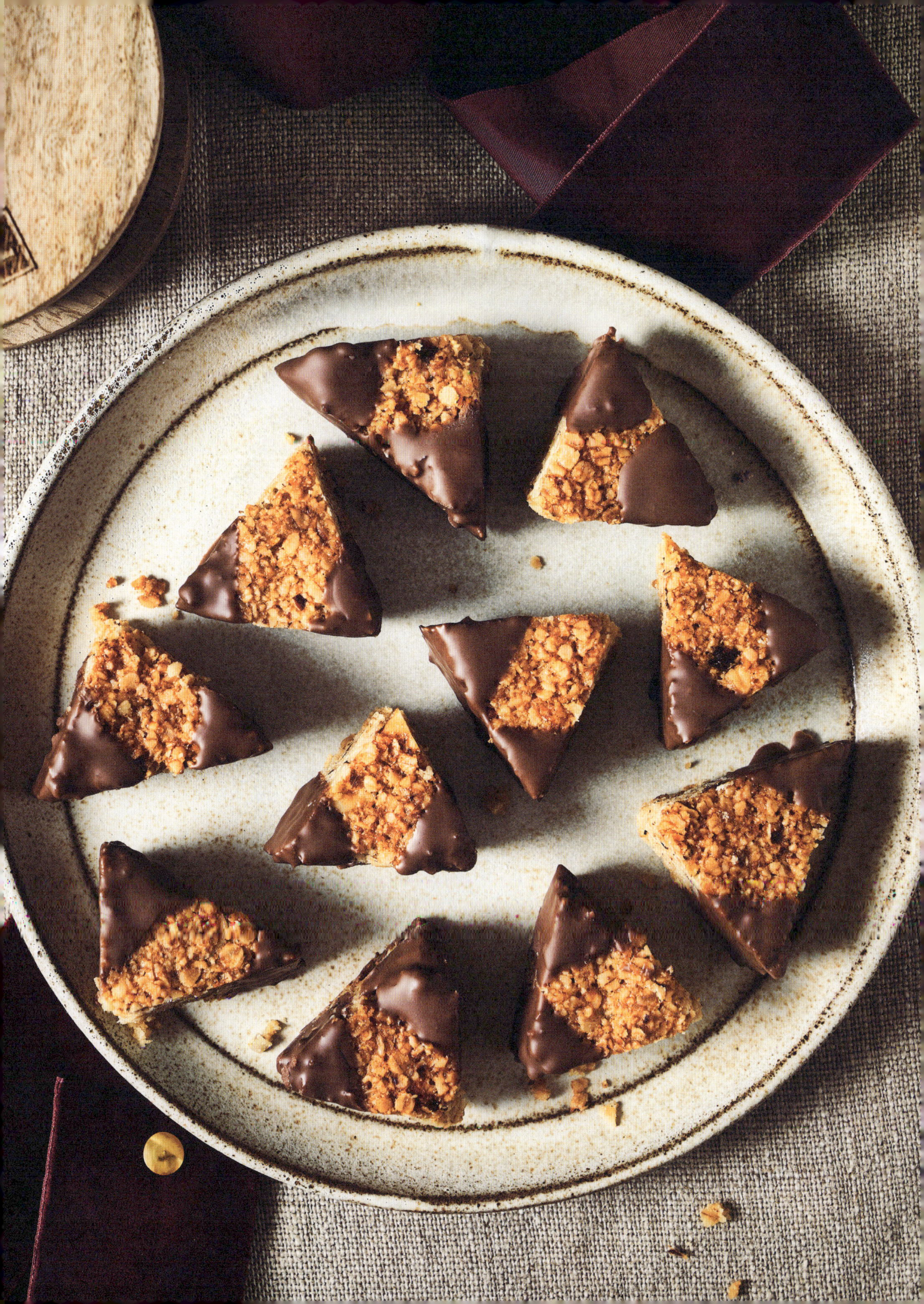

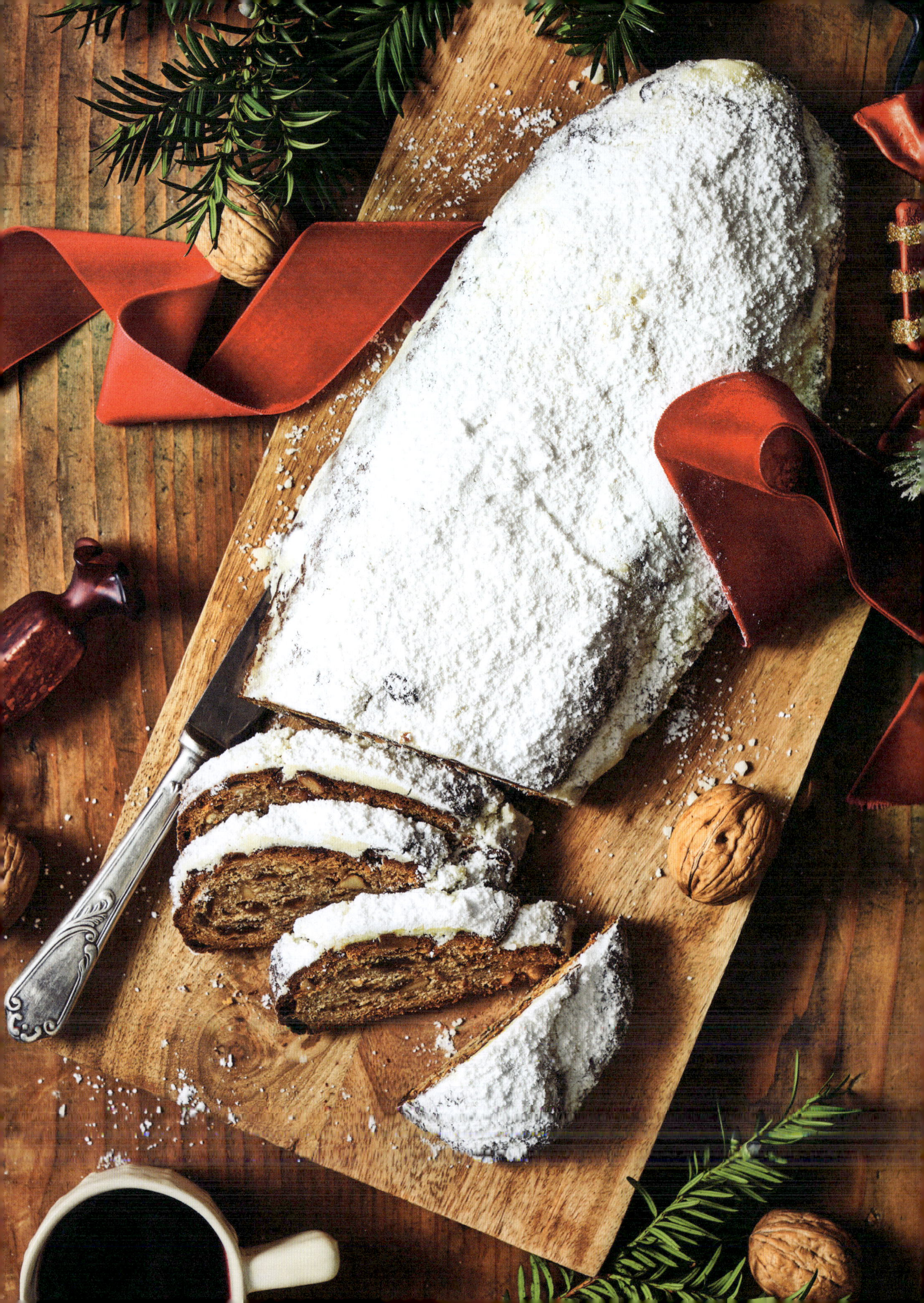

Traditional stollen

The day before you plan to bake, mix the sultanas, currants and rum in a bowl. Cover and leave to infuse.

The next day, sift the flour into a large bowl and make a well in the centre. Whisk the yeast with a little of the milk, then pour into the well with the rest of the milk. Sprinkle some flour from the edge over the liquid and knead into a dough. Cover and leave to rise at room temperature for 2 hours.

Chop the candied lemon peel, candied orange peel and both types of almonds. Add to the dough together with the granulated sugar, vanilla sugar, lemon zest, salt, clarified butter and the remaining milk and knead well. Cover and leave to rise at room temperature for 3 hours.

Preheat the oven to 200°C (400°F/Gas 6). Grease a baking tray with a little butter and dust with a little flour. Knead the dough well once more and divide into 2 portions. Shape these into long loaves. Score lightly lengthways and place on the tray. Leave to rise for 30 minutes.

Bake in the oven for 1 hour. Remove from the oven and leave to cool slightly. For the glaze, melt the butter in a small saucepan. Brush the stollen with the butter twice, then dust with both types of sugar. The stollen should be left to mature for at least 3-4 weeks before serving.

Tip: To make the clarified butter, put 800g (1lb 12oz) butter in a small saucepan over a low heat and heat slowly. The whey will settle at the bottom and the pure fat (the clarified butter) will float to the top. Carefully pour the clarified butter into a container and discard the whey.

Makes 2 stollen

For the bread

750g (1lb 10oz) sultanas
125g (4½oz) currants
125ml (4fl oz) rum
1.25kg (2lb 12oz) plain (all-purpose) flour
150g (5½oz) fresh yeast, at room temperature
375ml (13fl oz) milk, at room temperature
75g (2½oz) candied lemon peel
75g (2½oz) candied orange peel
5 bitter almonds or 2 teaspoons amaretto or almond liqueur
150g (5½oz) whole almonds
250g (9oz) granulated (white) sugar
20g (¾oz) vanilla sugar
½ tablespoon grated zest of 1 lemon
20g (¾oz) salt
600g (1lb 5oz) clarified butter, at room temperature (see Tip)
Butter and flour, for the baking tray

For the glaze

125g (4½oz) butter
40g (1½oz) granulated (white) sugar
125g (4½oz) icing (confectioners') sugar

Paula Dehmel

Christmas in the Pantry

There was a small hole under the doorstep. Behind it sat Keek the mouse, waiting. Keek waited until the master of the house had taken off his boots and wound up the clock, until the lady of the house had put her keys on the bedside table and tucked in the sleeping children once more, even until everything was dark and there was a deep silence in the house. Then Keek left.

It wasn't long before there was movement in the pantry. Keek had alerted the whole mouse family. There were Meek, the mother mouse, and her five little ones, and Uncle Grisegrey and Auntie Furry.

'Wife, here's something soft and sweet,' Keek called softly to Meek from the top shelf, 'the children will love it,' and he handed out some poppy seed pudding.

'Come here Grisegrey,' Furry chirped, peeking out from behind the flour box, 'I've got roast goose, delicious, I tell you, oat-fed meat with a perfectly crispy crust!' But Grisegrey was sitting in the corner of a new box of gingerbread, happily nibbling away and showing no intention of moving. The mouse children fought in the sandpit and were given soft poppy seed pudding.

'Daddy,' said the eldest, 'my teeth are sharp enough, I'd rather nibble, nibbling sounds so nice.'

'Yes, we want to nibble too,' chimed in all the mouse children. 'Poppy seed pudding is too mushy!' Soon they could be heard nibbling on roast goose and gingerbread.

'Don't make yourselves sick,' cried Furry, who was afraid that there might not be enough for her. 'You can die of an upset stomach!'

The little mice looked at their aunt in horror; they didn't want to die at all, that was a terrible thought. Father Keek calmed them down and told them about Gottlieb and Lenchen, the children who were lying in their beds with a wooden horse and a doll in their arms. He told them about the huge tree set up in the living room, decorated with lights and glittering tinsel, and how the whole house smelled wonderfully of fresh cake, which was unfortunately kept out of reach in the glass cupboard.

'Oh,' said Furry, 'don't talk so much. Let the children eat instead.'

But the little mice laughed at their round-bellied aunt and asked dear old Keek many more questions than he could answer. Eventually they insisted on having a Christmas tree too, and their loving mouse parents even ran off to the kitchen and returned dragging a branch cut from the big Christmas tree. What fun the mouse children had! The little mice squealed with delight and began to nibble at the green wood, but it tasted disgustingly of turpentine, so they gave up and climbed around the branch instead. Eventually they turned the whole pantry into their playground. They scampered here and there, every so often standing up on their hind legs and peering curiously over the shelves into every corner. They played hide-and-seek behind the tins of vegetables and the jars of preserves — what were they supposed to do with that stupid Christmas tree they couldn't even eat! But after the smallest had fallen into the pot of plum jam and had to be licked clean by Mother Meek and Uncle Grisegrey, they were forbidden to run around and had to sit still and nibble at the gingerbread again.

The next morning, the old cook was surprised to find the fir branch in the pantry, along with lots of crumbs and other things that didn't exactly belong in a pantry — you can guess what! When Gottlieb and Lenchen came into the kitchen to say good morning to dear old Marie, she showed them the mess and said: 'The mice had their own Christmas party in here!'

But the children whispered and laughed and went and got a flowerpot. They planted the branch in it and decorated it with sweets, cracked nuts, honey cake and pieces of bacon. Old Marie grumbled, but as the lady of the house looked on and laughed, she had to give in. She made sure everything else was safe and only left the hungry little mice their Christmas tree.

The children were delighted to find the mice's Christmas tree stripped bare on Boxing Day. How they would have loved to hear a thank you from the little critters!

'I'll never forget the delicious bacon,' said Furry, as Grisegrey nibbled on a hazelnut. But Keek and Meek were worried about their little ones, who had eaten too much gingerbread, and as you know, dear children, that's not good for the stomach!

Buttery quark stollen

Makes 1 stollen

250g (9oz) quark

200g (7oz) raisins

500g (1lb 2oz) plain (all-purpose) flour, plus some extra for dusting

100g (3½oz) candied lemon peel

50g (1¾oz) candied orange peel

15g (½oz) baking powder

200g (7oz) granulated (white) sugar

Grated zest of 1 lemon

2 eggs

2 tablespoons rum

400g (14oz) butter

150g (5½oz) slivered or flaked almond

Also

Icing (confectioners') sugar, for dusting

Preheat the oven to 180°C (350°F/Gas 4) and line a baking tray with baking paper.

Drain the quark and dust the raisins with flour. Mince the candied lemon and orange peel.

Sift the flour and baking powder onto the work surface and make a well. Add the granulated sugar, lemon zest, eggs and rum to the well and whisk to combine. Cut half of the butter into cubes and knead in, then incorporate the quark, raisins, almonds, candied lemon and orange peel. Knead everything until well combined.

Shape into a loaf, place on the baking tray and bake in the oven for 1¼ hours (test for doneness with a toothpick — it should come out clean). Just before the end of the baking time, melt the remaining butter in a small saucepan. Remove the stollen from the oven, brush with melted butter and dust with icing sugar.

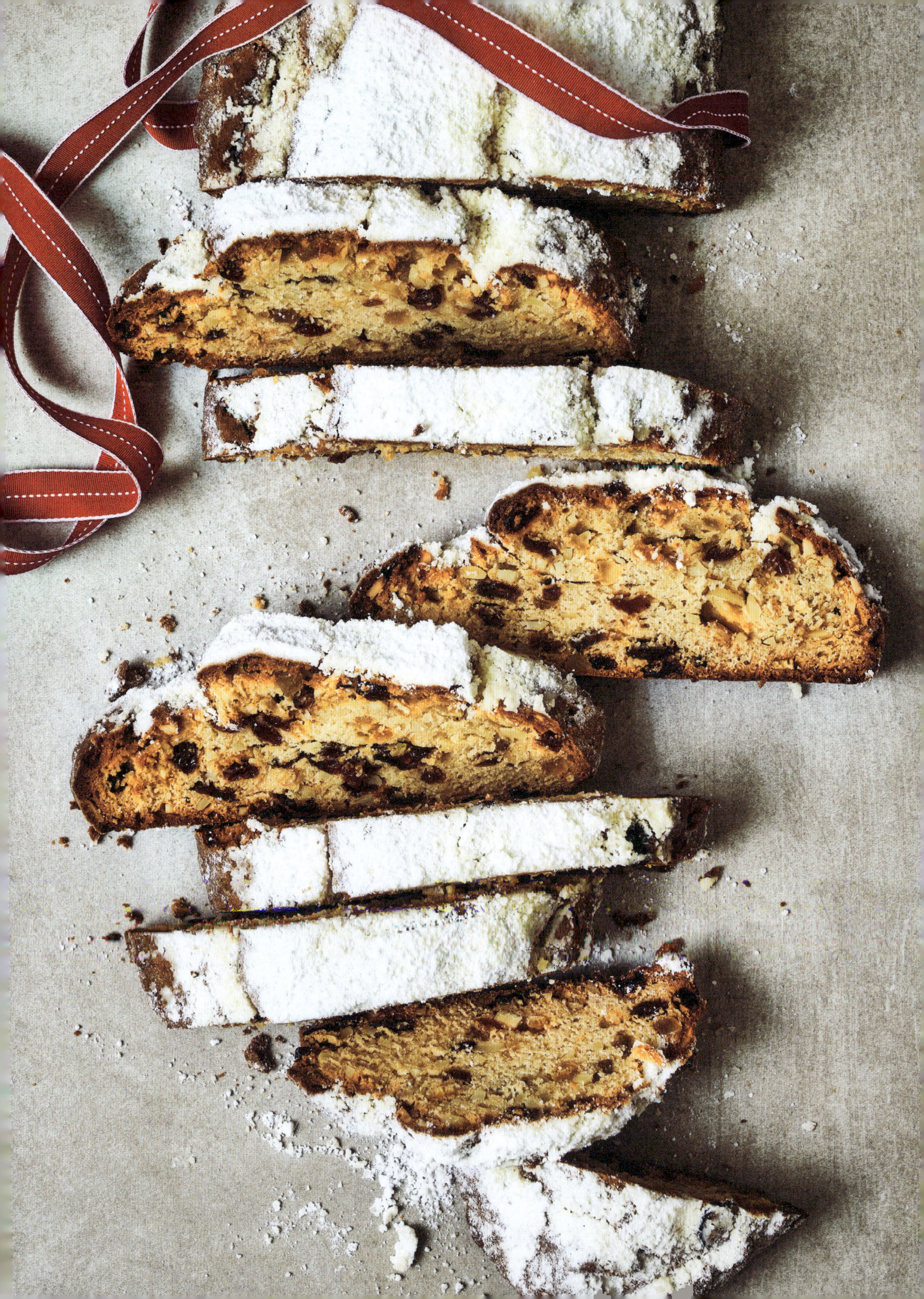

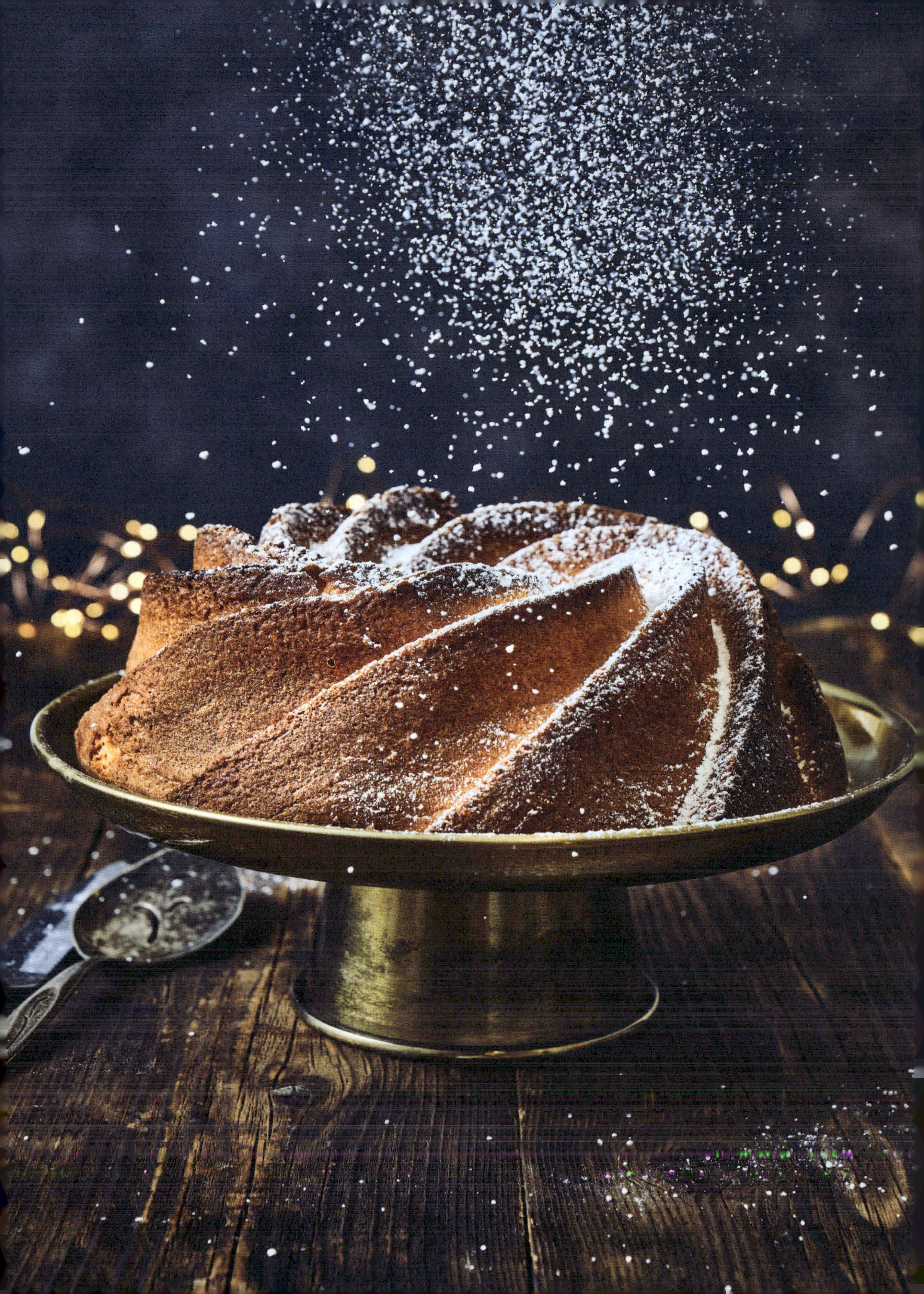

Lemon and yoghurt Bundt cake

Preheat the oven to 160°C (325°F/Gas 2-3). Grease the cake tin and dust with flour.

Sift the flour and baking powder into a large bowl. Add the lemon zest and sugar and stir to combine. Add the butter, yoghurt, eggs, milk and lemon juice and mix everything into a smooth batter.

Pour the mixture into the cake tin. Tap the tin on the work surface a few times to remove any air bubbles. Bake the cake in the oven until golden brown, about 45-50 minutes (test for doneness with a toothpick — it should come out clean). Leave to cool in the tin for 10 minutes, then remove from the tin and set aside to cool fully on a wire rack. Dust with icing sugar.

225g (8oz) plain (all-purpose) flour
15g (½oz) baking powder
Zest and juice of 1 lemon
225g (8oz) granulated (white) sugar
125g (4½oz) very soft butter
130g (4½oz) yoghurt
3 eggs
60ml (2fl oz) milk

Also

Bundt cake tin (22cm/8½ inches diameter)
Butter and flour, for the tin
Icing (confectioners') sugar, for dusting

Tree log cake

6 eggs

1 pinch of salt

120g (4¼oz) granulated (white) sugar

150g (5½oz) marzipan paste

200g (7oz) butter, at room temperature

100g (3½oz) icing (confectioners') sugar

10g (¼oz) vanilla sugar

100g (3½oz) plain (all-purpose) flour

100g (3½oz) apricot jam

2 tablespoons orange liqueur, to taste

200g (7oz) dark cooking chocolate

1 tablespoon coconut oil

Also

Round springform baking tin (24cm/9½ inches diameter)

Butter, for greasing

Double boiler

Preheat the oven to 250°C (500°F/Gas 9). Line a baking tin with baking paper and butter the sides.

Separate the eggs. Beat the egg whites and salt until stiff, then gradually whisk in the sugar. Finely dice the marzipan and combine with the butter, icing sugar and vanilla sugar in a large bowl. Beat the mixture until creamy. Gradually stir in the egg yolks, then fold in the beaten egg whites and flour.

Spread 2 heaped tablespoons of batter over the base of the baking tin. Bake for 4 minutes on the top rack of the preheated oven. Remove the tin from the oven. Spread another 2 heaped tablespoons of batter on top and bake for another 4 minutes. Continue until you have used up all the batter. The batter should yield about 10–12 layers.

Leave the cake to cool slightly before inverting it onto a wire rack. Remove the baking paper. Heat the jam over a double boiler, pass it through a sieve and stir in the orange liqueur to taste. Glaze the tree log cake with the mixture. Set aside to cool fully. Coarsely chop the cooking chocolate and melt in a stainless steel bowl over a double boiler together with the coconut oil. Glaze the cake with the chocolate and refrigerate until the glaze is dry. Slice to serve.

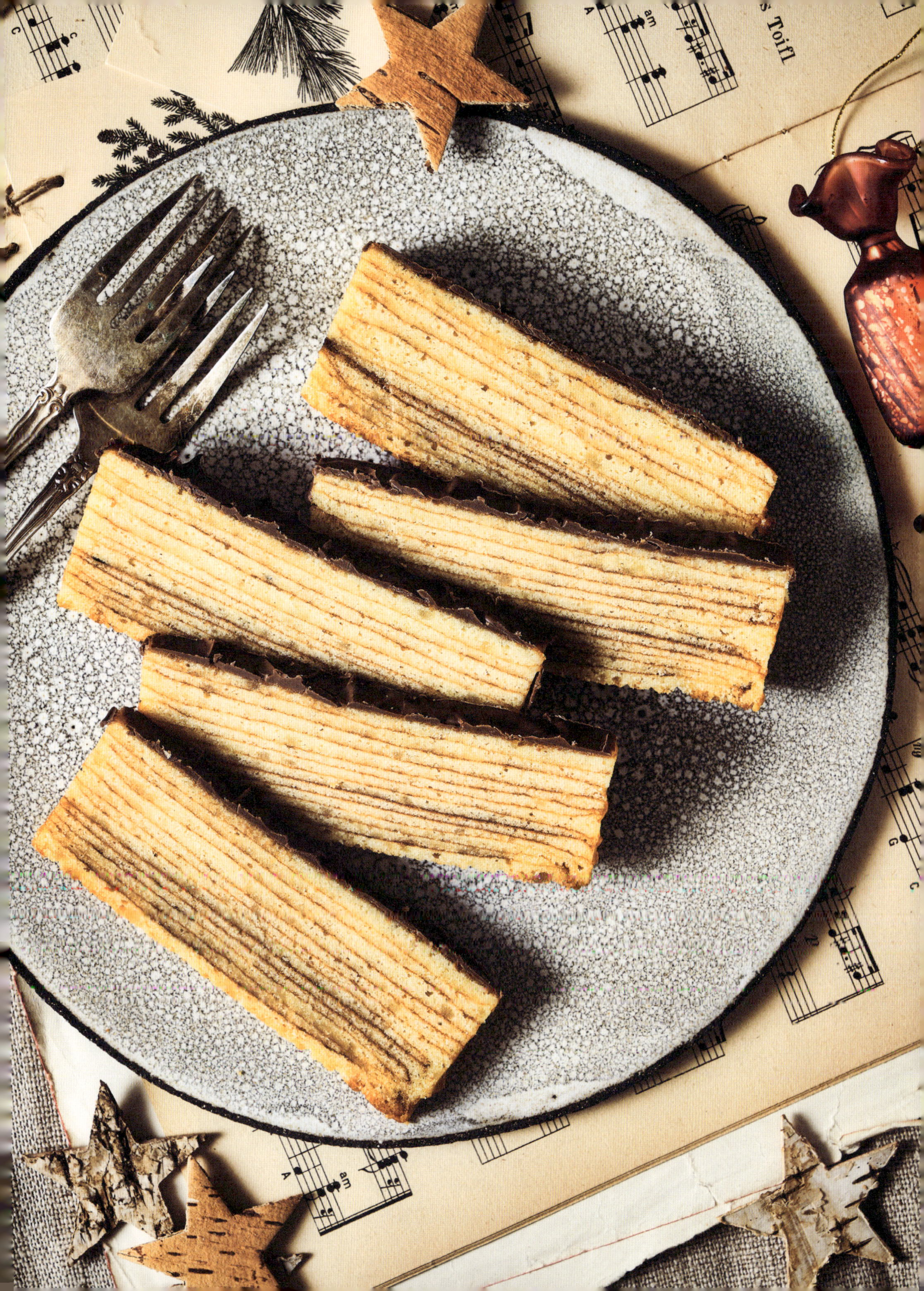

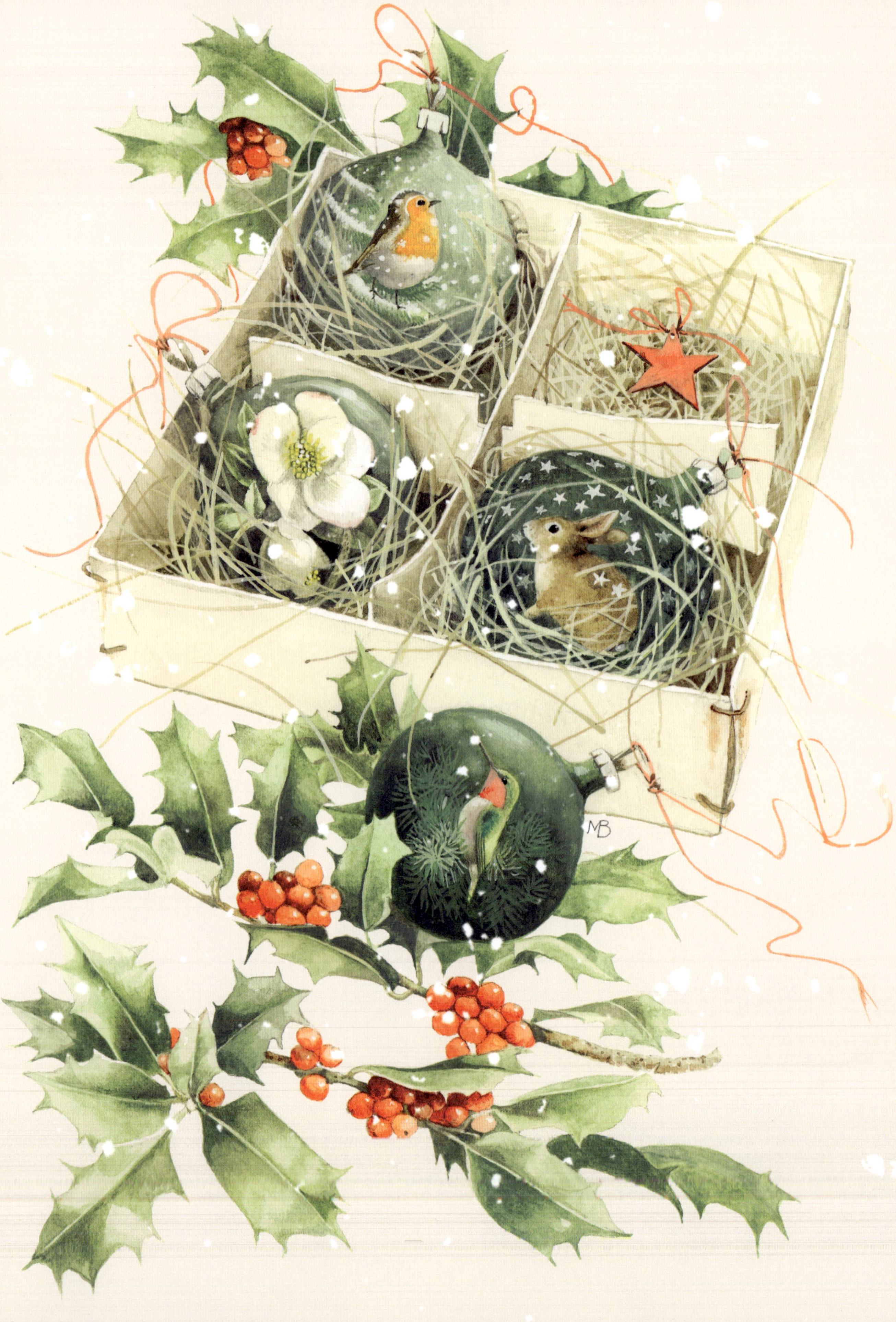
MB

Julius Kreis

Baking (extract)

Advent has a scent all its own. You can smell it in almost every home: Bark from nativity sets, twigs of fir, candles and, above all, the familiar aromas of Christmas baking in the kitchens and hallways: sugar and spiced Christmas cookies, candied lemon and orange peel, almonds, chestnuts, rum...
In an old house, there's still a yellowed, stained exercise book from great-grandmother's time. The writing is full of love and care, with little Biedermeier flourishes; it speaks of its time with old measurements and weights: a 'measure' of flour, ten 'lots' of sugar, a 'deca' of nutmeg. Everything is expressed in a somewhat cumbersome way: 'One takes ...', 'then do ...', 'stir everything together assiduously and well ...'

Then come recipes in a different handwriting: Grandmother added to the book, as did Mother. A long line of writings, a long line of cooks. Here and there, children's hands, long since old and gnarled, have added little scribbles. This is the book to consult for everything to do with marzipan, butter dough, hazelnuts, cinnamon stars, for three dozen Christmas delicacies.

Christmas baking must be done outside the daily routine of cooking. In the late afternoon or evening. Wonderful childhood memories: You'd come home in the afternoon on a frosty December day, your cheeks red with cold, your skates in your frozen fingers, and the smell of hot coffee would waft from the open door. There would be a sweet bun next to your mug, the kerosene lamp would be lit, but there was something else in the air: the tantalising smell of Christmas cookies! But Mother would chase us away from the table with a friendly scolding, carrying a bowl of dough and a cutting board, carrying candied orange and lemon peel, almonds and hazelnuts, and she'd start mixing, kneading, beating and cutting. The older girls were allowed to help. But we little ones could only look at the raisins, nuts and sugar with big, hungry eyes, and our fingers would tingle ... So Mother gave in and handed us all some nuts and raisins. They already gave us a taste of Christmas. Once the dough was rolled out, it was time for the exciting tasks of cutting out cookies and pressing marzipan into moulds. Even Father, who was usually so strict, joined in and with a good deal of fun. There they were set out, little stars and flowers, rabbits and birds, bells and hearts. And the marzipan was moulded into images of horses and riders, roses and tulips, roosters, deer and shepherdesses. The delicious smell in the living room evoked the magic of Christmas. Every time scraps of dough were rolled out again, we'd nibble a little bit of the sweet dough, which almost tasted better than the cookies it would become. People stayed up late on those evenings, and we could all hardly wait for the first cookies to come out of the oven, hot and fragrant.

Once the baking was done, all the cookies were placed in large boxes, which were kept on the highest shelf in the pantry, with us eagerly awaiting their release on Christmas Eve. Our young eyes would stare longingly at the boxes, and we'd beg Mother for a taste. Sometimes she would relent and give us a cookie for particularly good behaviour or hard work, but not without a sigh: 'You little gluttons — we won't have any left for Christmas!'

But every year there was still enough to fill our baskets to the brim, and how delighted we were when we recognised a piece we had cut out ourselves!

Christmas cupcakes

Makes 6 cupcakes (or 12 mini cupcakes)

For the batter

400g (14oz) raisins

240g (8½oz) chopped dried cranberries

120ml (4fl oz) rum

125g (4½oz) butter, at room temperature, plus a little extra for the tin

110g (3¾oz) brown sugar

1 tablespoon orange marmalade

1 tablespoon honey

Grated zest of ½ lemon

2 eggs

180g (6½oz) plain (all-purpose) flour

½ teaspoon each ground cinnamon, ground ginger and gingerbread spice

For the frosting

1 egg white

250g (9oz) icing (confectioners') sugar

3 teaspoons lemon juice

Also

1 cupcake (or mini cupcake) tray

Golden sprinkles and stars to decorate, as desired

The day before baking, put the raisins and cranberries in a bowl. Add the rum, cover and set aside to soak overnight.

The next day, preheat the oven to 150°C (300°F/Gas 2). Grease the cupcake tray thoroughly. In a bowl, whisk the butter and sugar until creamy. Stir in the marmalade, honey and lemon zest. Add the eggs one at a time, whisking continuously. Gradually incorporate the soaked raisins and cranberries, flour and spices.

Spoon the batter evenly into the cupcake tray wells, smoothing down the tops. Place the tray in the oven and bake the cupcakes for 35 minutes. Remove, leave to cool, invert onto a wire rack and then turn over again.

For the frosting, lightly beat the egg white. Gradually add the sifted icing sugar and whisk until smooth. Carefully stir in enough lemon juice to make the mixture a little more liquid. Glaze the cupcakes with the frosting, letting it run down along the sides.

Decorate with golden sprinkles and stars, as desired.

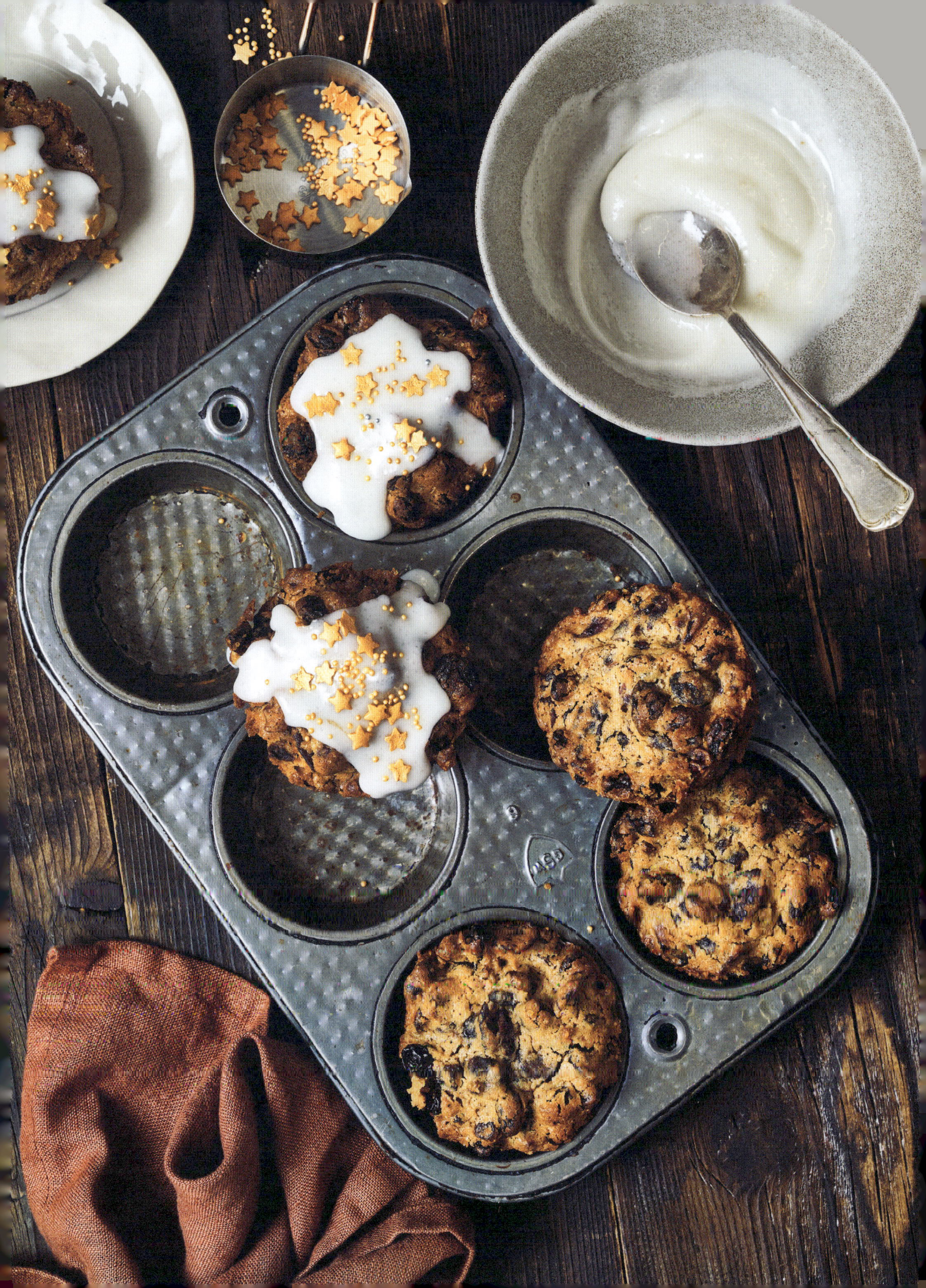

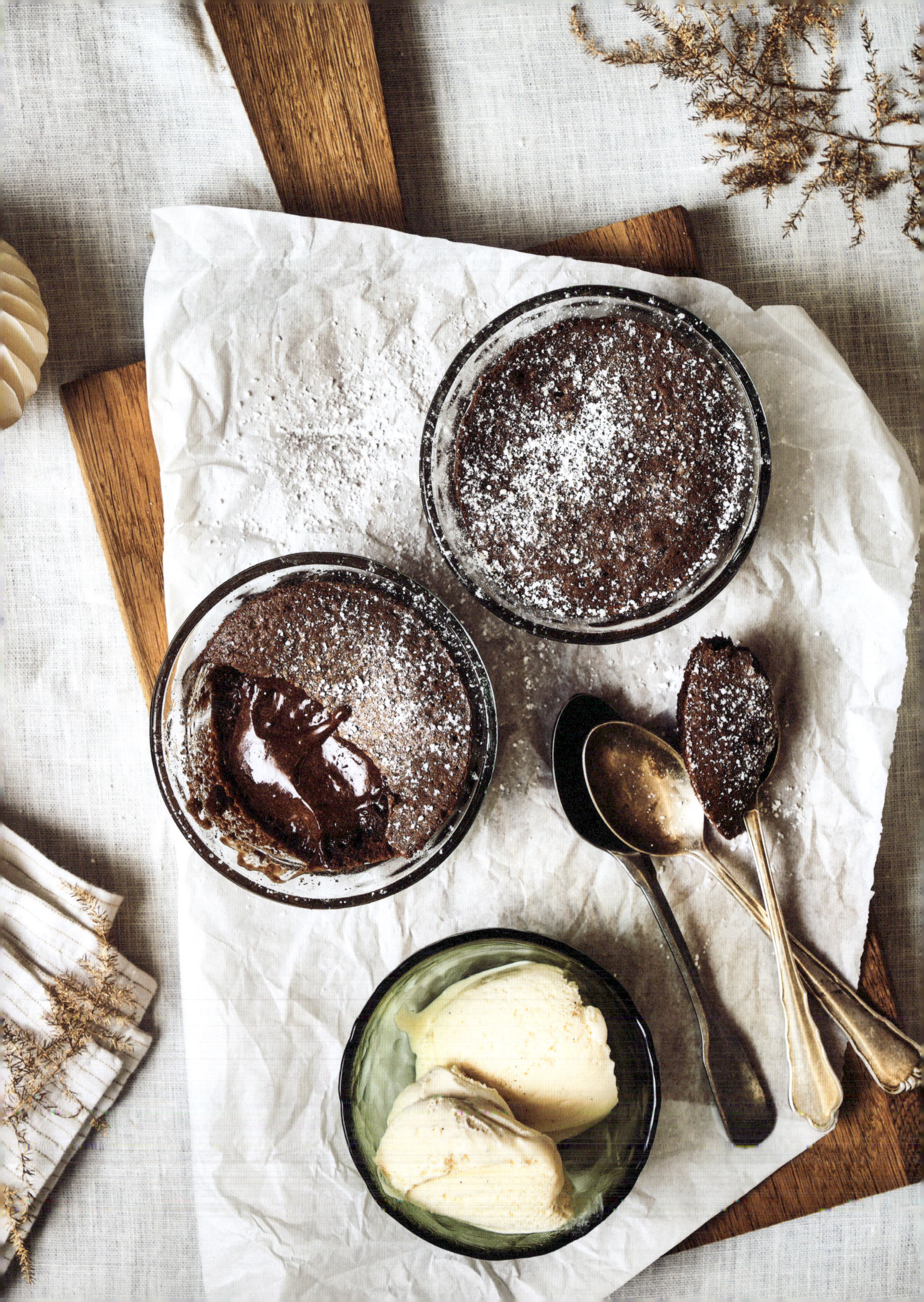

Festive mud cakes

Grease the ramekins and preheat the oven to 200°C (400°F/Gas 6). Coarsely chop the chocolate.

Melt the chocolate together with the butter in a stainless steel bowl over a double boiler, stirring constantly. Be careful not to overheat and ensure that no water splashes into the chocolate. Set aside.

Mix the flour with the cinnamon and ground cloves. Whisk the eggs and sugar in a bowl until foamy. Fold into the chocolate mixture. Gently fold in the spiced flour. Transfer the batter to the ramekins and bake for 10 minutes. The mud cakes should still be liquid inside.

Serve warm straight from the oven, dusted with icing sugar.

Tip: These cakes are delicious with vanilla ice cream.

140g (5oz) dark chocolate

140g (5oz) butter, plus a little extra for the ramekins

60g (2¼oz) plain (all-purpose) flour

½ teaspoon ground cinnamon

1 pinch of ground cloves

4 eggs

80g (2¾oz) granulated (white) sugar

Also

4 ovenproof ramekins, 125ml (4fl oz) each

Butter, for greasing

Icing (confectioners') sugar, for dusting

Double boiler

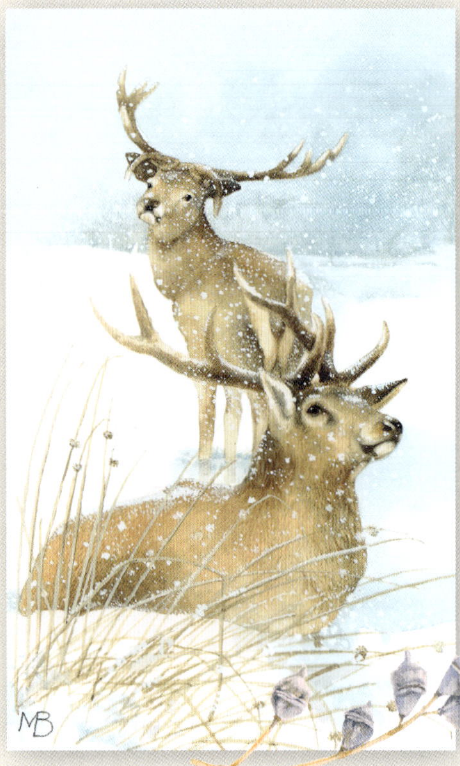
MB

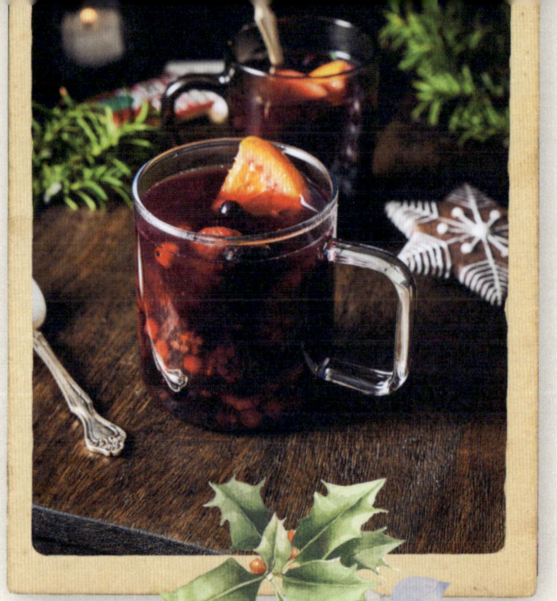

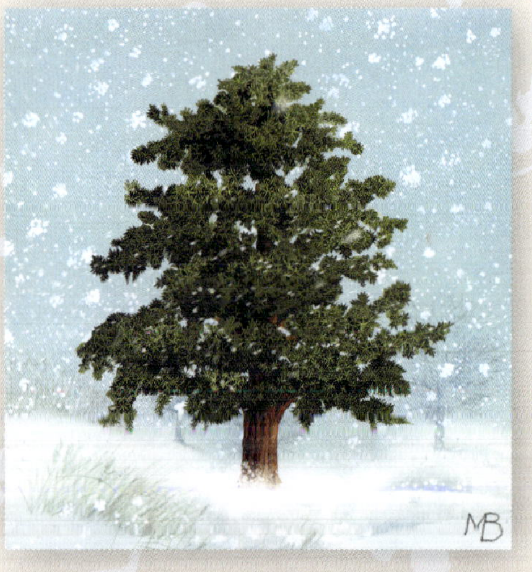
MB

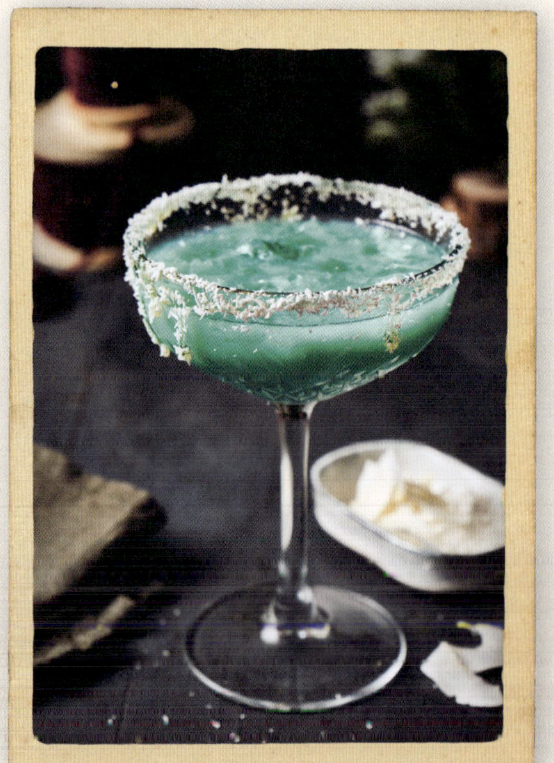

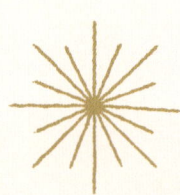

Festive drinks

Christmas forest berry punch

400g (14oz) mixed berries (frozen)
1 apple
1 orange
1 litre (35fl oz) blackcurrant juice
1 litre (35fl oz) cloudy apple juice
4 cinnamon sticks
6 star anise
750ml (26fl oz) red wine

Defrost the frozen berries.

Wash the apple and orange under hot water, pat dry, halve and slice.

Add the blackcurrant juice, apple juice, cinnamon sticks, star anise and orange slices to a large saucepan and heat gently until the juice is hot but not boiling. Add the defrosted berries, apple slices and red wine, heat for another 15 minutes over medium heat and serve immediately.

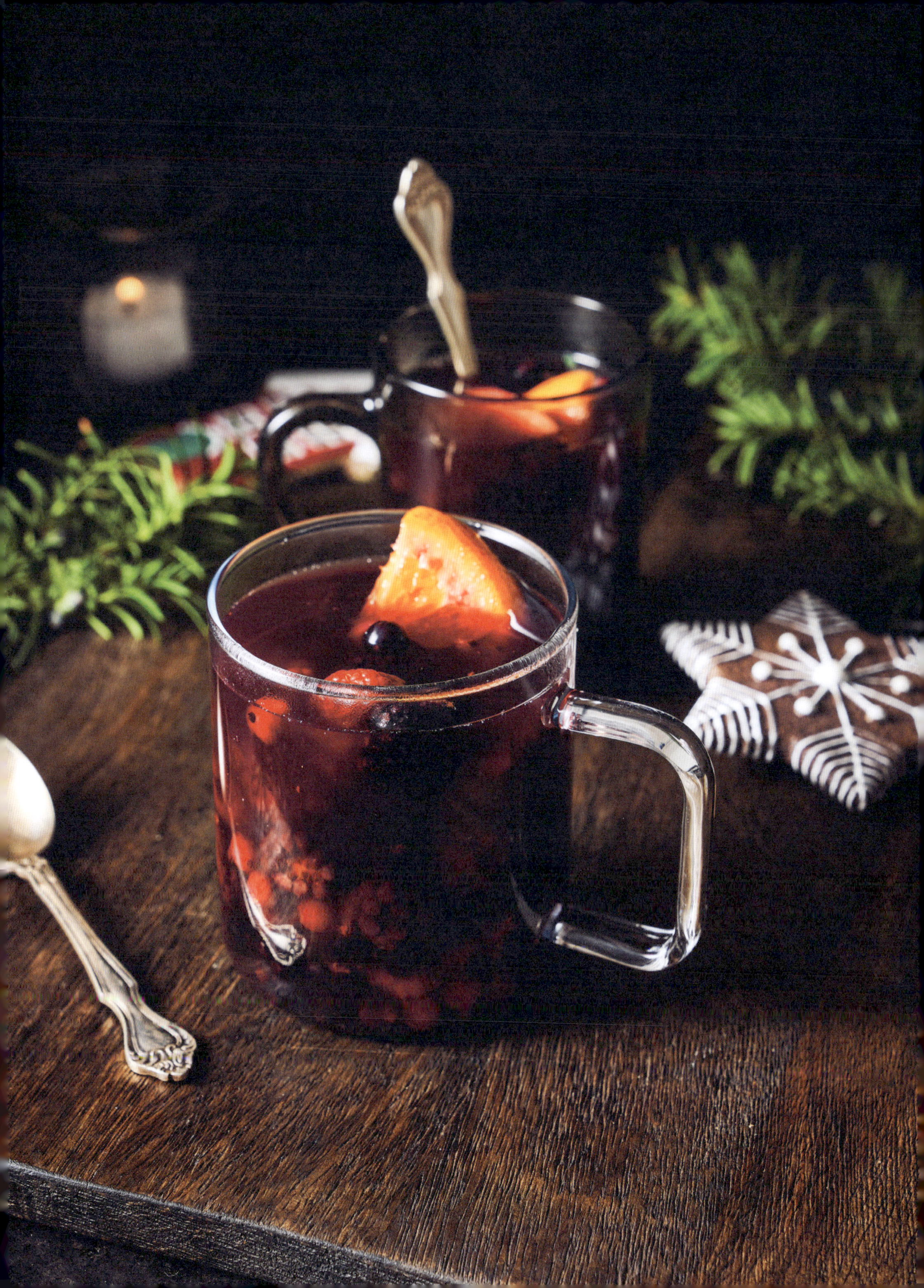

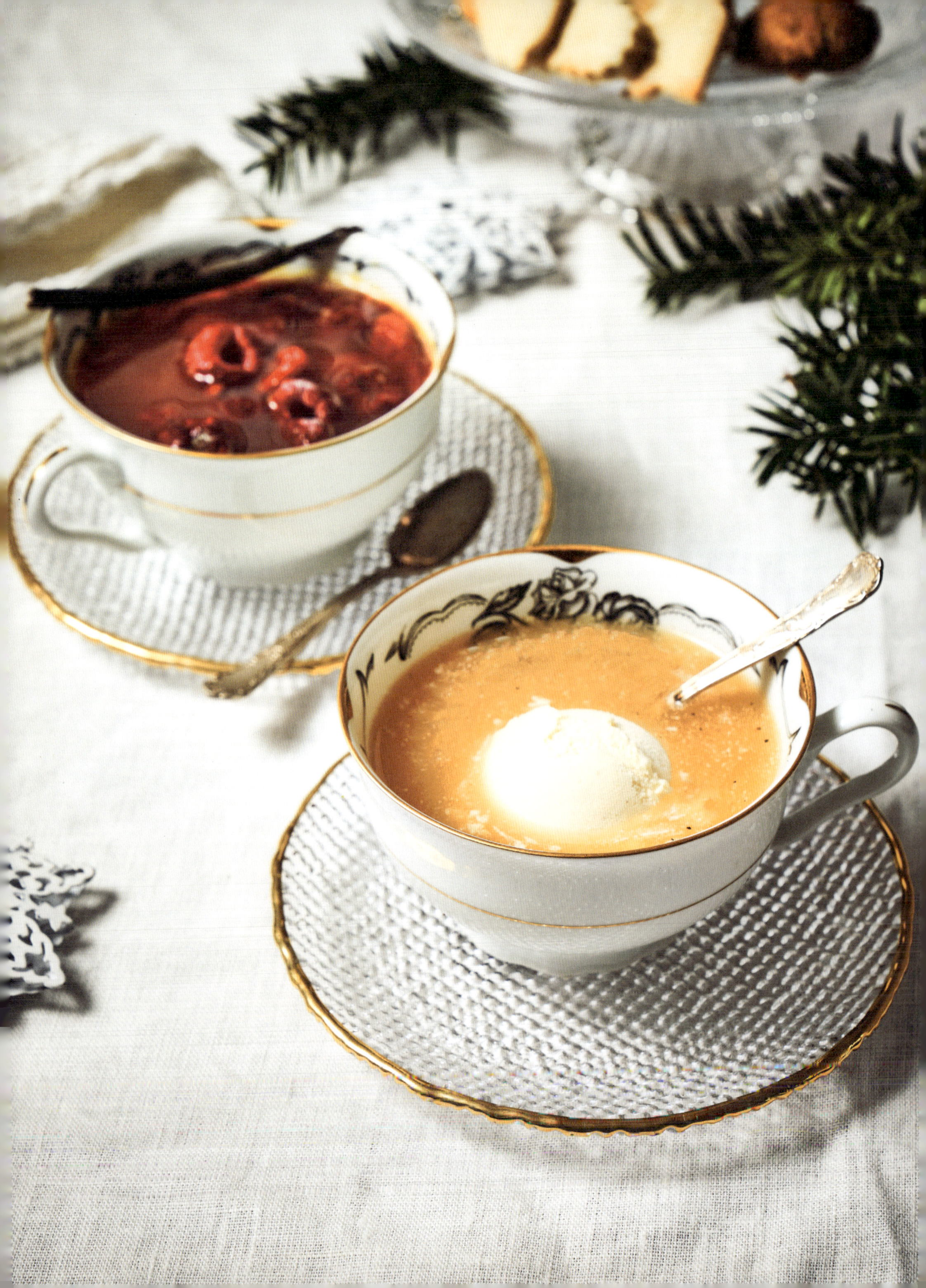

Mandarin punch

Defrost the frozen raspberries.

Halve and juice the lemons. Slice the vanilla pods open lengthways and scrape out the seeds.

Add the lemon juice, vanilla seeds and pods, mandarin and apple juices to a saucepan together with the spices. Heat the punch over low heat, but do not bring to the boil. Leave to infuse for 15 minutes. Remove the vanilla pods and spices with a slotted spoon. Stir in the honey.

Place a few raspberries in each serving cup or glass, top with the mandarin punch and serve warm.

Makes about 10 servings

Raspberries (frozen), for garnish
5 lemons
2 vanilla pods
1.25 litres (44fl oz) mandarin juice
500ml (17fl oz) cloudy apple juice
3 cinnamon sticks
3 star anise
10 allspice berries
3 cardamom pods
3 tablespoons liquid honey

Hot apple punch

Slice the vanilla pod open lengthways and scrape out the seeds. Slowly heat the apple juice in a saucepan with the nutmeg, cinnamon, cloves and vanilla seeds. Do not bring to the boil.

Pour the hot apple punch into serving cups or glasses. Add the vanilla ice cream and stir gently until it has started to melt, then serve warm.

Tip: If you like, add 20ml (½fl oz) rum or amaretto per serving.

Makes about 10 servings

1 vanilla pod
2 litres (70fl oz) apple juice
2 pinches of freshly grated nutmeg
2 teaspoons ground cinnamon
½ teaspoon ground cloves
10 scoops of vanilla ice cream

German flaming punch

Makes about 10 glasses

2 oranges
1 lemon
2 litres (70fl oz) red wine
3 star anise
3 cloves
2 juniper berries
2 cinnamon sticks
1 spoonful of sugar cubes
350ml (12fl oz) rum (min. 50%)

Also

Punch pot
Fondue burner
Tongs for the sugar cubes

Wash the oranges and lemon under hot water, pat dry, halve and cut into slices. Place in a large saucepan together with the wine and spices and heat over medium heat, but do not bring to the boil. Allow the fruit and spices to infuse in the warm liquid. Transfer the wine mixture to a punch pot and place on a fondue burner.

Tightly pack the sugar cubes onto a large metal spoon and pour the rum into a jug. Place the spoon of sugar over the punch and drizzle with rum. Carefully light the sugar cubes to flambé, keeping a safe distance. Caution: The flame may shoot up! When the rum has almost burnt off, slowly pour the remaining rum over the cubes and tip the sugar into the punch. Never pour the rum directly from the bottle onto an open flame!

Serve the flaming punch in punch glasses and enjoy warm.

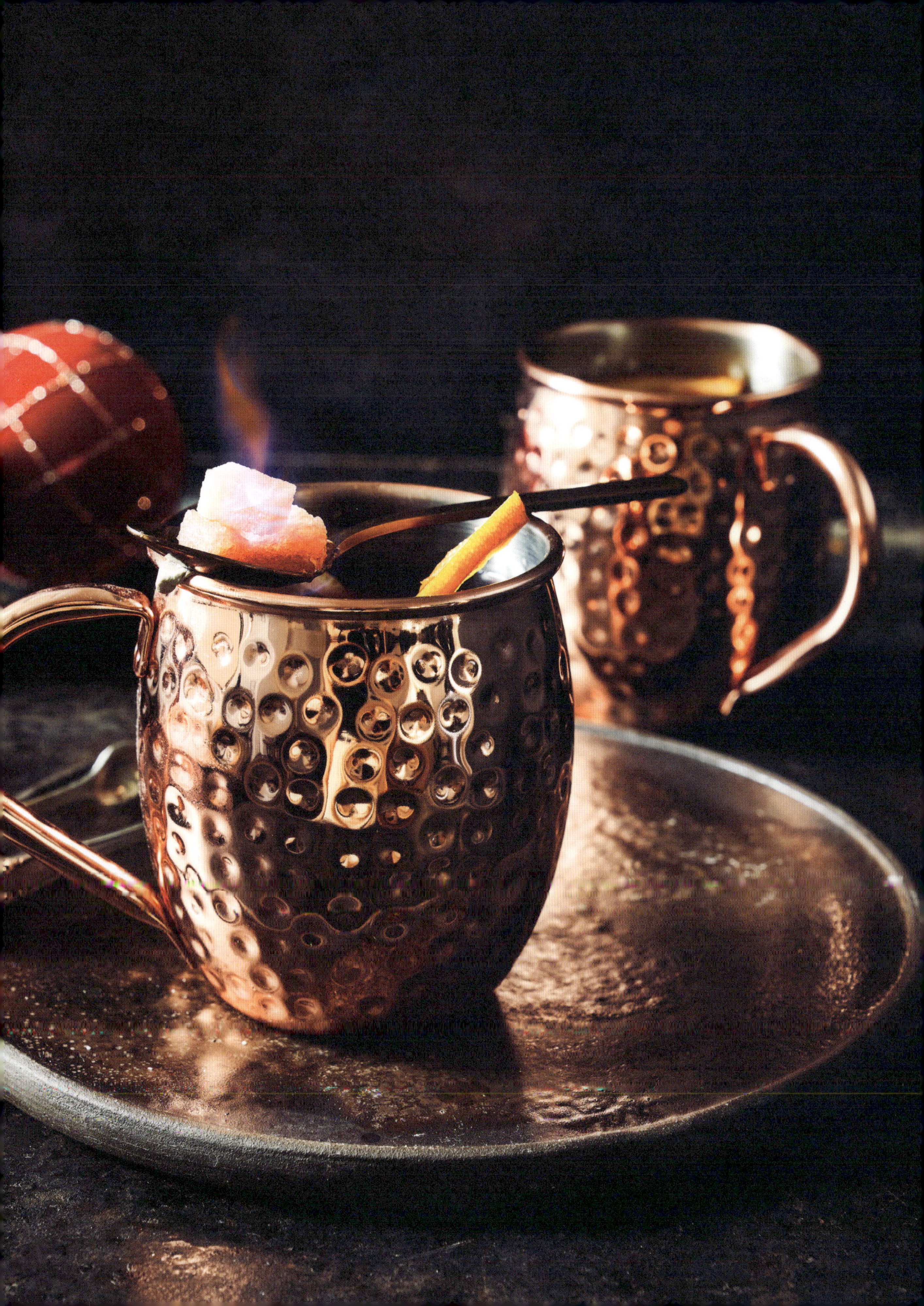

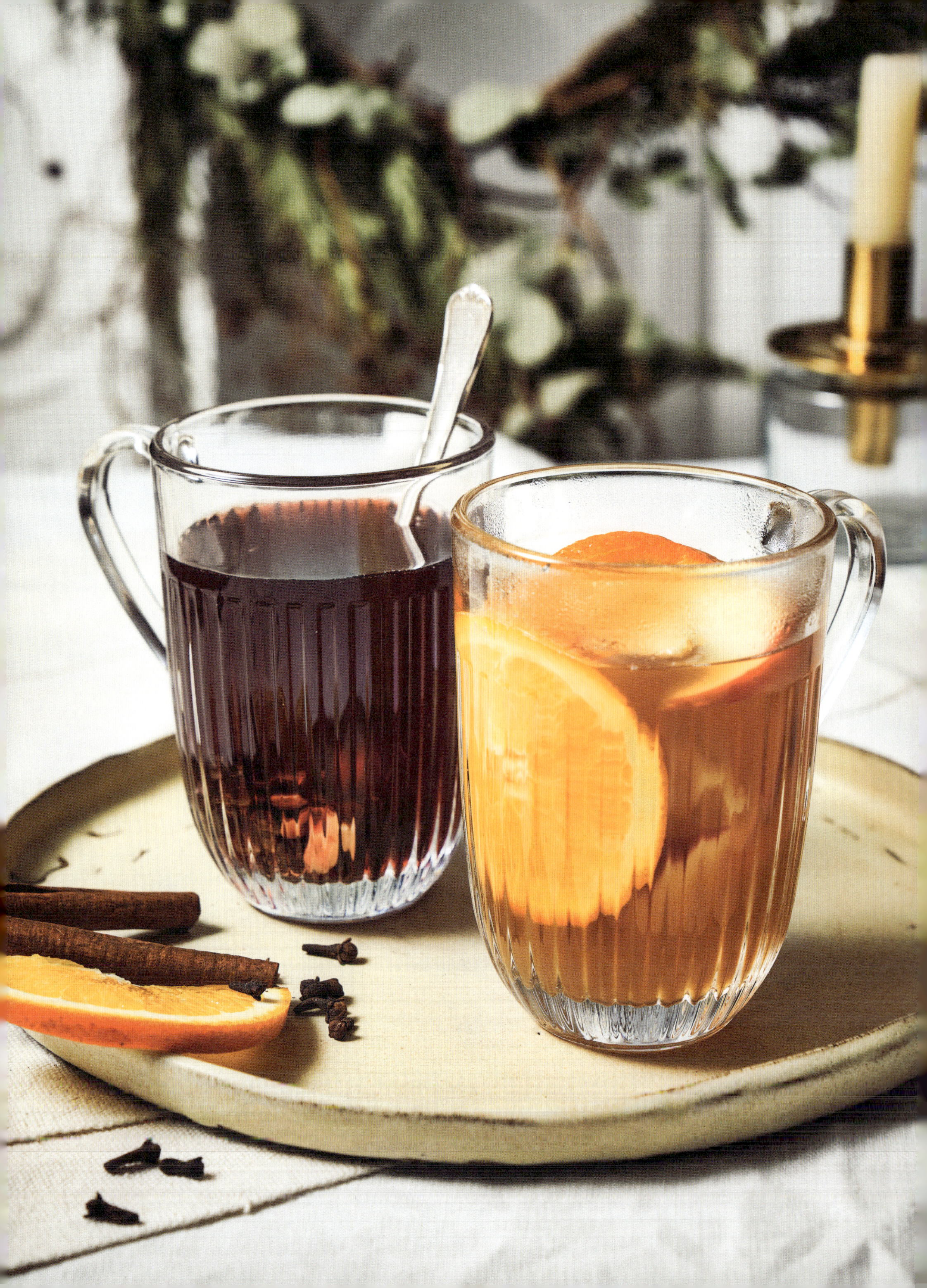

White mulled wine

Wash the oranges under hot water and pat dry. Peel the ginger. Cut everything into slices. Wash the apples, pat dry, cut in half and remove the cores. Cut into slices and transfer to a bowl. Pour over the amaretto and leave the apple slices to infuse for 30 minutes.

Add the white wine, apple juice, orange and ginger slices to a large saucepan with the honey and cinnamon sticks. Heat everything slowly, but be careful not to bring the wine to the boil. Add the amaretto and apple slices to the mulled wine and heat everything through again.

Pour the white mulled wine into glasses and serve warm.

Makes about 10 glasses

4 oranges
1 piece of ginger (6cm/2½ inches)
3 apples
200ml (7fl oz) amaretto
2 litres (70fl oz) white wine
600ml (21fl oz) cloudy apple juice
8 tablespoons liquid honey
4 cinnamon sticks

Red mulled wine

Mix all the ingredients in a saucepan, cover and leave to infuse overnight. When ready to serve, bring the wine to a near simmer, but do not let it boil.

Strain off the spices, sprinkle with almonds and sultanas and serve hot.

Makes about 10 glasses

1 litre (35fl oz) red wine
125g (4½ oz) brown sugar
1 teaspoon lemon zest
2 cinnamon sticks
1 teaspoon ground ginger
5 cloves
4 cardamom pods or ½ tablespoon ground cardamom
2 pieces of dried bitter orange peel

Also

60g (2¼ oz) blanched almonds
60g (2¼ oz) sultanas

Christmas sangria

Makes about 10 glasses

1 pomegranate
2 tart apples
2 oranges
500g (1lb 2oz) peaches (tinned)
1.25 litres (44fl oz) red wine
200ml (7fl oz) Calvados
250ml (9fl oz) apple juice
250ml (9fl oz) cranberry juice
5 tablespoons brown sugar
2 cinnamon sticks
2 cloves

Halve the pomegranate. Remove the seeds and set aside. Wash the apples and pat dry, then cut into quarters. Remove the cores and cut the quarters into bite-sized pieces. Peel the oranges and cut into pieces. Strain the tinned peaches, reserving the juice. Cut the peaches into pieces and place in a bowl together with the apple and orange pieces and the pomegranate seeds.

Add the wine and Calvados to the bowl together with the apple, cranberry and reserved peach juices, the sugar and spices. Mix well. Cover the bowl with cling film and refrigerate for at least 2 hours. Remove the spices with a slotted spoon.

Divide the sangria and fruit among glasses and serve chilled.

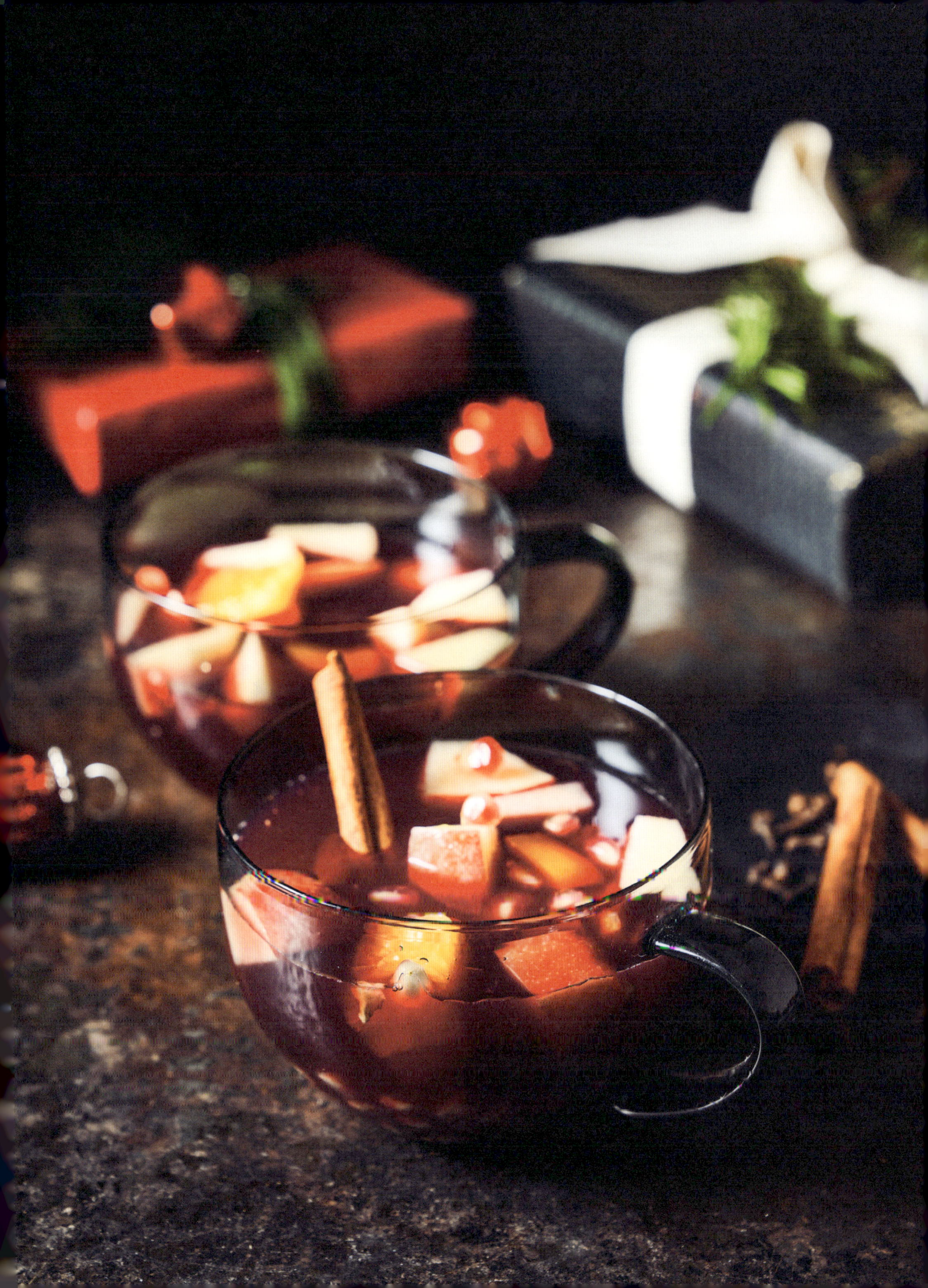

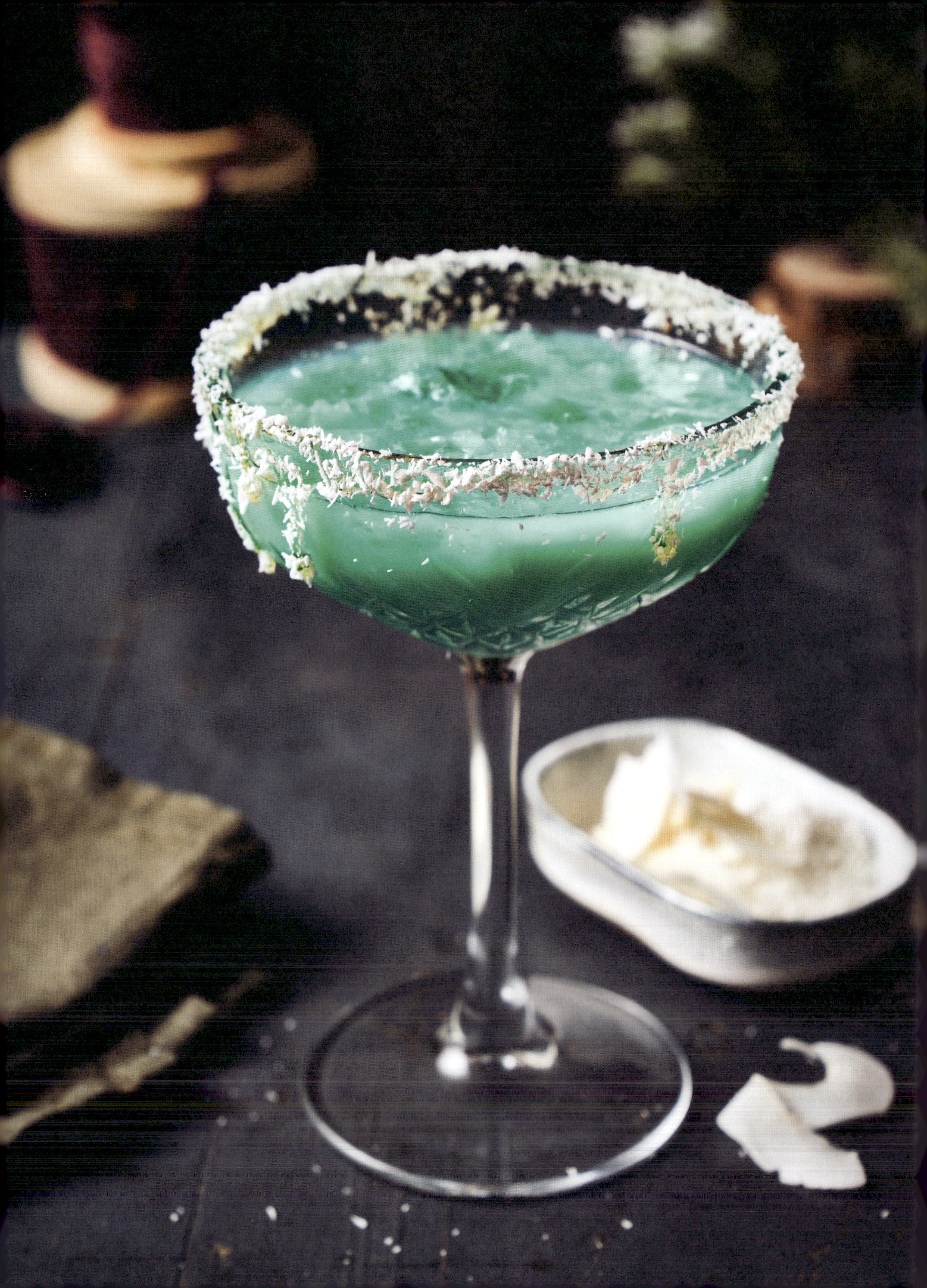

Jack Frost cocktail

Put all the ingredients for the cocktail in a blender and blend well.

For the coconut rim, place a little honey and the coconut on separate plates. Dip 4 cocktail glasses first into the honey and then into the coconut.

Pour the Jack Frost cocktail into the glasses and serve immediately.

Tip: Vary the amount of crushed ice according to your preferred taste.

For the cocktail

160ml (5¼fl oz) pineapple juice
80ml (2½fl oz) vodka
80ml (2½fl oz) Blue Curaçao
80ml (2½fl oz) cream of coconut
150g (5½oz) crushed ice

For the coconut rim

Liquid honey
Desiccated or finely shredded coconut, for garnish

Clementine and rosemary prosecco

For the rosemary syrup

1 bunch of rosemary sprigs (about 50g/1¾oz)
2 clementines
300g (10½oz) granulated (white) sugar

For the prosecco

120ml (4fl oz) clementine juice
60ml (2fl oz) lime juice
60ml (2fl oz) rosemary syrup
260ml (9fl oz) prosecco

Rinse and shake dry the rosemary. Set aside 4 small sprigs for garnishing and pick off the leaves from the rest. Chop the leaves coarsely. Wash the clementines under hot water and peel off thin strips with a zester. Set aside a few strips of zest for the prosecco.

For the syrup, bring 500ml (17fl oz) water to the boil in a small saucepan. Add the sugar and mix well. When the sugar has dissolved, add the chopped rosemary and the clementine zest. Cover and simmer over a low heat for 1 hour. Allow the syrup to cool and then pass the liquid through a fine sieve. Transfer the syrup into a sterilised bottle and seal airtight. It will keep in the fridge for several weeks.

For the clementine and rosemary prosecco, divide the ingredients among 4 champagne glasses and stir carefully. Serve garnished with a sprig of rosemary each and the remaining clementine zest.

Tip: Use a non-alcoholic prosecco for an alcohol-free version.

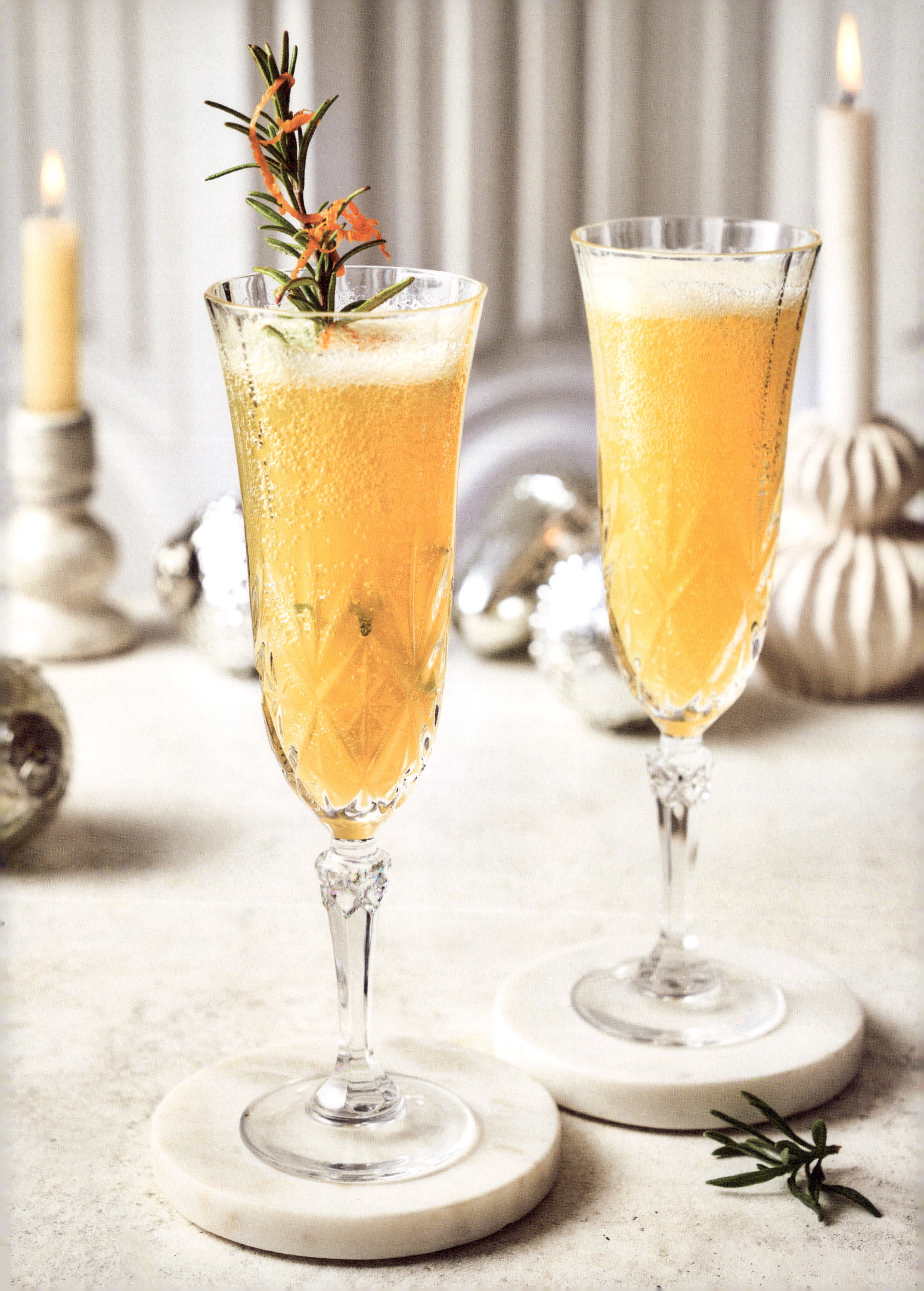

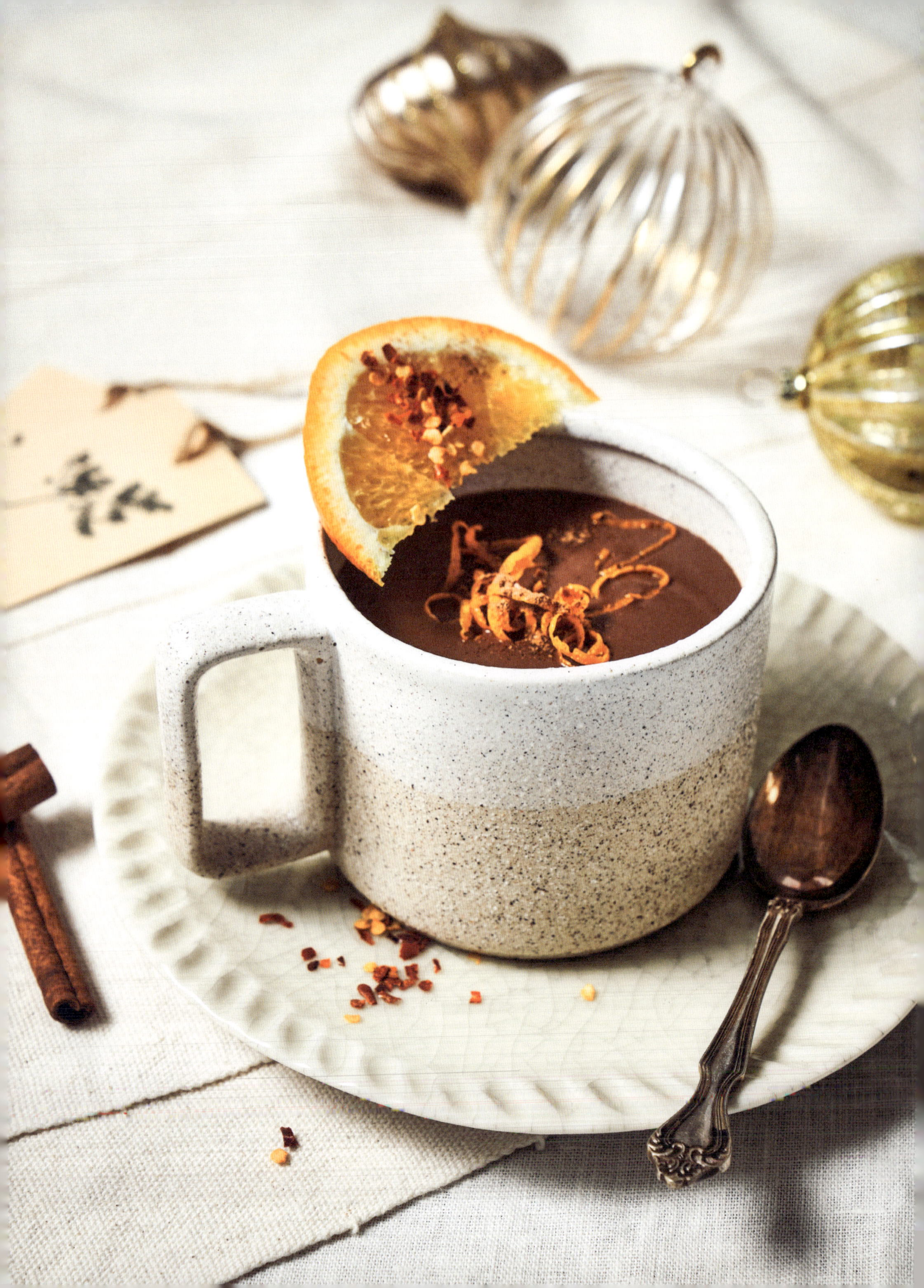

Orange and chilli hot chocolate

Wash the oranges under hot water, pat dry and finely zest. In a small saucepan, bring the milk, half the orange zest, the chilli flakes and cinnamon to a boil. Remove the saucepan from the heat.

Break the chocolate into small pieces and stir into the hot milk to melt. Add the Cointreau and sweeten with the honey. Mix everything well and strain through a sieve.

Pour the hot chocolate into 4 mugs and serve sprinkled with chilli flakes and the remaining orange zest.

Tip: For a non-alcoholic orange and chilli hot chocolate, omit the Cointreau. Add a little more milk and chocolate, if you like.

2 oranges
1 litre (35fl oz) milk
½ tsp chilli flakes, plus a little extra for sprinkling
1 teaspoon ground cinnamon
200g (7oz) dark chocolate
80ml (2½fl oz) Cointreau
4 tablespoons liquid honey

Also

4 orange wedges, to garnish

Index of recipes

A
Almond shortbread nests 129
Amaretto dessert 114
Apricot crumble gingerbread 145

B
Beetroot carpaccio 23
Black-and-white biscuits 138
Bread dumpling with mushroom ragout 53
Butter biscuits 128
Buttery quark stollen 156
Button mushroom cream soup 13

C
Carrot hummus with cumin 37
Chestnut ice cream with vanilla and Amarena cherries 92
Christmas cookie custard 106
Christmas cupcakes 164
Christmas forest berry punch 170
Christmas sangria 178
Cinnamon stars 127
Classic potato cake 31
Clementine and rosemary prosecco 182
Coconut macaroons 132
Cranberry shortbread 144
Cream of parsnip soup with thyme croutons 10
Crispy pork belly with vegetables and potatoes 72

D
Duck breast with spiced orange red cabbage 75

F
Festive bruschetta two ways 41
Festive mud cakes 167
Fillets of lamb with rosemary and mashed celeriac 66
Flourless chocolate gingerbread 147

G
Garlic and porcini mushroom pull-apart bread with a feta and mushroom spread 38
Gentleman's pudding 117
German flaming punch 174
German gingerbread biscuits 146
German roast goose with gingerbread sauce 81
Gilthead bream in salt crust with pine nut butter and lemon and thyme potatoes 63
Goat's cheese with orange honey and roast tomatoes 20

H
Hazelnut rounds 133
Honey parfait with mulled wine plums 96
Honeyed balsamic carrots with hazelnuts and yoghurt 26
Hot apple punch 173

I
Italian roast goose, Parma-style 80

J
Jack Frost cocktail 181

L
Layered domino biscuits 137
Leg of lamb with goat's cheese and herb salad 69
Lemon and yoghurt Bundt cake 159
Lemon sorbet 109

M
Mandarin punch 173
Mousse au chocolat 105

N
Nut roast with sweet potato and chestnut mash 54
Nut triangles 150

O
Orange and chilli hot chocolate 185
Orange mascarpone cream with slivered almonds 110

P
Pannacotta with caramel sauce 102
Pecan biscuits with chocolate filling 141
Pepper-crusted fillet of beef with sweet potato rosti 84
Pumpkin and beetroot Wellingtons with kale pesto 50
Pumpkin gnocchi with beetroot in sage butter 49
Pumpkin risotto with sage butter and caramelised chestnuts 46

R
Radicchio and rocket salad with cranberries and walnuts 14
Red mulled wine 177
Roast goose with potato dumplings and red cabbage 76
Roast pumpkin with rocket and feta 28
Roasted maple pears with almond praline and yoghurt 95

S
Saffron and almond butter 37
Salmon with potatoes and pea pesto 60
Spiced biscuits 134
Spinach and salmon quiche 34
Sweet fluffy dumplings with poppy seed butter 121
Swiss cheese fondue 87

T
Traditional stollen 153
Tree log cake 160

V
Vanilla crescents 126

W
White chocolate and coconut parfait with red fruit jelly 118
White chocolate cream with raspberries 99
White mulled wine 177
Winter salad with bacon-coated prunes 17
Winter vegetable gratin 57

Index of ingredients

A
Apple
- Christmas forest berry punch 170
- Christmas sangria 178
- German roast goose with gingerbread sauce 81
- Hot apple punch 173
- Mandarin punch 173
- Roast goose with potato dumplings and red cabbage 76
- White mulled wine 177

B
Beef
- Pepper-crusted fillet of beef with sweet potato rosti 84

Beetroot
- Beetroot carpaccio 23
- Pumpkin and beetroot Wellingtons with kale pesto 50
- Pumpkin gnocchi with beetroot in sage butter 49

Berries, mixed
- White chocolate and coconut parfait with red fruit jelly 118

Blueberries
- Gentleman's pudding 117
- Radicchio and rocket salad with cranberries and walnuts 14

Bread
- Bread dumpling with mushroom ragout 53
- Festive bruschetta two ways 41
- Garlic and porcini mushroom pull-apart bread with a feta and mushroom spread 38
- Nut roast with sweet potato and chestnut mash 54
- Swiss cheese fondue 87

Brioche bun
- Cream of parsnip soup with thyme croutons 10

C
Carrot
- Carrot hummus with cumin 37
- Crispy pork belly with vegetables and potatoes 72
- German roast goose with gingerbread sauce 81
- Honeyed balsamic carrots with hazelnuts and yoghurt 26
- Nut roast with sweet potato and chestnut mash 54
- Winter vegetable gratin 57

Celeriac/celery
- Crispy pork belly with vegetables and potatoes 72
- Fillets of lamb with rosemary and mashed celeriac 66
- German roast goose with gingerbread sauce 81
- Winter vegetable gratin 57

Cherries
- Amaretto dessert 114
- Chestnut ice cream with vanilla and Amarena cherries 92

Chestnuts
- Chestnut ice cream with vanilla and Amarena cherries 92
- German roast goose with gingerbread sauce 81
- Nut roast with sweet potato and chestnut mash 54
- Pumpkin and beetroot Wellingtons with kale pesto 50
- Pumpkin risotto with sage butter and caramelised chestnuts 46

Chickpeas
- Carrot hummus with cumin 37

Chicory (witlof)
- Winter salad with bacon-coated prunes 17

Chocolate
- Chestnut ice cream with vanilla and Amarena cherries 92
- Festive mud cakes 167
- Gentleman's pudding 117

Mousse au chocolat 105
Orange and chilli hot chocolate 185
White chocolate and coconut parfait with red fruit jelly 118
White chocolate cream with raspberries 99

Clementine
Clementine and rosemary prosecco 182

Cooking chocolate
Flourless chocolate gingerbread 147
Layered domino biscuits 137
Nut triangles 150
Traditional stollen 153
Tree log cake 160

Crème fraîche
Garlic and porcini mushroom pull-apart bread with a feta and mushroom spread 38

D

Duck
Duck breast with spiced orange red cabbage 75

F

Feta cheese
Garlic and porcini mushroom pull-apart bread with a feta and mushroom spread 38
Roast pumpkin with rocket and feta 28

Fish
Gilthead bream in salt crust with pine nut butter and lemon and thyme potatoes 63
Salmon with potatoes and pea pesto 60
Spinach and salmon quiche 34

Forest berries
Christmas forest berry punch 170

G

Goat's cheese
Festive bruschetta two ways 41
Goat's cheese with orange honey and roast tomatoes 20
Leg of lamb with goat's cheese and herb salad 69
Radicchio and rocket salad with cranberries and walnuts 14

Goose
German roast goose with gingerbread sauce 81
Italian roast goose, Parma-style 80
Roast goose with potato dumplings and red cabbage 76

Gouda cheese
Bread dumpling with mushroom ragout 53
Garlic and porcini mushroom pull-apart bread with a feta and mushroom spread 38

H

Horseradish
Cream of parsnip soup with thyme croutons 10

J

Juniper berries
German flaming punch 174

K

Kale
Pumpkin and beetroot Wellingtons with kale pesto 50

L

Lamb
Fillets of lamb with rosemary and mashed celeriac 66
Leg of lamb with goat's cheese and herb salad 69

Lamb's lettuce
Beetroot carpaccio 23
Winter salad with bacon-coated prunes 17

Leek
Crispy pork belly with vegetables and potatoes 72

German roast goose with gingerbread
   sauce 81
Winter vegetable gratin 57
Lentils
Pumpkin and beetroot Wellingtons
   with kale pesto 50

M
Mascarpone cheese
Amaretto dessert 114
Orange mascarpone cream with slivered
   almonds 110
White chocolate cream with
   raspberries 99
Mushrooms
Bread dumpling with mushroom
   ragout 53
Button mushroom cream soup 13
Classic potato cake 31
Festive bruschetta two ways 41
Garlic and porcini mushroom pull-apart
   bread with a feta and mushroom
   spread 38

O
Orange
Christmas forest berry punch 170
Christmas sangria 178
Duck breast with spiced orange red
   cabbage 75
Fillets of lamb with rosemary and mashed
   celeriac 66
German flaming punch 174
Goat's cheese with orange honey and
   roast tomatoes 20
Orange and chilli hot chocolate 185
Orange mascarpone cream with slivered
   almonds 110
White mulled wine 177
Winter salad with bacon-coated prunes 17

P
Parmesan cheese
Italian roast goose, Parma-style 80

Nut roast with sweet potato and
   chestnut mash 54
Pepper-crusted fillet of beef with sweet
   potato rosti 84
Pumpkin gnocchi with beetroot in sage
   butter 49
Pumpkin risotto with sage butter and
   caramelised chestnuts 46
Salmon with potatoes and pea
   pesto 60
Parsnip
Cream of parsnip soup with thyme
   croutons 10
Pear
Festive bruschetta two ways 41
Roasted maple pears with almond praline
   and yoghurt 95
Peas
Salmon with potatoes and pea pesto 60
Plums
Honey parfait with mulled wine
   plums 96
Winter salad with bacon-coated prunes 17
Pomegranate
Christmas sangria 178
Winter salad with bacon-coated prunes 17
Pork
Crispy pork belly with vegetables and
   potatoes 72
Italian roast goose, Parma-style 80
Winter salad with bacon-coated prunes 17
Potatoes
Classic potato cake 31
Crispy pork belly with vegetables and
   potatoes 72
Fillets of lamb with rosemary and mashed
   celeriac 66
Gilthead bream in salt crust with pine
   nut butter and lemon and thyme
   potatoes 63
Nut roast with sweet potato and chestnut
   mash 54
Pumpkin gnocchi with beetroot in sage
   butter 49